W9-ACI-506

Lives of Our Own

The Invisible Scar: The Great Depression
and What It Did to American Life from Then to Now

Born Female: The High Cost of Keeping Women Down

The Crowding Syndrome: Learning to Live
with Too Much and Too Many

Everything a Woman Needs to Know
to Get Paid What She's Worth

The Case Against College: What Families Should Know
About the High Cost of a College Education
and Whether It's Really the Springboard to Success

Enterprising Women: Their Contribution
to the American Economy, 1776–1976

What Women Want

The Two-Paycheck Marriage: How Women at Work
Are Changing Life in America

The Good Years: Your Life in the Twenty-first Century

Second Careers: New Ways to Work After Fifty

Lives of Our Own: Secrets of Salty Old Women

Lives

of

Our Own

SECRETS OF

SALTY LD WOMEN

Caroline Bird

Houghton Mifflin Company

BOSTON   NEW YORK

1995

For information about permission to reproduce selections from this
book, write to Permissions, Houghton Mifflin Company,
215 Park Avenue South, New York, New York 10003.

Library of Congress Cataloging-in-Publication Data

Bird, Caroline
Lives of our own : secrets of salty old women / by Caroline Bird.
p. cm.
Includes bibliographical references and index.
ISBN 0-395-65234-0
1. Aged women — United States — Biography. 2. Middle aged women —
United States — Biography. 3. Aged — United States — Psychology.
4. Middle age — United States — Psychological aspects. 5. Life
change events — United States — Case studies. 6. Ageism —
United States — Case studies. I. Title
HQ1064.U5B385 1995
305.4 — dc20   94-44262
[B]   CIP

Book design by Anne Chalmers
Set in Fournier

Printed in the United States of America

MP 10 9 8 7 6 5 4 3 2 1

TO THE MEMORY OF MY
GREAT-GRANDMOTHER SAWIN

Acknowledgments

My first debt is to the hundreds of openhearted older women who were willing to share the "secrets" of their new lives with the readers of this book and patiently correct my accounts of what they told me, especially Toby Ansin, Joleen Bachman, Rena Bartos, Ingrid Beall, Susanna Bedell, Jean Benear, Elizabeth Bingaman, Euna Blake, Olga Bloom, Madeline M. Blue, Joan W. Blumenfeld, Lydia Bragger, Helen Breed, Ruth Brinker, Anne Browner, Reva Buck, Ann Buckingham, Marjorie DeMoss Casebolt, Marianne Cashatt, Ruth Combecker, Dorothy S. Conlon, Cynthia Coupe, Bettie L. Crane, Helen Crosswait, Gail Deaver, Carrie Barefoot Dickerson, Phyllis Diller, Anita Wilkes Dore, Joan Ellis, Maddie Glazer, Jane Gould, Lois Gould, Grace Graves, Berniece Greetham, Doris Grumbach, Dr. Ruth W. Hayre, Lucy Hendrickson, Mary Hess, Marguerite Hibbard-Taylor, Helen Holmes, Phoebe Hoss, Dana Hull, Ruth Humphrey, Helen Johnston, Marge Kalina, Barbara Kelley, Ruth Kinnard, Leslie Koempel, Vilma Kohn, Jeanne Kretschmer, Patricia Larsen, Lila Line, Rice Lyons, Angela Martinez, Laura Jean Masters, Sue Mathias, Shirley McKittrick, Margaret McQuarrie, Caroline Miller, Margo Miller, Mildred Miller, Alice Miskimin, Barbara Morris, Esther Nelson, Sheila Newman, Mary Burke Nicholas, Cecelia O'Meara, Avis-Ann Strong Parke, Florence Parrish, Ellen Paullin, Fay Porter, Jane Poulton, California B. Quint, Jean S. Remke, Shirl Rendlen, Hania W. Ris, Gloria Ross, Joan Rowland, Constance Lee Rowley, Ann B. Rupsis, Phyllis Sanders, Joan Schine, Jean Way Schoonover, Dot Smith, Fay J. Smith, Irene Stambler, Emily Anne Staples, Clarice A. Strasser, Audrey Tegethoff, Jacqueline Thea, Isabella Threlkeld, Mary Jean Tully, Louise Ulrich, Genevieve Vaughan, Elizabeth Verssen, Dr. Virginia Vollmer, Frances Weaver, Margaret Weinstock, Mary Ann Williams, Hazel Wolf,

Jane K. Woodward, Nancy M. Wright, Frances Young, and Wilma Young.

My friend Bard Lindeman put me in touch with many of these women by writing about my project in "Prime Time," his nationally syndicated newspaper column. He was ever ready with an elusive fact or the name and phone number of someone who could supply it.

Gilbert Brim, director of the MacArthur Foundation Research Network on Successful Midlife Development, encouraged me and gave me an overall view of research on aging. Others who helped me get started were Dr. Ron Abeles, associate director, Behavioral and Social Research, National Institute on Aging; Maxine Forman, manager, Women's Initiative, American Association of Retired Persons; Lou Glasse, president of the Older Women's League; Barbara Haber, curator of printed books, the Arthur and Elizabeth Schlesinger Library on the History of Women in America; and Dr. John Rowe, president of Mt. Sinai School of Medicine.

More authorities than I can name took time out to give me specific information. I would like to give special thanks to the following among them.

Dr. Elliott Howard, internist and cardiologist associated with Lenox Hill Hospital and author of the popular book *Health Risks*, adapted his quiz on health habits to older women.

On the treatment of older women at work, I received help from Martin Sicker, director, Work Force Programs, AARP, and from the plaintiff's employment attorneys Virginia O'Leary of Oakland City, Indiana, Judith P. Vladeck of New York City, and Francine Weiss of Washington, D.C. Like everyone else who has written about discrimination in employment, I leaned heavily on the research of the late Dan Lacey, publisher of *Workplace Trends*.

On the image of older women on television, I am indebted to George Gerbner, dean emeritus of the Annenberg School of Communications at the University of Pennsylvania in Philadelphia, and Treesa Drury, director of advertising standards for the AARP.

Special information on the new role of older women in philanthropy came from Joanne Hayes, consultant in fund development;

Caroline Miller, assistant director, Department of Planned Giving and Endowment, United Jewish Appeal–Federation of Jewish Philanthropies; Sondra C. Shaw, director of development, Wisconsin State Historical Society; and Gloria Steinem.

Assistance in locating women, maintaining a database of well over three hundred names, and tracking down data in the library came from Maureen Cassidy, Anita Makar, Lauren Muffs, Chris Perkins, Liz Reardon, Leisa Russell, Molly Sinclair, and Roberta Walsh.

Finally, I owe a special debt to Patricia Haskell, editor, agent, book producer, and friend of many decades, whose prompt and unfailing advice kept me on the torturous path from a glint in the eye to a book you can hold in your hand.

Contents

Lives of Our Own

SECOND HALF,
SECOND CHANCE

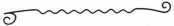

THIS BOOK IS FOR and about older women who want to create new lives for the quarter-century of active years that now lie ahead for most women in their fifties — women who want to make the unexpected, uncommitted years on their own count as much as, and sometimes more than, the years they spent caring for others.

Eleanor Roosevelt is my inspiration. Her book *On My Own* describes the new life she started after she took the White House elevator down for the last time. And we call ourselves salty old women not because we like to call a spade a spade (though most of us do), but because however responsive and caring we are to those around us (and most of us are), we hardly fit the stereotype of sweet little old ladies.

We are mainly older women whose marriages are behind us. Although you don't hear much about us, we are a bigger part of America every year. We hide ourselves even in the statistics.

We've all heard about the rapid rise in the number of older people, but I was surprised to discover how fast our particular segment of older people is increasing. In 1990 there were 12,896,000 formerly married women over fifty-five. Between 1987 and 1990, when the number of people over fifty-five rose by 2 percent, the widowed, divorced, or separated women among them rose a whopping 37 percent, an increase that amounted to a million women a year. The reasons seem to be not only that there are more older people and that widows live longer than widowers, but that more older women than in the past are single because they have been divorced or separated.

At a time when every splinter group is labeled, we don't know what to call ourselves. Our problem is with the word "old." However many birthdays we've had, we don't think of ourselves as old. Sometimes we look around a room and are surprised to find that so many of our friends are growing gray. Why are we spending time with these people? They're not like us. They're old!

Old can sometimes be good for a man, but never for a woman. A man is a "man" or a "gentleman" to the end of his days. Attendants who call female patients by their first names wouldn't presume to address their male patients that way. In the South, people can call you a "good old boy" to your face, even if you're young, but one is not so easily a "good old girl."

Old is so bad for a woman that we rush to say "young lady" for women of any age — especially those who are obviously old. The only self-respecting reply is the one Maggie Kuhn, who founded the Gray Panthers, gave to President Ford: "Mr. President, I am not a young lady. I am an old woman." But few of us have the courage.

"Old" is a word you're not supposed to use with "woman." When age has to be mentioned, we talk uneasily about a woman "of a certain age," of "indeterminate age," or "the *wrong* side of fifty" (italics ours). But few of us feel that these euphemisms apply to us personally. We describe others but seldom ourselves as "mature," "senior citizens," "golden-agers," or in their "twilight years." Survey data tell us that most older women regard themselves as young for their age.

"Older women," as in Older Women's League (OWL), begs the question. Older than what? Older than you are now? The older woman that a high school boy boasts of dating may be all of twenty-two. Like other kind terms, "older women" will eventually wear out and be replaced by something that doesn't sound like a euphemism.

The problem is that old is not a number. It's a role, a stereo-type, or a state of mind. But whatever it is, it's taking longer to get there all the time. At the beginning of the Common Era, most people didn't survive into their fifties, and at that age, Cicero wrote his remarkably perceptive essay on old age. In the nine-teenth century, Bismarck set the age of retirement at sixty-five for a very practical reason: so few attained that age that the tax-payers could afford to pension them. Now so many are vigorous through their sixties and seventies that you may not regard your-self as old when you are over seventy-five. "Youth creep" is what the sociologists call it.

This isn't a book about "age passing," or how to look younger than you are. Women who devote all their time to this game are subscribing to the feminine mystique, which values women pri-marily for their youth, beauty, childbearing ability, and attrac-tiveness to men. In her own way, each woman mentioned in this book has made the revolution from within that put Gloria Steinem in touch with her body in her sixth decade.

This is a book about women who want to use the freedom of their later years to create new roles for themselves, often by doing badly needed work that no one else is doing. Don't married women find new roles in their later years? Of course they do. But there are several reasons why the widowed, divorced, and separated are the ones to watch.

For starters, being left alone after the first flush of youth is supposed to be the worst possible thing that can happen to a woman. Public attention has rightly focused on poor old women who need help because they've been left alone, while those of us who con-tinue to be active and gainfully employed are glad to escape spe-cial notice. But it's just those women who have had to learn to live by themselves in their later years who have the most to teach. Most older women in this position didn't choose to live on their own, but when freedom was forced upon them, they learned how to make the most of it.

No rules! No roles! No meals to get! Nobody to consider but

myself! I can do anything I want! At times this is scary even for those of us who are relieved to be out of our marriages. Growth isn't steady or painless, and once we've achieved one goal, another seems to loom ahead. Very few of the older women interviewed for this book said they'd really like to go back and relive any earlier period of their lives, even when their marriages had been happy.

But however we're doing, older women of the 1990s have an advantage our mothers didn't enjoy. We've been through it before. Ageism — going by age when it doesn't matter — is much like sexism, and every woman over fifty-five knows what it means to be classified on the basis of sex when it doesn't matter. In fact, many of us can recall the shock of discovering how we ourselves tried to fit the stereotypes of the feminine mystique that was keeping us down.

Now that we are older, we do the same thing. Being even just an older woman, not an old one, is so bad that most of us don't like to talk about it. Unlike Jews and blacks, older women do not have strong organizations to represent them. Jews have long had their Anti-Defamation League and blacks the National Association for the Advancement of Colored People. All old women have in the way of defense organizations are the relatively weak and new Older Women's League and the Gray Panthers, and most of us don't sign up. Like the Jewish humorist, we don't want to join a club that would take us in.

A lot of us felt that way about the women's movement of the 1970s. Other women were suffering from sex discrimination, but we kept away from them because we thought we had been lucky enough to find our own ways around it. The successful businesswomen I interviewed in 1967 for the *Saturday Evening Post* didn't even understand what I meant by sex discrimination. Most of them said, "But in my business, it helps to be a woman!" And they were right. They were supervising women telephone operators or selling or writing about fashion and beauty or selling securities to widows.

Was this discrimination? At first I thought I had no story. It took me a long time to see that these women were successful because they were reinforcing one of the cultural restrictions on women: managing them in the female ghetto of low-paid occupations; helping them to attract men with clothes and cosmetics; confirming them in the belief that they lacked the skill and knowledge to manage their own money.

Just as a fish doesn't know it's stuck in the sea, I didn't realize at first that I was in the female job ghetto with them: I had been sent out to interview them *because I was a woman.* (In the end, the male editor who had thought up the story turned it down; because, he said, I was an exception, I just didn't understand that most women didn't want careers.) But during the turbulent decade that followed, every young woman was forced to think about herself in terms of the issues that feminists were raising.

Now, in the 1990s, it's happening again. Women are liberating themselves, this time from the double whammy of age and sex. We are beginning to see how the stereotypes of age are foreclosing our futures. But because we have been through it before, the new revolution ought to go faster.

We know that the first thing we have to do is define the stereotypes that keep us down, find out how true they are today, what damage they are doing, and what purposes they serve. Then we have to explore the possibilities of a world in which they no longer apply.

And how do we fight? Those of us who are veterans of earlier revolutions know firsthand that the hardest battle is the one we have to fight with ourselves. Many blacks still doubt that black is beautiful. Many women still think they are equal at work and privileged at home.

As before, each of us has to begin with herself. Each of us has to question what her efforts to "stay young" are doing to her. We dye our hair, lift our eyelids, and puff out our breasts with dangerous gels in order to keep our bodies forever thirty. The price of staying young is arrested development. (Would any of us choose to remain forever six years old?)

But the physical insult to our bodies isn't the worst of it. The effort to stay young can be a vicious form of self-induced mental retardation. It encourages us to throw away all the things we've learned that make us uniquely ourselves, as if they didn't matter. If we succeed in stopping the clock, by the time we're past menopause we've conceded that our lives are over.

To save ourselves, we have to give up the ideal of eternal youth, look squarely at the surprisingly compensative biological changes we can expect in the decades after menopause, and realize that what we hate about growing old is the spin our culture puts on these changes.

Each of us has to learn for herself that the conventional wisdom about youth is wrong. Every year of our lives, from the playpen on, we gain some abilities and lose others. The women we admire for staying young are women who never stop growing. And in talking to hundreds of these women, I've found that we all build on what has happened to us before, as birds build a nest out of the odd bits of this and that they find lying around.

In the past few years I've talked to several hundred women who have made new lives for themselves after they've been left alone. At first I wanted to create a kind of back fence over which we could talk about the ways we've invented to cope with our new situation and find a pattern in the miscellany of new roles we've created for ourselves. I looked for women making new lives in every area, so that every woman could read about someone who would make her say to herself, "Oh, I could do that!" or "So that's how she did it!"

It didn't work out exactly as I had planned. There weren't as many widows as I had hoped to find following Eleanor Roosevelt into politics. And many women who had made exemplary new lives for themselves reminded me uncomfortably of the exceptional women who were always mentioned back in the 1960s when I was trying to find out whether women were discriminated against in business. If the personal is the political, maybe we need to do more for one another than exchange our tactics. Maybe we need a strategy.

In 1968, *Born Female* served as a handy source for the data pioneer feminists needed to make their case with employers, legislators, courts, and the media. In 1995, I hope that *Lives of Our Own* will pass the ammunition we'll need to break the suspicious and self-defeating silence about independent older women.

PART I

The Rest of Your Life

My great-grandmother Sawin was a preacher's daughter who organized the first school in Madison, Wisconsin. She lived to be a hundred years old, and according to family legend, it was her birthday that killed her. The children in the school named after her brought her a hundred roses. "People aren't supposed to live to be a hundred years old!" she said to my grandmother. And a week later, without any sign of illness, she just stopped living.

It's not a fairy story. I have a picture of her surrounded by the lethal roses, and another one, taken shortly before, with my four-year-old self beside her chair. "Grandma in the chair," I am said to have called her.

Her long life and painless death sound like a morality tale, but what's the moral?

My father was her favorite grandchild. To him, the moral was that the traditional virtues of women are rewarded. When he told the story, he would go on to talk about how she had spent her whole life doing for others. And he'd tell about how she would get up at four in the morning to make him a strawberry shortcake before he started out on what people used to call a century bicycle race — one hundred miles.

Then my mother would remind him about how Grandma Sawin had bankrolled their courtship with sums of money that were truly phenomenal coming from a woman whose only cash income was the $12 a month she received as the widow of a veteran of the War of 1812. And if this sounded like a dig about my father's poor money management, he could go on to talk about how nobody had ever heard Grandma Sawin complain — a dig at my mother's willingness to ventilate her grievances.

As for me, I've never been able to forget the story, but the moral keeps changing. When I was in psychoanalysis during the

1950s, my great-grandmother's impossible virtue symbolized the stern, repressive culture responsible for my neuroses. She was a woman so repressed that she died when she thought it was the right thing to do!

In the 1960s, when I began to rebel against the traditional role of women, the stories about her sounded like the myth-making of an oppressive patriarchal culture. Never thinking of herself! Always doing for others, especially males! (Would she have risen at four to make a strawberry shortcake for her granddaughter?) A victim who didn't know it! If she was all that happy, she shouldn't have been.

Now that I am older, there are many morals to be drawn from the stories about her, which continue to haunt me.

- Repressing complaints can be emotionally cost-effective. Maybe she knew what therapists are now just discovering, that "letting it all hang out" is as apt to make your troubles worse as to purge them. After listening to the tell-all stories of victims of disabling accidents, sex abuse, date rape, and even sex and age discrimination in the workplace, I've sometimes wondered how much of the personal it's fair to ask any one person to sacrifice to the political.
- You have to cope with what's in front of you. Grandma Sawin was a coper, not a helpless victim. The Indians who peeked into her log schoolhouse didn't bother her; she said, "I had more trouble with the white men." But she didn't seem to have much trouble with either.
- She had a lot going for her in achieving a long life, much of which escapes a great many of the liberated women of my generation: no liquor, tobacco, or drugs; the physical activity of daily life on the frontier; an unquestioned role and care to the end of her days in the bosom of a supportive family; recognition for her service to the community; a sound constitution, without which she would never have survived her first birthday on the frontier.

◎ The mind controls the body. New Age thinkers and voodoo doctors are on to something we've been ignoring. If you are not supposed to be alive, you can easily die. Grandma Sawin read her large-type Bible every day. She believed that "the years of our life are threescore and ten, or even by reason of strength fourscore." The roses did her in because they reminded her that she was in a stage of life that wasn't supposed to be.

Now that I'm going on eighty, I've finally made peace with my great-grandmother. Her life no longer means any one thing, but, to paraphrase Shelley, like a dome of many-colored glass, it has left a stain on the white radiance of eternity.

1

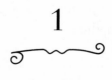

MORE

OF YOUR YEARS

ARE AHEAD

IF YOU ARE EXCITED by the prospect of exploring the un-charted territory that lies ahead, the good news is that your future is going to be longer than you were brought up to expect, and it gets a little longer every year that you live. If you were fifty in 1992, you could expect to live another thirty-one years — and those who turn fifty after you may have even more.

This is relatively new. Life expectancy *at birth* has been in-creasing for over a century. It zoomed in the 1960s, when anti-biotics saved children and young adults. But the experts always pointed out that while more people were surviving to sixty-five, the Social Security definition of "old," you couldn't expect many more years than sixty-five-year-olds had always had once you got there. If you were an exceptional individual, you might live longer than the average, but nothing could be done to increase the average human life span. That's the view you absorbed when you were young.

Nobody talked much about it. As recently as the 1980s, census tables sometimes displayed data by age groups up to seventy-five, lumping everyone over seventy-five into a limbo, not because they were all alike (actually, the older you get, the more you differ from your age mates) but because the table-makers didn't think anyone was interested in them. But in the 1993 *Statistical Abstract*, they added a group "75 to 84," so "85 and over" became the highest age group.

After World War II, demographers began to notice that old

people were living longer, too — particularly old women. In 1950, a sixty-five-year-old woman could expect 15 more years of life. By 1987, she had 18.7 years ahead of her, a gain of almost 4 years, about twice the gain (from 12.8 to 14.8 years) for men.

Instead of rejoicing, policymakers greeted the gains as catastrophes. Pity the young, who are going to have to pay higher Social Security taxes to support all these useless old people! Pity the poor old widows, doomed to hang on for more and more useless years alone! Always helpful, family-oriented women's magazines ran articles on "How to Keep Your Husband Alive."

Lengthening lives raise a lot of questions. Demographers projecting the future costs of Social Security want to know how long life expectancies can continue to rise. Social scientists studying women want to know why we live longer than men, and what's going to happen to this gap in the future. The speculation has been frankly partisan. Betty Friedan credits women's increasing control over their lives. I'm a feminist who is inclined to think that we age better than men because we've had more experience juggling and switching roles. But in the backlash against women in business, conservatives have gleefully predicted that women climbing corporate ladders will soon enjoy the privilege of dying like men. (Actually, of course, bosses of either sex aren't as apt to have heart attacks as the people whose necks they breathe down.)

Psychologists and psychotherapists have other questions. At every age, the death rate is higher for those who have lost a mate than for those who are still married. The hazard is higher for men than for women, and is highest in the year the marriage ends. But is it the *trauma* of the loss that kills, or is there something lethal about the *status* of being divorced or widowed?

There are many conjectures about why losing your husband shortens your life, but no one seems to have bothered to test them by comparing the lifestyles of widows who die sooner with those who live to a ripe old age. If the handicap is cultural, it may even now be changing. More older women work. More have Social Security. Fewer are penniless and dependent.

For each of us, of course, the good news is more personal.

What about me? Do any of the experts have any clues about how many more years I can expect to live? Do the experts have any clues about why some women live to be so much older than others?

There are no good answers. We know surprisingly little about later life; most census tables don't display death rates by single years of age over eighty-five. Yet it is just at the higher ages that individual differences take over. Whites generally live longer than blacks, but once they are into their eighties, blacks are the ones who live longer. The Delaney sisters, who were 104 and 102 when their memoirs became a bestseller, belonged to the minuscule group of college-educated blacks of their generation who seem to be virtually indestructible.

Even scholars are headed for the terra incognita of later years, so they've filled in the blanks, as early mapmakers used to do, with dragons and griffins based on the tales told by the oddball travelers who have been there. Published studies of one kind or another show that you will live longer if you

> belong to a church
> eat breakfast
> think your health is good, whatever the doctor finds it to be
> are a woman born under the sign of Gemini
> have avoided caffeine
> don't smoke
> don't drink
> like your work
> score high on intelligence tests
> enjoy or used to enjoy sexual intercourse
> exercise in your leisure time
> weigh within 20 percent of your recommended weight
> respond creatively to change
> are less anxious than you used to be
> are adaptable and flexible
> integrate new things and ideas into your life
> want to stay alive.

It's easy to detect the spin on these possibilities. Older people were tested because someone was trying to promote one of these behaviors. Even in the 1990s, what we "know" about those who survive into their later years tends to be the result of an attempt to verify anecdote or myth with studies of woefully inadequate populations.

To pin down any predictor, you'd have to start with a random sample of babies, find a way to measure each and every suspected predictor, and keep detailed records every year on everyone until the last one died. None of us would live to see the answer. Until someone comes up with the funds and the patience for more than a century of mind-numbing record keeping, the best guesses are going to come from the clinical judgment of physicians who have been following a large clientele of patients for years.

Dr. Elliott Howard is just such a physician. An internist and cardiologist at New York's Lenox Hill Hospital who has a large private practice, he and his father, a health educator, have been interested in preventing illness by teaching their patients to live healthier lives. In 1986, Dr. Howard's book *Health Risks* presented a detailed questionnaire that encouraged readers to rate their vulnerability. When I asked Dr. Howard for his clinical judgment, he identified twelve items that can predict the length of a woman's life. He also set up a scoring system that a woman can use to add or subtract years from her remaining life, according to standard actuarial tables.

Dr. Howard finds that the biggest life shortener after age fifty-five is smoking more than two packs of cigarettes a day. The next most serious predictors are smoking less than two packs a day while drinking alcohol several times a week, abnormal heartbeat or EKG readings, and diabetes. Risks that become serious over time are a diet long on beef, bacon, processed meats, whole milk, butter, cheese, ice cream, and other saturated fats; blood pressure higher than 190/110; a cholesterol:HDL ratio greater than 5:1; a parent who had heart disease before the age of forty; being more than 40 percent over ideal weight; and a combination of bad health habits and a relative who suffered from osteoporosis, or thinning of the bones. Other negative factors include feeling depressed most of the time and never engaging in physical activity such as walking, gardening, sports, or other exercise.

The ancient Greeks thought of themselves as facing the past, because that was all anyone could ever really know, while the future was an unknown that was always creeping up behind them. For us it's the other way around. We are always facing the future and putting the past behind us.

We don't know what is ahead of us, but we have every reason to expect that the rest of our lives will be longer and better than the later lives of the women behind us.

2

WHAT REALLY HAPPENS
WHEN YOU GROW OLD

WE DON'T LIKE to think about what we'll be like when we're really old, but let's take a few minutes to think about it anyway. What can we reasonably expect to happen to us?

To begin with, we don't know when anything is going to happen. We can't go by other people. The older a person gets, the more likely she is to deviate from the averages we read about. I missed a few periods at forty-five and thought it was menopause, but when I got around to going to the doctor, he found I was pregnant, and to his surprise I was wildly delighted about it — apparently another deviation from the average.

About all we can count on is a slow decline in physical ability punctuated by increasingly frequent ailments requiring medical attention, slow changes in lifestyle and goals to adapt to physical limitations, and continued growth in nonphysical capacities such as reasoning ability, skill at coping, and ability to understand ourselves and other people.

Whenever they come, the changes caused by age alone are minor annoyances that take a woman by surprise. You discover for yourself that you tire sooner and get out of breath more easily; that it's harder to get in and out of coats, see in the dark, adjust to a sudden bright light, catch what people say when they drop their voices, get out of the way of a speeding car, remember what you were doing after an interruption, and answer the phone while the television is on. You notice that there's a bigger difference than there used to be between your good days and your bad ones.

The declines sneak up so gradually that you notice them at first only by what you find yourself doing to make up for them. I realized that my eyes didn't see so well in the dark when I decided I needed a night-light in the hall to the bathroom; that my hair was thinning when I woke up with a mouth full of hairs from my pillow after a night of tossing; that it took longer to get up out of my easy chair when I decided to set the answering machine for four rings instead of three; that my energy varied more widely during the day when I found myself snapping at people who interrupted me in the precious morning hours; that my fingers were growing stiff when I found myself taking a second look at the easy jar openers in mail-order catalogues.

I wondered why I found myself missing a step in a routine operation like dressing or getting breakfast, and why the days seemed to go by faster than they used to do. When I skipped the step of recorking the wine bottle before putting it back on its side in the fridge, I cleaned up the mess and thought it all out. My body was slowing down and could no longer keep up with the timetable for physical routines that was still inside my head. And come to think of it, I no longer tried to cross streets against the light.

Little puzzles clear up. I now know why old people are seldom late for appointments. It's not that they have time on their hands — actually, it's the other way around; they have to be careful about what they do with their dwindling energy — but that they start earlier because they know they can't sprint to make up for an unanticipated delay. And when I wondered why I was tired of the soft blues and greens I used to like, I was told that older people often turn to bright colors because the lens of their eyes thickens, so the shorter wavelengths of blues and greens have a harder time getting through.

A lot more is going on than most of us notice: gradual changes in eyesight, hearing, reaction time, balance, short-term memory, hair color, joint mobility, temperature regulation, sleep patterns, muscle strength, blood pressure, heart rate, endurance, and susceptibility to some diseases. Bones thin. Arteries stiffen. Women imagine the whole world notices when their waistline thickens, their breasts droop, their skin wrinkles, their hair thins, and it gets harder to keep weight off.

Not all the changes are visible. You probably notice that your internal thermostat doesn't work as well as it used to because you find yourself wearing a sweater when the kids are running around in shorts. But you don't notice that you aren't as thirsty as they are on a hot day, so you don't drink as much water as you need. That can be dangerous, because when it's hot or you're overheated, your kidneys don't concentrate waste in your urine as well as they used to do. Instead of conserving the water you need in your body, you keep losing water down the toilet, whatever the weather. So you ought to force yourself to drink water, whether you feel like it or not.

If you're bored with this list by now, it's because none of us wants to hear these messages from our body. Gloria Steinem recalls the moment "when I realized I could only count on going sleepless for one night — and not two — when I needed to meet a deadline." The eye doctor told her she was getting far-sighted. A strange hairdresser commented that her long hair was thin. Like everyone else's, her reaction to the first bodily signals was denial, and then defiance. She was too busy to do anything about them.

Busy or not, most of us find some way to deal with the minor annoyances so we can go on forgetting them. Most older women say their health is good. And except for the tiny minority in nursing homes, most women eighty-five and over say they can take care of their personal needs and home chores without help. Among them are women who have to take medicine every day to keep their blood pressure down or who are getting around on an artificial hip or who are able to read because their cataracts have been removed. In their minds, a medical condition doesn't count if it isn't keeping them from doing what they have to do.

It now appears that real disability rates for people over sixty-five actually declined in the 1980s. The National Long-Term Care

Survey followed a sample of Medicare recipients and found that the total number of people over sixty-five had increased faster than the number of people over sixty-five who were actually disabled or needed help with everyday life.

Maybe we're beginning to see the payoff for better health habits and medical advances like cataract operations, but some of the credit may go to the growing availability of alternative ways of doing what the gerontologists call the "activities of daily living" — things like washing yourself all over, going to the bathroom, dressing, cutting your toenails, getting in and out of bed and up and down stairs, as well as doing such necessary chores as shopping, cooking, housekeeping, and banking. When you talk with women over seventy-five who insist they are doing everything they used to do, they tell you about the easier ways they've found.

When bathing, for instance, many of us have switched to showers to avoid getting in and out of a slippery tub. Luckily, my old-fashioned Afro hairdo is a time-saving wash-and-wear model that shampoos handily while I'm showering. And thanks to the strategically located grab bars I've installed in and around the shower, I expect to be able to keep myself reasonably clean without outside help as long as I can walk. And I've installed a raised toilet, which makes it easier to go to the bathroom.

When dressing, we automatically pass up tight jackets, back zippers, and small buttons that are a trial to stiff shoulders and fingers. I've bought a necklace with a big hook clasp I can connect even at the back of my neck. Wide palazzo pants can be as fancy as a dress and save you from pulling pantyhose up over your hips. Looser and bigger are always better, and so is fewer. It's hard on my shoulders to pull on socks and panties, especially when it's hot, but nobody notices if I go without them in summer.

Cooking for one is no sweat if you stock your freezer with fancy frozen dinners and single portions of a favorite recipe you've made up on a day when you feel like cooking. Eating alone can be boring, but I plan supper around the evening news — a good excuse for shutting the computer down for the day. In the morning I tear out sheets of the paper with interesting articles before getting breakfast, and then I prop them up in a transparent plastic bookholder to read with my orange juice and cereal.

Shopping isn't the fun it used to be, but there are ways to take the muscle out of it. I began shopping by catalogue when even good stores installed racks you have to paw through yourself. Ordering several sizes and styles lets you do the trying-on at home for a bit of postage, which is cheaper in gas and time than hassling through the store.

There used to be alternatives, but everyone now has to get groceries by pushing a cart around a supermarket. Years ago I had my handyman build a ramp from the garage to the back door so I wouldn't have to lift heavy bags up steps, and getting them inside is even easier since he took it upon himself to liberate a shopping cart from a supermarket parking lot for my personal use. But the bags have been getting heavier and heavier. Now that a home delivery milk service has started up in Poughkeepsie, I don't have to go to the store so often. If I plan it right, I can buy enough on one trip to last me three weeks. I go on a day when there's somebody at home to unload the bags the supermarket people have loaded into the car. By the time these occasional forays get to be too much, some young marketing genius will be offering "phone and deliver" grocery shopping and imagining that he has invented it.

I could go on, but the point is that, if you make an exception of grocery shopping, there has never been a time when it was easier to compensate for the decline in breath and muscle that used to make it hard for old women to live alone. Word processors are easier on the body than the manual typewriter on which I wrote my first books. Cars have power steering and brakes. You no longer have to hang out the clothes or stoke the furnace. Telephones have amplifiers. Many new houses are landscaped with a ground cover that doesn't have to be mowed.

Then there are all the marvelous devices, many of them offshoots of space technology, that watch over you. Not only burglar alarms, but wireless transmitters you wear around your neck that automatically phone for help if you fall. Alarms that go off or that relay a signal by phone when the fridge door isn't opened for twenty-four hours. A chair on a track that climbs the stairs. A seat cushion lift to raise you out of your chair.

And comforts! Beds were never like this. Motorized to prop you up ever so much more comfortably than pillows. Heated bed-pads that warm you exactly to the temperature you crave at the moment. Adjustable lights that swivel and brighten to your taste. Remote controls that activate television, VCR, radio. And more, much more just around the corner.

You have to watch these things, though. Some technological wonders are better than others. None of the gadgets for opening small bottle tops that are screwed on too tight for you to open with the strength in your hands work better than a pliers with a mouth wide enough to get around the cap. Cars with automatically locking doors are fine until you forget to take your keys out of the ignition and then can't get into your car without calling an auto mechanic.

Okay, I can hear you saying. I'll be more comfortable. But that's not much to look forward to. In classic psychology, old age is mentally as well as physically downhill all the way. You can slow and make up for the declines, but you can't reverse them, and nothing happens that could possibly be described as intellectual growth. The fountain of youth is a myth, and so is Betty Friedan's Fountain of Age.

In her book of that title, Friedan reports that B. F. Skinner, the great behaviorist, was particularly cross with her for organizing a seminar on "Growth in Aging," insisting that age and growth were contradictory terms. But I recall reading somewhere that in his later years, the inventor of the famous Skinner box for experimenting with infants devised an ingenious bedside desk so that he could roll over and write when he woke up in the middle of the night. Was the invention of this desk what he called "behavioral conditioning to offset the effects of decline like hanging your umbrella on your doorknob to remember to take it along in the event of rain," or was it evidence of intellectual growth?

Psychologists no longer agree that intellectual ability inevitably declines in old age, but it's hard to prove it one way or the other. Most psychological tests and the thinking that went into them grew out of attempts to predict which men would make the best soldiers and how many children would need extra help at school. They were intended for the convenience of bureaucracies that went by the averages. We know that today's older people don't do as well on some of them as today's younger people, but we have just begun to track individuals in their later years to see what really is likely to happen to any one person.

The tests psychologists have devised in an attempt to be precise sound artificial. "Fluid" intelligence — the ability to see similarities in patterns that aren't even related to anything in life — appears to decline, but "crystalline" intelligence, which depends on past experience, seems to increase. And I was gratified to read that *verbal* abilities continue to rise, especially among people who use words all the time in their work. Maybe I'm becoming addicted to the crossword puzzle because I'm getting better at it.

The problem is that such tests are less helpful in predicting the behavior of older people than of young people because older people differ so much from one another. Some improve their scores, some do worse, and others go up and down over the years, so it's not too hard to find what you are looking for in the data. P. B. Baltes, a proponent of late-life growth, speculates that widowhood may trigger mental and personal growth, and a lot of women I've talked with say that's exactly what happened to them.

Some aging changes in females must be due to rogue genes that aren't policed by evolution, because natural selection couldn't affect what used to happen to the few female mammals who survived after their reproductive years were over. But the main reason you differ from your age mates at seventy more than you did at twenty is that different things have happened to you. Folklore tells of shocks that "turn hair white in a single night," and all of us have watched presidents of the United States age visibly in photographs taken during their first few months in office.

Sober research confirms that our bodies and minds respond together. Health and vitality can decline dramatically in the months following the death of a spouse, and caretakers often remark on an eerie lack of aging in people confined for decades in mental institutions where nothing happens to them. In 1969, when the neurologist Oliver Sacks jolted victims of sleeping sickness out of decades of lethargy, one of his patients, Miss R., looked forty years younger. She had raven-black hair, her face was unlined, and she sang the tunes and spoke the language of a flapper. "I *know* it's '69," she told Sacks. "I *know* I'm 64 — but I *feel* it's '26. I *feel* I'm 21."

There is a genetic timetable for what happens to our bodies from birth to death, but as human beings, we "grow old" the way we "grow up." We continue to respond to challenges in ways that increase our control. We continue, in other words, to learn by experience.

All old women aren't alike, so you can never be sure in advance what kind of old woman you are going to turn out to be, but here are some of the changes women attribute to their aging.

I don't miss activities that take more energy than they are worth.

I've discovered how many things I can do without.

I'm better at seeing the woods instead of the trees.

I'm more tolerant and open-minded.

I like myself better than I did when I was younger. (A *New Woman* survey found that women over fifty were more pleased with their lives than women under thirty, and though they were fatter than young women, they were less likely to worry about it.)

I'm less involved in the lives of my children and more worried about the world.

I'm less interested in money beyond what I need to live.

I'm less thrilled by successes and depressed by failures.

To be specific about this old woman, what have I learned, how have I grown since my husband, Tom, died, when I was sixty-six?

Here are some random observations, offered in the spirit of O. E. Hebb, the Canadian psychologist who reported his observations on himself in *Watching Myself Grow Old*.

I've invested in technology that saves energy. I bought my first computer and learned how to use it as Tom lay dying. The bland concentration that it required kept my mind focused on something emotionally neutral. Since then I've gone through several improvements, fuming each time about how long the transition takes. Luckily, the world is full of young hotshots you can hire to sit beside you and teach you. It is a symptom of my advancing age that I no longer really mind how they must privately snicker at my gaffes.

I've become compulsively neat. It started as a reaction to Tom's incorrigible messiness, but it's turned out to be a serendipitous defense against the loss of short-term memory. You don't have to remember where you put your keys if you always put them in the same place.

I've become a bit set in some of my ways. With no one to consider but myself, I've put the daily activities of dressing, bathing, cooking, eating, and exercising on automatic pilot. The down side, of course, is that I've forgotten how to make breakfast for company. The up side is that I no longer have to think about diet and exercise.

I've learned to cut through details faster, though there do seem to be many more details to cut through.

I spend less money on things (fashions, furnishings) and more on people (drivers, cleaners, helpers).

I've learned to let people help me. Robin Walsh is a reference librarian who can dredge anything up out of the Vassar College Library in no time at all. I miss the shock to the nerves of stumbling on other (and distracting) material and the sheer joy of being in my favorite place in the world, but you have to accept losses with your gains.

As my energy declines, I've learned to make better use of it. I don't go to meetings unless I can justify spending the time. I don't read a lot of topical books that I can cover by watching *Booknotes* on C-Span while eating my dinner. (This saves my eyes, which get blurry now toward the end of the day.)

I pass up the glow I used to get from outbursts of righteous indignation. I have other uses for the energy.

I've learned to wait, like the man in "September Song." A lot of things come your way if you just let the old earth take a couple of turns.

I've learned not to cry *ouch* before I'm hurt, and that I can stand a lot more than I think I can. Both tricks are good ways to cope with pain.

I'm learning to shut up and listen. (But I still have a long way to go.)

I've become better at my craft. I'm less worried about pleasing editors and more worried about pleasing myself.

I find myself marveling more at how good people are. For every well-publicized maniac who shoots up a train, millions routinely help other passengers with small acts of kindness, and in the event of disaster, thousands will risk their lives to rescue strangers. What binds us together is stronger than what pulls us apart.

I believe — and I admit that it is an article of faith — that humans are problem-solving animals. The process may be built into our nervous system at a level almost as deep as the reflex that pulls a finger out of the fire. Answers always lead to new questions, because the process itself is programmed into us. If you are reasonably successful in solving one challenge, you raise your sights to tackle a harder one, but if you fail, you drop back to simpler ones.

What this means is that if you have been successful in dealing with the practical challenges of work and family that preempt your middle years, you go on to deal with rarer challenges. Successful artists and scientists break new ground. Business and political leaders retire from making money and putting out fires and start worrying about long-term policy. In 1994, former president Carter undertook, on his own initiative, to visit North Korea and succeeded in getting the stalled talks with South Korea restarted.

That same year, he averted bloodshed in Haiti by persuading the military junta there to accept American intervention. Free of the restraints that hamper a sitting president, he may have averted two wars in a single year. And even those who retire to improve their golf game bring a notorious intensity to a challenge that isn't as simple as it sounds.

The short answer to what's going to happen to us when we're really old is that we're going to be more like ourselves. We grow by adapting to the challenges thrown at us, until at the end, each of us is a curiously wrought, unique organism, one that never was before and will never be again. Too bad it's snuffed out at the end, but consider the enormity of the alternatives!

I happen to believe that the ultimate questions, like "Is there an afterlife?" and "What started the universe?" are mostly artifacts of our programming. They can't be answered, and I'm one of those dull people who lose interest in a question unless there's a way to get a useful answer — at least while answerable questions directly related to our survival are piling up on our plates.

If you hold this view, then successful agers — those who aren't crippled by failure earlier in life — are the most interesting people on earth and the best hope of the human race for continued survival in the future.

Especially when they are old women.

PART II

New Lives:
The Silent Revolution

Back in 1940 when France was falling, I was living in the French Quarter of New Orleans and afraid I was pregnant. Heroism was in the air, so I tried the local remedy for bringing on a period: a pint of whiskey topped off by a stiff dose of castor oil while soaking in a hot tub. Holding my head, for reasons that must have made sense at the time, was a young man who had fled to the Quarter from his Old South family.

"Whatever will become of me?" I asked him when I began to hope I would die.

He sized up the situation and spoke firmly: "You will live to be a Salty Old Woman and the terror of all about you."

"How nice," I thought. And lived.

— "Growing Up to Be a Salty Old Woman," by Caroline Bird; *Ms.*, August 1983

3

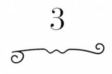

THE
SALTY OLD WOMEN
AROUND US

LOSING A HUSBAND makes a woman feel, at first, as if she is or ought to be invisible. Even if it's really a blessed relief, even if you hated his guts, even if you think you don't care, you don't feel real. "Empty" and "numb" are the words that most often come to mind.

Dr. Joyce Brothers, the advice columnist, thought she was taking the death of her husband of thirty-nine years in stride, but when she backed the Porsche she had bought for his birthday out of the driveway, she began to cry and thought of driving the car over an embankment to stop the pain. She eventually wrote about it and received thousands of letters from women thanking her for reassuring them that they weren't going crazy, because they felt the same way.

Margaret Weinstock was another widow who thought she was doing fine at first. "I had felt surprisingly in control after my husband's death and confidently went out of town to a professional conference, as previously planned, within a month thereafter," she wrote me. "But after I got out of the Boston subway to the hotel headquarters, my wallet was missing. That opened the floodgates and made me feel completely out of control of my then-complicated life. I had not been afraid to go out of town alone before."

Irene Stambler thought her marriage was happy until her husband of twenty-four years and father of their four children told her he wanted to live with another woman, but she didn't actually cry until she got to the supermarket and found she couldn't fill even one cart with what she needed for herself alone.

Clarice Strasser couldn't bear to stay alone in the big house where she and her husband had reared their children. After he died "suddenly on a beautiful day," she just locked the door and rented an apartment in New York City.

Gloria Ross "couldn't stand to be either with people or alone" after her husband died.

California Quint always loved to travel, so when her bedridden husband died after a four-year illness, she had the biggest garage sale of the year in Redding, California, took the train to New York, and caught a freighter to Australia.

Barbara Kelley describes the moment of her divorce as a "plunge into a cold mountain lake." She was the one who wanted it. She felt that it was time to take responsibility for her own happiness. But she lives in Westport, Connecticut, a town of couples, and divorce was scary. Her friends dropped her "as if I had AIDS." The divorce left her without a house and with only enough alimony to pay a small mortgage, "but I didn't mind scaling down when I considered the alternative." In a whirlwind of activity, she moved into a small house, went back to college to get a graduate degree, joined the Unitarian Church, and created a paying job for herself at the hospital where she had been a volunteer. She remembers the first flush of independence as "the most stimulating period of my life."

The psychic work of bereavement is to fill the hole, to take back the energy that was tied up in the relationship that's gone and invest it in something or somebody else. In spite of their initial reactions, all these women shifted gears and went on to new roles that they say are the most rewarding of their lives.

These are typical of the women past menopause who have created a new life for themselves after losing a husband to death, divorce, or a nursing home. A salty old woman celebrates her liberation from the dependence and caution of the childbearing years with what Margaret Mead called "postmenopausal zest" while growing, changing, and creating a lifestyle and role that fit her better than the life she led with a partner.

Some older women have always refused to commit social suttee when they're left on their own. The quintessential salty old woman was Eleanor Roosevelt. When she left the White House for the final time, she already knew what she did *not* want to do. "I did not want to run an elaborate household again," she wrote in *On My Own*. "I did not want to feel old — and I seldom have."

When President Truman asked her to represent the United States at the newly formed United Nations, she objected at first that she wasn't qualified. But when he persuaded her that it was her duty, she went on to use what she had learned about politics at home to further the ideals of brotherhood and compassion that had been growing for decades inside her. It was only when she was on her own that she could grow into a unique individual — in her case, one of the few who have literally changed the world for the better.

Eleanor Roosevelt wasn't alone in this. We expect women to achieve later than men, after the childbearing years. Especially for homemakers, women's unexplored potential builds up in the middle years to explode in the postmenopausal zest Margaret Mead described. Instead of following the male pattern of peaking in middle life and then declining a bit, women achievers are more likely to keep moving on and up, gathering steam as they break out of a cocoon of domesticity to explore new territory.

Like Eleanor Roosevelt, Brooke Astor, one of New York's most creative philanthropists, was a child of privilege whose early married life was not always happy. But when she inherited a fortune from her third husband, Vincent Astor, she used what she had learned about philanthropy from her second husband, the stockbroker Charles Marshall, to put the stamp of her own personality on a city that is hard to influence. Instead of relying on "experts," she started personally investigating every one of the one hundred New York projects she now funds and serving on charitable boards that had theretofore been all-male bastions.

Like Eleanor Roosevelt, Brooke Astor developed a style of her own to explore the possibilities of her unique situation. Only an Astor with an unexpected talent for management could have organized the financial rescue of the New York Public Library. Only a lover of gardens with money could have relieved the barren stoniness of midtown Manhattan with the unexpected little parks between skyscrapers that she calls "outdoor living rooms." But most of all, this patrician who is now in her eighties is enjoying herself. The author of a novel about a love affair between an older woman and a younger man, she is proud of her ageless beauty. Mindful of the impact of her persona, she does not hesitate to visit unspeakable slums in dramatic fashionable clothes designed especially for her. "They don't expect just any old woman," she explains. "They want to see Mrs. Astor."

Astor reminds you of that other dowager, the Queen Mother of England. A story that circulated in the 1980s suggests that the Queen Mother then felt freer to speak her own mind than she had when she was the consort of a reigning king. "I don't know what you old queens are doing down there," she is reported to have shouted down the tube to the devoted gays who staff her kitchen. "But this old queen up here would like a gin and tonic."

Famous salty old women of the past outgrew a series of husbands and lovers, learning something from each of them. Colette was seventy-one and crippled with arthritis when she published *Gigi,* her most famous novel, but she learned the writing craft from her first husband, an older Parisian journalist who locked her up in her room and forced her to write fiction that he published under his own name. After thirteen years of this slavery, she left him to write on her own. Husband No. 2 was one of her editors, who complained that she wrote "too much about love." That was probably only natural, because she was having an affair with a much younger man, who may have provided material for her novels about this kind of match and who eventually became Husband No. 3.

Coco Chanel didn't marry the long list of men who helped her grow, but like Colette, she made her greatest contribution when she was seventy-one. Starting before 1910 with a millinery shop, which was patronized by the other mistresses of the two men who shared the expense of keeping her, she moved up the social scale through liaisons with powerful and wealthy men like the Grand Duke Dmitri of Russia, the British Duke of Westminster, and Pierre Wertheimer, a rich German Jew who helped launch her perfume. Changes of regime didn't stop her. During the German occupation of Paris, she became the mistress of a Nazi general, who allowed her to stay at the Ritz. And in 1954, after years of exile in Switzerland, she reopened the famous House of Chanel to launch the easy, understated, wearable look that has made simple dressing a classic fashion ever since. In a sense, of course, she was always on her own.

These stories should remind us how lucky we are that we no longer have to pursue a talent through a succession of bedrooms, but they also teach us that the capacity for a constructive response to the challenge of the end of a relationship continues long after our childbearing years are over. And now that it is socially acceptable for women to end a marriage that keeps them from growing, more women are exploring the possibilities of growth at later and later ages.

The shock of midlife divorce bumps some women up to a new level of achievement. Without this propellant, Ann Richards might not have become governor of Texas, Phyllis Diller might not have become a nationally known comedian, Frances Lear might not have created a magazine for mature women, and Madeline Albright might not have become our ambassador to the United Nations.

Early in this century, "Ma" (Miriam) Ferguson was elected governor of Texas to fill out her husband's unexpired term, but divorce was the life event that propelled Ann Richards into the governor's seat in 1990. During the 1950s, she married her high school sweetheart, raised four children, and taught school. In the 1960s she volunteered in local Democratic campaigns, and in 1976 she was elected county commissioner, after her husband declined the nomination. Holding office in her own right was the beginning of the end of her marriage. After her divorce, in 1984, she used what she had learned about strategy, fund-raising, administration, and public speaking to craft an image that capitalized on her personality. Brilliant phrasemaking ("Poor George, he can't help it. He was born with a silver foot in his mouth") and the wise-old-woman look of her halo of white hair and profusion of wrinkles (deliberately unretouched in photographs) raised her to the shortlist of potential presidential candidates.

Phyllis Diller put aside her dream of becoming a concert pianist to marry a salesman and bring up their five children, but when he lost his job, she had to go to work. It was he who saw where her true genius lay and persuaded her to audition for a job as a nightclub comic. Her jokes about the trials of domestic life as a suburban housewife launched her on a career that now earns her $1 million a year from movies, television, nightclubs, lectures, and books such as *Phyllis Diller's Housekeeping Hints*, *Phyllis Diller's Marriage Manual*, *The Complete Mother*, and *The Joys of Aging and How to Avoid Them*.

Diller describes her humor as "tragedy revisited," a way of coping with a problem by redefining it as ridiculous. The therapy worked for millions of women who shared Diller's frustrations with her family, her housekeeping, her looks, her seventeen surgical attempts to improve her appearance, and her relations with her mythical husband, "Fang." Her book *Phyllis Diller Tells All about Fang* prompted her first husband's relatives to sue her. A second marriage, to a singer, ended in 1975.

"My two husbands didn't have their own lives," Diller explains, citing the classic competition between a woman who is on her way up and a husband who is on his way down. "Equal is great, like Helen Gurley Brown and her husband. They both have careers, they're both busy. They see each other about two days a week. Freedom is the secret."

At seventy-six, Diller has a live-out beau and no desire to remarry. "But he doesn't want to, either. He's at my house all the time, but we still have our freedom. We each have our own mansion." She continues to wow audiences with her jokes, now on aging, while she goes back to playing the piano and forward to a whole new career in painting.

Frances Lear describes herself as a victim of the feminine mystique who liberated herself from a long-standing marriage in order to find her own identity. At sixty-two, after twenty-eight years of living in the shadow of her husband, the fabulously successful Hollywood producer Norman Lear (*All in the Family* and *Maude*), she divorced him and used her share of their fortune to start a magazine for older women. In celebration of her newfound personhood, she called it *Lear's*, a name to which she felt she had a right because of her long collaboration with her husband, who used her as the prototype for Maude in his sitcom about a feminist.

Lear had no experience in publishing or even in business, but she did have a divorce settlement of $112 million and a burning need to succeed on her own. She describes what happened in her autobiography, aptly titled *The Second Seduction*. "After nearly going mad from the grief of loss — not from the loss of my marriage but from the fact of loss — I understood that my life, at least for the time being, depended upon finding a way out of investing everything in one man." After a great deal of expensive trial and error, and to the surprise of editors and marketers, she succeeded in breaking what *Time* called the "wrinkle barrier." Although *Lear's* never attracted enough advertising to earn a profit, it reflected a positive image of older women to a half-million readers until Frances Lear folded it in 1994 to start a television company and make a video advising women on how to manage their money.

Madeleine Albright had all the ingredients for a starring role in international affairs when her husband of twenty-three years left her for a younger woman. The multilingual daughter of an anti-Communist Czech refugee who brought her to the United States when she was eleven, she grew up knowing about central European politics and went on to get a Ph.D. in Russian affairs at Columbia. Marriage to Joe Medill Patterson Albright, *Newsday*'s Washington bureau chief, taught her about how news is made and brought her skills as a political volunteer and fund-

raiser to the attention of Democratic party leaders. But it was
the shock of her divorce that forced her to put all these pieces
of her life together. Her subsequent research for universities and
think tanks led, after the fall of communism, to testimony on
Capitol Hill and appearances on the MacNeil/Lehrer television
news show. In 1993, President Clinton appointed her to Eleanor
Roosevelt's old job as ambassador to the United Nations.

There's something disturbing about the spectacle of a woman
thriving after the end of her marriage. Were Lear and Albright
running on the adrenaline of women scorned? Were Richards
and Diller harpies who outgrew and then shamelessly deserted
the fathers of their grown children? Whatever the circumstances
of a divorce, tradition finds a way to blame it on the wife. All
four could as easily be feminist heroines who broke out of marriages that were keeping their talent under wraps.

No one, least of all the players, knows what really happens inside
a marriage, much less who's to blame for its breakup. But one
thing can be determined from the outside: whatever the causes
and whoever holds the moral high ground, in real life divorce
usually hurts an older woman more than it hurts an older man.
Heroines or villains, these women have demonstrated that it is
possible for a woman to put together the random pieces of her
early life to create a place in the world that is uniquely her own,
and that, of course, is the reason we are talking about them here.
Career success is one of the ways in which women use later years
on their own to actualize themselves.

But not all salty old women are rich, famous, or privileged.
In 1992, ninety-two-year-old Clarice Humphrey became the oldest person ever to register to vote for the first time in the state
of Alabama. It was one of the first things she did after the death
of her husband, who didn't believe in women's voting and "always
took care of voting" for both of them. She voted for Bill Clinton.

Some of the most influential older women have been black.
Whatever the reason (perhaps the heritage of slavery has been
more crippling to men), older women have often spoken up for

the African American community. Think of fragile Harriet Tubman, who left her freeborn husband behind to lead black slaves to freedom, as surefooted as the elephant matriarch that tests the path for the pack. After her husband died, she remarried a black Union soldier twenty-two years her junior.

Think of Sojourner Truth, who used her legal enfranchisement to leave her still enslaved husband and five children to preach against racism and sexism. Although she was illiterate, her powerful words still move us: "I have plowed, and planted, and gathered into barns, and no man could head me — and aren't I a woman?"

Unlike white women, black women have always had to earn money and have often been able to get better jobs than their men, so it has been easier for them to become leaders in business. It is an interesting footnote to history that the first black American to become a self-made millionaire may also have been the first American woman to attain that distinction. Mme. C. J. Walker developed her hot-comb method of grooming African Americans' hair when she was an illiterate single mother with $1.50 in her pocket. She later married Walker, a newspaper sales agent who taught her advertising and mail-order methods, but she divorced him when he failed to support her vision of a national business.

Black women find it easy to extend their concern and care to children beyond the immediate family. A good example is "Mother" Clara Hale, the founder of Harlem's Hale House, for the addicted babies of drug users. After her husband died, Hale supported her three children by taking other children into her own home. At sixty-five, shortly after retiring from paid foster care, she started taking in addicted babies and caring for them at her own expense. She demonstrated that old-fashioned holding and rocking and cherishing could see these babies through the agonies of withdrawal. When she was seventy, she was able to raise enough money to set up a brownstone home for them. She continued to care for the little addicts and to run up and down the five flights of stairs to her own room on the top floor until her death, at eighty-seven.

The fight against racism and sexism is a favorite late-life role for feisty African American women. When Barbara Harris was in college, she marched with Martin Luther King, Jr. at Selma. She went on to work for social justice in the Protestant Episcopal Church while earning her living as a public relations executive at the Sun Oil Company. As soon as ordination became possible for women, she started studying for the ministry. In spite of her divorce, in 1989 she became the first woman bishop in the long history of the church. In high-heeled shoes and with spiky mauve fingernails, the Right Reverend Barbara Harris projects a contemporary image. "Forget the ring, sweetie," she told a woman who wanted to kiss her gold-and-diamond bishop's ring. "Kiss the bishop."

In 1993, another divorced black woman was doing her best to broaden the image of the United States Senate, a body as traditionally male and white as the Episcopal House of Bishops, on which it was modeled. Instead of keeping quiet and "going along," as freshmen are supposed to do, newly elected senator Carol Moseley-Braun of Illinois captured the television cameras by rising to protest the renewal of an obscure patent application for the United Daughters of the Confederacy, a southern organization that continues to use the Confederate flag as its insignia.

Some of the most independent, inventive, and flexible women are disabled. After her divorce, Barbara Sagarin found she could make a good living driving a San Francisco cab. Hand surgery forced her out of the business, but not out of driving, which made it possible for her to live independently. She persuaded the authorities to give her a special permit for a gadget that makes it possible for disabled people to drive with one hand. She used to carry her groceries up to her second-floor apartment one bag at a time by sitting down on each step.

Talk to Mary Cashatt on the telephone and she sounds like any other widow minding a five-year-old granddaughter. Since her retirement on a pension from thirty years of work with the

Commonwealth of Virginia, she has earned money for travel and extras by doing consulting jobs for church and government agencies in her area of expertise. In her later years alone, she is passing on to others the unique achievement of her work and life.

Mary is paralyzed from the waist down. Her spinal cord was cut in an automobile accident during her senior year in high school, but this total disability didn't stop her from achieving college, career, friends, romance, marriage, motherhood, and grandchildren. A special intercom allowed her to participate in her high school classes by phone, and at graduation she delivered the valedictory address from a wheelchair. After an intensive rehabilitation program, she learned how to bathe, dress, go to the bathroom, and fold a wheelchair into the back of a two-door car well enough to attend the university near her home.

After college, she taught English and did psychological testing at the Woodrow Wilson Rehabilitation Center in Fishersville, Virginia, where her wheelchair was no oddity. There she fell in love with the intern chaplain, a divinity student suffering from multiple sclerosis. They married after his graduation from seminary. She had no trouble getting pregnant and delivering a son, or using her strong arms to lift him out of a drop-side crib, and by devising a wide strap that circled her wheelchair, she was able to hold him on her lap and even take him along to the supermarket. When her son was ready for school, she went back to her job, and when illness forced her husband to retire, she was able to support and care for the family. After her husband died, she and a girlfriend spent three weeks traveling in China. How did she manage her wheelchair in a strange country? "I'm not shy," she says. "I don't mind asking for help."

Such women are pioneers who have continued to grow to the very end of their lives. They have a lot to teach other women, but very little is known about how they differ from age mates who think their lives are over.

It isn't easy even to find them. They don't think of themselves as image-busters or pioneers. They aren't organized, and they don't fall easily into categories, because each of them is celebrating what is most unique about herself. Only when we encourage them to talk about what is on their minds do we learn about their new, self-generated agendas.

Not the least of the problem of finding them is that they are all around us. Like the hidden figures in picture puzzles, they are lost in a big picture about something else, so you can't detect them unless you know what you are looking for. You have to be willing to see them apart from some category in which they prefer to see themselves.

What I tried to do was to find and talk to enough women who were doing something worth passing on to other women that I missed as little as possible. I didn't know what those things would be in advance, so I cast a wide net. Some of the two hundred I eventually accepted as pioneers were women who answered appeals in Bard Lindeman's syndicated newspaper column, "Prime Time," and a half-dozen specialized publications like the Peace Corps *Hotline*. Some were friends or friends of friends. Almost everyone I interviewed referred me to others. And like some of the women in this chapter, a few were national figures whose careers are on the public record.

As I talked to the first ones, I listened to what they had on their minds, searching for recurrent themes. If I thought they had something to pass along, I invited them to join the database. Almost everyone I invited agreed to talk to me by phone, to fill out written questionnaires on topics about which they could be especially helpful, to give me basic data about themselves for the purpose of analysis, to field my calls back for specific information, and to trust me to check with them before attaching their names to any of the experiences they shared with me.

I wasn't looking for a true cross-section of the population of older women on their own, and I didn't get one. These women were clearly more privileged than the average in every measurable way. According to the census, 48 percent of female households over fifty-five who are living alone have less than $10,000 a year in total income, compared with only 13 percent of the women in this book, and 22 percent have more than a high school education, compared with a whopping 89 percent of these women. In addition, these women were much more apt to continue working for money after what is regarded as normal retirement age. The census reports that only 8.4 percent of women over sixty-five are in the labor force, compared with 49 percent of these.

When I saw how skewed my sample was becoming, I made an effort to recruit women in every income, educational, occupational, racial, and geographic category, so my sample would include as many options as possible. And it wasn't as hard as I had feared to find lifestyle pioneers who were poor, black, disabled, or without a college education.

4

CUSTOM-MADE

ROLES

"All the world's a stage,
And all the men and women merely players:
They have their exits and their entrances;
And one man in his time plays many parts,
His acts being seven ages."
— Shakespeare, *As You Like It*

EVERYONE NEEDS a part to play in some human drama —
an identity, a handle, a public label, a quick way to explain herself
to a stranger. Although Shakespeare allocated roles by age, he himself
and a few favored men of his time began to choose their roles
instead of playing the roles assigned to them. But choice has come
more slowly to women.

Losing the role of wife is harder than losing the role of husband. Even women who think they are liberated find it hard to
kick the habit of going along with what women are supposed to
do. Too many still accept the retired role, the sick role, the client
role, the victim role — parts traditionally assigned to them in
scenarios created by employers, pension systems, doctors, and social workers.

Psychologists now suspect that it's bad for our mental health
to let other people define us. In 1986, the sociologist Phyllis Moen
and her coworkers at Cornell University's Life Course Institute
reinterviewed 313 women whom they had first interviewed as young
married mothers in 1956. They found that the more roles the
women played, the higher they scored in satisfaction and self-

esteem. The multirole women were even healthier and longer-lived than those with fewer roles.

The six roles the Cornell researchers counted — worker, church member, friend, neighbor, relative, and club or organization member — weren't mutually exclusive, and they didn't interfere with a home-centered lifestyle. Their value seems to have been that they gave women confidence in themselves and practice in switching roles, which came in handy later on, when their homemaking years were over.

And that's what I found, too. The women who fare best when they are left alone in their later years are acting in plays of their own choosing, sometimes in parts for which they don't look the type, and increasingly in roles that aren't even on file with Central Casting. Here are some examples.

INTERNATIONAL VOLUNTEER

Martha Peterson worked as a music teacher, social worker, literacy leader, and medical technologist during the forty-two years of her marriage, but after her divorce she devoted time to finding herself as a single woman with the help of religion, psychology, and activity. She spent 1990 as a Peace Corps volunteer in Pakistan, taught Bible for four weeks in the Ukraine during 1992, and was teaching English at Hebei Teachers College, Shijiajuang City, People's Republic of China, in 1994.

HISTORIAN

California Quint was named by her father, who went to California in 1909 and fell in love with his adopted state. She was always interested in local history and served at one time as president of the local historical society. She worried about the unsorted mess of eight thousand books, papers, and photographs that well-meaning people had bequeathed to the society, which didn't have the funds to take care of them. So when her husband became an invalid shortly after she retired from the state highway department, she used the time she had to spend at home volunteering to help sort the documents. Some of them turned out to be priceless; for instance, photographs taken before the construction of Shasta Dam showed what the area looked like before it became Shasta Lake.

California bought the historical society four computers and enlisted her computer-minded brother to help set up a system. She has taught close to a dozen volunteers, including four or five who are over seventy-five, how to use the computers. The photographs are classified by date and place, for the convenience of divers exploring the lakebed as well as the descendants of people who lived on land that is now inundated.

EXPLORER

Dot Smith had always dreamed of mountains while helping her husband raise sheep on a New Zealand farm. When he died, she left the farm in the care of a grown son and took off for Peru, Nepal, Sikkim, and Tibet, then went on to hunt for rhododendrons in China. At sixty-seven, in spite of a hip replacement, she signed on as a member of the general crew of a sailboat expedition to investigate pollution in Antarctica.

PHILANTHROPIST

Ruth Hayre was a teacher in the Philadelphia schools and became the system's first black high school principal. After she was widowed and retired, she established a fund at Temple University to provide college tuition for 119 students of the sixth-grade classes of two schools, who will be admitted to college when they complete high school.

ACTRESS

Helen Breed confined herself to amateur theatricals while her husband was alive, but at the age of sixty-five she started doing parts in Off-Off-Broadway productions, giving herself five years to make a place for herself in paid, professional theater. In 1982, a little more than five years later, she appeared in *The Holly and the Ivy* at the Roundabout Theater in New York. She went on to nine or ten screen parts, most notably as one of the older women in *The Witches of Eastwick*. At eighty-two she was "appearing" in TV commercials, doing voiceovers with her faultless upper-class diction.

ATHLETE

Berniece Looney was an All-American long-distance swimmer who collected 135 medals and 35 trophies. After World War II cheated her out of competing in what would have been the 1944 Olympics, when she was at the top of her power, marriage and three children sidelined her into coaching and teaching for more than thirty years.

They weren't good years. One son killed himself before his eighteenth birthday, and the other died of a brain aneurysm two months after his daughter was born. When her husband took up with a younger woman, Berniece divorced him, and found herself deserted by the friends she had known when she was part of a couple. In order to have something of her own, she started to coach and swim at Y's (she thinks that the exercise helped her sleep at night and roll with the punches).

Then, when she was fifty-seven, while coaching adults for the North Carolina Senior Games in Wilmington, she decided to compete herself in the 55–59 age class. Not only did she win, but she met and soon married sixty-one-year-old Don Greetham, another competitor, who had recently lost his wife. She went on to compete in senior meets and win one gold medal after another, just as she had done before her marriage. She and Don now train together. They are "real jocks," say their grown children.

IMPRESARIO

Olga Bloom is a professional violinist who often wished that the public could enjoy the intimate chamber music that her musician friends played with one another for fun at her home. So when she saw an ad for an old coffee barge, she and her husband mortgaged their house in Brooklyn to buy it and make it over into an acoustically perfect little low-rent concert hall for small neighborhood audiences. Then, when they had gotten as far as docking it illegally at the Fulton Ferry Landing, Tobias Bloom suddenly died.

Rather than give up the dream, Olga rented out her home, moved onto the barge, and started working on it. When nearby longshoremen saw a tiny woman in her fifties swinging a hammer, they volunteered to help. "It was like the reverse of *Mephisto*," she told a reporter. "I sold my soul to God, and then everything I needed came just when I needed it." Bargemusic, Ltd., as she called her venture, attracted government and private funding that allows Olga to give low-cost concerts twice a week all year round to an audience of 130. Like the minister of a small congregation, Olga can shake hands with every member of the audience.

These are only a few of the women who have found fulfilling new roles they never played while they were wives.

Women who used to play bridge on free afternoons are now known all over the country as competitors in tournaments arranged by national associations. Women who used to go birdwatching on Sunday mornings near home have become environmentalists, exploring species they never knew existed in order to help preserve them. Women who were casual knitters, quilters, pot makers, or jewelry makers while they were raising families are selling and exhibiting at craft fairs all over the country. Women who loved dolls or antiques have become authorities known to all other collectors. Museum docent, whistle blower, genealogist, rock climber — it's hard to find anything in the whole wide world that isn't conferring a new identity on some older women.

Of course, these women are all unusually successful. They wouldn't have talked to me if they didn't think they had secrets to pass on to others. So it is fair to ask whether there is a pattern in the new roles they've found that will encourage other women to explore the possibilities of their later years alone.

It's fair to ask, perhaps, but hard to answer. Existing classifications, set up for younger people, aren't much help. A routine office job can be the same old rut to a woman who earned half the family income throughout her marriage but an exciting adventure to a lifelong homemaker. The line between profit and nonprofit gets vague in later life. Does a hobby of collecting antiques become a business when a woman begins to earn money as an appraiser? And what about women who invest their energy in an autobiography which they hope will explain their lives not only to themselves but to their children?

I finally decided to come up with my own labels for a woman's identity, conferring a role not according to what it looks like from the outside but, in part at least, by what it means to the woman who has adopted it. If she is in the labor force, is she working primarily for the money, the pleasure of the work, the good it can do, the recognition that goes with it, or because it proves something about herself? Everyone's motives are mixed, so my categories are inevitably untidy, but they begin to spy out the possibilities.

The most popular *motive* among the women in this book is helping people outside the family. Those who want to do good by changing people's opinions I classified as working for change. Since nest eggs so often wind up in the hands of older women, some of those women have found a new role in philanthropy. Some older women use their new freedom to seek adventure or go into politics. Many more find a new direction in paid work, in practicing an art or a craft, or in becoming a better person through life review, travel, study, or psychotherapy.

These, then, are my classifications: Seeking Adventure, Doing Good, Working for Change, Sharing Wealth, Breadwinning, Practicing a Profession, and Creating Art.

SEEKING ADVENTURE

Wilma Young was dying to get out of the car and dive into the woods on the Alaska Highway, but she was alone and afraid she might meet a bear. She had always wanted to explore the wilderness and primitive societies, but her husband didn't share her interest, so she had contented herself with reading about them. When he died unexpectedly, she thought of joining the Peace Corps, but she had never been on her own away from family and friends and wondered whether she could hack it.

Alaska looked like a test. It was reasonably close to home, and the prevailing language was English. She enrolled in Elderhostel courses about Alaskan Indian life in Juneau, Sitka, and Fairbanks, visited an aunt in Montana, and struck north alone in her car.

Somewhat to her surprise, she found it exhilarating to drive along without a trace of humankind in sight. Even when she was scared, she wasn't lonely. At one camp stop, she persuaded a couple from Massachusetts to go hiking with her. They saw no bears. She gave herself a Brownie point for coping.

As the road wound on, she learned that she liked her own company — preferred it, really — and could manage on her own in emergencies. Unexpectedly, she lost her fear of death. She had always worried a lot about the actual experience of dying, and a course for hospice volunteers about what actually happens hadn't been much help. But in Alaska she learned how death was built into the cycle of hunting and fishing life. Native Alaskans accepted it matter-of-factly, and their calm was catching. She now thinks of dying as a normal part of living. Confident in herself, she came home and joined the Peace Corps.

Wilma Young is no freak. It is thought that men are generally more willing to take risks than women, but psychologists can't establish that age has anything to do with it. When presented with a series of choices, older respondents are as likely as young ones to choose the risky alternatives. And not only is there no support for the myth that people grow timid with age, but it can work the other way around.

Lois Gould remembers herself as a timid city girl afraid of falling, climbing, throwing and catching, the dark, sliding down a banister, being called on, and jumping rope — a girl who closed her eyes when a ball was thrown her way. Then, after twenty-two years of marriage, with two grown sons and seven published novels, she felt an uncontrollable urge to get out of the city and go alone to the wild northwestern coast of Ireland, where, she'd heard, the rain blows sideways.

Her friends thought she was crazy, but she did it and she loved it — even when her car sank deep in mud, with its front end dangling over a chasm for hours; even when the wind filled her teeth with sand and slammed her car door shut. Once, driving along the foot of a cliff, she wondered whether she could climb it, and with no one around to knock sense into her head, she got out of the car and did it. She rescued a baby seal. She tried to rent a lonely coast guard station. She wrote and walked and climbed and got lost and made friends with strangers. She loved it so much that now, although she returns every now and then to New York, she spends most of the year in Ireland.

Why? When *New Choices* magazine asked her to explore the phenomenon, she found that she wasn't the only late-life adventurer. An acrophobic fifty-one-year-old woman told her that she had forced herself to go up on a Ferris wheel twice in the same week and then moved on to kayaking, roller skating, and quitting her dull, safe job for challenging volunteer work.

Gould thinks older women need to take risks to pick up the unfinished business of their adolescence. After they've raised their children and done all they are supposed to do, they look around and say to themselves, "Well, I've done it. Now let's see, where was I before all this started?" She thinks this "second childhood" is good for them.

Betty Friedan notes that late-life adventuring isn't confined to rich males. In *The Fountain of Age*, she records that she was struck by "how often, especially for women, the opening to new adventure in age came with the loss of a certain kind of economic security or social status, through widowhood or divorce." But she doesn't say why.

Margaret Mead's "postmenopausal zest" is the most plausible explanation. A tomboy loses some of her daring at puberty, when her hormones program her to protect her body, but she gets it back when her childbearing years are over. This burst of energy can be a marital problem if it occurs when a husband's declining testosterone level is inclining him to a life of domestic cocooning, but when he's out of the picture, there's nothing to keep the woman from doing something he would have vetoed.

Jane Woodward's husband was an invalid who thought scuba diving was too dangerous for her. After his death she went on a snorkeling binge that took her to obscure islands in the West Indies. And she liked the thrill so much that she kept doing it. At seventy-two, in spite of foot surgery that "slowed me down a bit," she was diving fifty feet with a fifty-pound oxygen tank on her back in order to qualify as a certified scuba diver before exploring the challenging waters of the Great Barrier Reef in the South Pacific.

Like adolescent boys, newly liberated older women like to test themselves. They like to prove, mostly to themselves, that they can still do it. That's what you hear when you listen to Wilma Young or Dot Smith or Berniece Greetham. But there are other motives, of course. Just getting away is enticing for widows like Jane Woodward and California Quint, who have been tied down at home caring for an invalid husband. And almost all of these women have felt a dash of "Now it's my turn" and "If I'm ever going to do any of the outrageous things I've thought of doing, it's now or never."

If ever a woman deserved a turn for herself, it was Jeanne Kretschmer. More conscientious and more burdened than most, she brought all the skills of coping for others to a career of adventure as dazzling as the final burst of a fireworks display.

Jeanne married after two years of college and worked long, hard hours helping her husband develop the Detroit Business Institute, a very successful chain of business schools. When she was fifty-one her husband died, leaving her with seven children and a business to run. The first few years she was tied down managing the business and caring for the three youngest children as well as her ailing parents. But after the nest emptied, she turned the day-to-day management of the schools over to one son and got out of his way by moving to Fort Lauderdale to help another son start a business of teaching and writing about marine navigation.

Jeanne didn't move to Florida for a life of quiet retirement. She was ready for something new. She'd been on a boat only twice before, but she thought it would be fun to live on one, so she bought a trawler named *Papa John* and moved onto it with her dog, Missy.

"A dog is a very good companion when you are first on your own," she says. "You have to walk the dog. That keeps you in shape, and you get to meet the most interesting people who also have to walk their dogs." (While keeping in shape, Jeanne the businesswoman recouped some of the expense of the trawler by letting her son use it to teach coastal navigation.)

Look for something new and you're apt to find it. Tim literally sailed into Jeanne's life. He docked his chartered boat next to hers and accepted her invitation to attend a course she and her son were giving in celestial navigation. Tim was a few years younger, divorced, and newly retired. It didn't take long for them to fall in love and decide to sail around the world together.

They were not, however, entirely daft. Although a newcomer to sailing, Jeanne was a quick learner with two requirements for long-distance sailing: she was never seasick and she could cook under adverse circumstances. Tim had raced sailboats in his youth and was a fanatic about details, so they spent five months outfitting a thirty-eight-foot sloop, the *Epoch*.

The year Jeanne was sixty, they set sail, just the two of them. From Fort Lauderdale they sailed to the keys, across the Caribbean to the Panama Canal (where they were assigned to a lock with a big freighter, which nearly ran over them), and on to the wide Pacific.

It takes more than romance for a crew of two to sail across the Pacific. For starters, they couldn't sleep together at night because one of them had to stand watch, but with four hours on and four hours off, neither of them ever got a full night's rest. Jeanne kept herself awake on her watches by writing verses about their adventures. They survived a cyclone in Tahiti, only to encounter others in Australia and Sri Lanka. They were stuck for a month on a South Sea island where checks and credit cards couldn't be converted into French francs, the only currency the local merchants would accept.

They were in no hurry. In the Southern Hemisphere, the winter months are typhoon season, so they spent the first winter ashore in French Polynesia, the second in Australia, the third in Sri Lanka and Bombay, the fourth in the Mediterranean. They didn't feel cut off, because in most of their ports they were only an airplane ride away from their children.

To everyone's surprise, Jeanne's serious-minded daughter Liz followed in her mother's footsteps. After her college graduation, she agreed to return to Australia with her mother for a few weeks' vacation before starting her career. But her mind was changed by a young South African on a schooner docked just behind the *Epoch* on the Burnett River. Liz moved onto the schooner, and the two young people sailed it to South Africa, where they were married.

The adventure ended as unexpectedly as it had begun. Jeanne and Tim never made it all around the world. They left the *Epoch* at Mallorca and traveled separately to the States for a visit, but Tim unexpectedly died the day he got home.

Back in Michigan, Jeanne was down but not out. Volunteer work was too tame. More challenging was a Peace Corps recruiting ad on television that promised "the hardest job you'll ever love." But would they take a sixty-seven-year-old woman?

Jeanne persuaded them. She had proven her ability to get along with all kinds of people, she let them know she was taking Spanish lessons in case they were worried about her ability to learn languages, and her experience in teaching and administering business was just what the Third World needed. She spent the next two years in the Fiji Islands, living in a primitive hut without plumbing or furniture while coaching the Fijians in the arcane art of keeping books for their small businesses of selling local handicrafts to tourists. Now in her seventies, she lectures on international development and works for the American Field Service, helping young people adapt to studying in a foreign culture.

"The hardest job you'll ever love": that challenge has captured the imagination of older women ever since Lillian Carter wrote about her Peace Corps service in India after she was widowed. The Peace Corps is choosy about its volunteers; applicants have to pass a tough medical examination and are screened for mental, physical, and moral qualities. But unlike private employers, the Peace Corps doesn't use age as a proxy for characteristics that are hard to measure, such as adaptability, and it does consider individual differences in making assignments. Jeanne had a skin disease that made her susceptible to malaria, so she wasn't sent to places where that disease was common.

The Peace Corps can be a poor woman's passport to adventure. For older women who qualify, it offers physical, emotional, and social challenges, a chance to help others, and, because of its age-equal policies, a chance to do professional work that private employers hesitate to give to older beginners.

Two widows in their fifties were surprised at how well they adapted to living for months without electricity or running water. During her three years in Tonga, Gloria Ross lived on what she could cook on a one-burner Primus stove, washed her jeans, towels, and sheets by hand in a plastic bowl, got around on a bike, and kept in touch with the outside world through a radio that transmitted only a few hours a day. And she loved it. "We wrote letters. We interacted with our neighbors. I reread paperback books. The real culture shock was coming home to find everyone glued to television."

For Cynthia Coupe, the loneliness was more difficult to bear than the privations. She missed having someone around to talk to every day who was going through the same thing. Still, she agrees with Gloria Ross that the culture shock of coming back — Peace Corps people call it the "reentry" — is harder than getting into the foreign culture to begin with. Every Peace Corps returnee experiences it differently. A lot depends on where you live, Cynthia says, and your financial situation, and your prospects for employment at home.

Working in exotic parts of the world is so attractive that people with money and time are willing to pay for the experience. Vilma Kohn, the widow of a research scientist, has made volunteering with scientific expeditions a permanent way of life. When her husband died after a short illness, she was fifty-seven, her four children were out of college, and she was studying for a master's degree in anthropology. "Grieving went on," she writes, "but the need to study for exams and to prepare written reports on various archeological topics kept me anchored in the world. His death left a void that hasn't been filled, but life, as the song reminds us, goes on."

At sixty-seven, Vilma is a volunteer archeologist who maps, surveys, excavates, and catalogues all over the world. Her new career provides a steady diet of exotic places, new people, the thrill of discovery, and learning about vanished cultures. Digging can be tedious work, but she never stays long enough in any one spot to be bored. For instance, she worked for a few weeks in Buenos Aires digging into the early history of the city with a project in urban archeology, then went on to the totally different challenge of restoring early Incan textiles in Chile.

But for sheer adventure and the thrill of danger, it's hard to beat exploring the world beneath the seas, in places whose names send most people scurrying for a big atlas. Vilma has studied reef growth in the Canary Islands, hundreds of miles west of Morocco in the Atlantic, and off Bonaire, an island in the Dutch Antilles, north of Venezuela. She has traced octopuses in the Tuamotus, an archipelago west of Tahiti in the Pacific, collected fish for the New York Aquarium in the Red Sea and on the Great Barrier Reef, and excavated a Dutch trading ship full of clay pipes that went down in the seventeenth century off the coast of the Dominican Republic. What has she liked best? It's hard to compare, she says, because the attraction is that each adventure has its own flavor.

Women hooked on archeology continue digging under adverse

conditions well into their seventies. It's painstaking, labor-intensive work, and it isn't for everyone. Vilma Kohn is especially well qualified because she has never stopped going to school. She earned her Ph.D. in zoology between her second and third children, went to law school when she was forty-one, acquired her certification in scuba diving at fifty-one, and has since taken specialized courses in archeological techniques and learned Spanish in preparation for South American digs. Credentials are important, because access to scientific expeditions is controlled by university or museum academics. The academics in the scientific field know what's available, and a great many are listed by an organization called Earthwatch, in Watertown, Massachusetts.

Volunteers are needed all over the developing world, but the opportunities are hard to find and arrange. Dorothy Conlon was a secretary in the Foreign Service in Taipei back when she had to give up her job to marry a Foreign Service officer. She came to relish the culture shock of living in a new country every few years, and after her husband died, she looked for a way to volunteer overseas. After months of hunting, she went to Bangkok to teach English under the auspices of WorldTeach in Cambridge, Massachusetts. She paid her own airfare but got housing and the $140 a month Thailand pays its teachers. Similar small nonprofit services are springing up to make such matches.

You can volunteer to work abroad even if you don't have a scarce skill or a lot of time or money. Would you like to spend three weeks repairing classroom furniture in Indonesia or giving Indonesian schoolchildren computer software and showing them how to use it? Global Volunteers of St. Paul will arrange it, including accommodations in a guesthouse with indoor plumbing, for $1,775 plus airfare. If you prefer, you can spend a similar tax-deductible vacation working for local people on any of a broad array of projects in another developing country, an emerging democracy, or even in a poor community in the United States.

Adventure is so big a pull that the travel industry makes money on "risk recreation" experiences such as river rafting, which parallel the Outward Bound programs, designed "to help young people and adults discover and extend their own resources and abilities by confronting them with a series of increasingly difficult challenges." A consumer researcher for the risk recreation business thinks that reckless activities compensate for what people aren't achieving on their jobs. This sounds like a young male reaction, but older women raft down the Colorado River too.

When Betty Friedan was in her sixties, she joined "Going Beyond," an Outward Bound expedition designed for people over fifty-five. She hoped to find out how older people take risks and seek adventure in ways they couldn't when they were young. She managed rafting down a whitewater river and surviving twenty-four hours alone in the woods, but she balked at rappelling down a cliff and had to be unceremoniously rescued from the challenge.

"I just didn't feel in control winging around that cliff," she confessed to Brian Lamb of C-Span. "And I thought, I don't have to test myself this way anymore." What she had learned about herself was that she had the moral courage to resist the peer pressure on which Outward Bound relies.

Friedan's experience suggests that vibrant older people continue to take risks, but their adventures aren't necessarily physical. Feminist psychologists say that women are more willing than men to take the risks of speaking their minds and sharing their feelings with other people. If so, these are the kinds of risks that almost every woman finds herself taking more often as she grows older. Our youth-oriented culture dismisses the frankness of old women as an embarrassment, but traditional cultures seem to have found a use for it. In their legends, it is the old women who stand up and speak truth to power.

DOING GOOD

After she was widowed, Lucy Hendrickson became the Salvation Army of the small California town where she had lived all her life. Anyone who wanted to get rid of old furniture was welcome to dump it in her big wooden chicken house. There she also stored items she picked up at flea markets to feed her hobbies of restoring furniture and making quilts. Sometimes she sold her handiwork for extra money to finance travel abroad, but most of the time she gave it away to people in need.

Age did not stop her. When arthritis kept her from making regular quilts, she found a way to make blankets by patching material together and tying it with yarn. At ninety, when she had to stop traveling, she waited for people to come to her.

"I find people in need," she wrote me. "Like one family recently. Lost all in a Texas flood, came here to California with three children and found an old trailer to sleep in. A worker from Mental Health called me about them and asked me to help. I used my phone. One of my retired friends is a good carpenter, so he's helping them restore a twelve-by-twenty-four-foot trailer and make built-ins. Another family offered a washer-dryer — still works, but they got a new one. So on and on. Life is beautiful and I thank the Lord daily for health and ideas and determination and life."

The tradition of neighborly help is surprisingly strong among older women, even in cities. Ruth Brinker, a sixtyish widow who grew up in South Dakota, now lives in San Francisco, but she still feels "compelled when someone in trouble comes across my path. Usually it's small things, people in the neighborhood."

When she discovered that a friend with AIDS was going without food because he was too weak to cook, she started using the pay she received for working at Meals on Wheels to prepare and deliver a hot meal and a bag lunch to seven AIDS patients every day. Newspaper accounts brought help, donations, and recognition by the Giraffe Project, a small foundation dedicated to publicizing individuals who "stick their necks out" to help others.

Helping, listening, counseling, nurturing, training, coaching, comforting, inspiring, making a difference in someone's personal life — these are the roles that have always been most attractive to older women. Only now what used to be neighborly help is provided through increasingly specialized nonprofit organizations.

There are a lot of people who need help. Poor children. Single mothers. Drug addicts. Refugees. Cancer patients. Battered wives. School dropouts. Shut-ins who need a lift to the hospital. Caregivers who need an afternoon off. People who never learned to read. The list keeps growing.

You may have to hunt for it, but whatever you want to provide, there's someone who needs it and can't pay for it. More than ninety different occupational tasks were being done on a volunteer basis by *Modern Maturity* readers who responded to a questionnaire in the April-May 1988 issue. Somewhere in the United States, even retired doctors, lawyers, and business executives are donating their skills to people or causes they feel are worthy.

Why do older people do it? More than half of the older people queried for a Commonwealth Fund study of 1992 — and even more of those between sixty-five and seventy-four — say that helping other people has become more important to them in the past few years. Ask them directly and you may get a noncommittal answer. They do it to keep active, because they have the time, because someone asked them, or simply because volunteering has become a habit.

At seventy-five, Virginia Kerns continues to volunteer because she has "always done it," she writes from Tucson. "I don't consider myself some 'do gooder.' . . . Rather I'm a 'point of needer.'" She helps victims of family abuse and chairs a group that gives small scholarships to students in medical fields. A lot of her age mates are still at it, too. At an informal fifty-eighth reunion of Vassar '35, one of my classmates offhandedly mentioned volunteering for the Lighthouse as a companion for a totally blind woman, while another turned out to be volunteering as a teacher in a maximum security prison.

For some, of course, helping those in need is a religious duty, but the compulsion isn't confined to the religious. When Lewis Thomas, the famous biologist, was dying, he told the *New York Times* essayist Roger Rosenblatt that he didn't believe in an afterlife and was dubious about the existence of God, but he was sure that the meaning of his life lay in what he had been able to do for other people, which is the way many women feel about their lives.

Volunteering to help others is by far the most popular new role for older women. When they are left alone, they almost intuitively reach out to do for others what they used to do for their families. Many of them realize that in helping others, they are helping themselves. A nurse freely admitted that she "couldn't have made it after my husband died if I hadn't had something to do every day." At seventy-five she was contributing thirty-six hours a week to the blood bank, Alzheimer's patients, and the mentally retarded.

Helen Holmes is a business school graduate who at seventy-six has become what she calls a "professional volunteer." She tried office work after her husband died but didn't like being tied down, so she decided to explore the world through volunteering. She has volunteered in hospitals, nursing homes, and the Social Security office. When she decided she would like to get into "personal volunteering," she went to "a lovely nursing home, where I now assist the activity director with the ladies who are in this beautiful home."

Volunteering for the Peace Corps is especially attractive to women forced to face life alone because it has the added attraction of taking them away from a sad scene and into an exotic part of the world. President Kennedy designed the Peace Corps for idealistic youth, but 10 percent of the volunteers it now sends overseas are over fifty. For women who have been closely tethered to home, the experience can be literally life-changing.

The first half of Marjorie DeMoss Casebolt's life followed a predictable course. She married after getting her college degree in home economics, did some substitute teaching while her four sons were small, and, as they grew older, taught consumer education in a vocational school in Tacoma, Washington. But when she was in her late fifties, her husband became restless. The "geriatric safari" they took to Africa didn't cure his midlife crisis.

Financially, the subsequent divorce left Marjorie secure. She continued to live in the waterfront home they had shared in Wauna, Washington, renting out the beach cabin to young people in exchange for help with lawns and gutters. But socially she was relegated to the limbo of older divorced women, where she even received an insulting proposition from a male friend of her former husband's.

All this changed when she joined the Peace Corps. In Guatemala, all her existing skills were desperately needed. She weighed and measured babies and taught nutrition, food preparation, and public health classes. But she also developed valuable new skills. She learned Spanish well enough to write radio jingles for public service announcements and four children's books, which were later used in Peace Corps training. She now raises enough money to send nineteen Guatemalan children to junior high school. She came home more self-confident, fifteen pounds lighter, politically more liberal, and with a new identity she is describing in a book that she will call *Margarita,* the name by which she was known in Guatemala.

Volunteer work wasn't exactly what Jean Schoonover had planned for her retirement. She had worked hard all her life, made all the money she could possibly need, and won just about every honor the public relations profession has to bestow. She had been looking forward to a life of unaccustomed leisure with her husband, Ray, their three children, and the grandchildren, who had begun to arrive. But in 1990, just as they were about to retire, Ray contracted lung cancer and died.

Alone in the New York townhouse in which she and Ray had raised their children, Jean was besieged by nonprofit organizations soliciting her help. Just by saying yes, she found herself involved in fields she had only glimpsed from afar. One day she might be developing a seminar for the National Executive Service Corps on management issues of interest to nonprofit organizations. Another day she was into limnology, the study of freshwater lakes, for the North American Friends of the Israel Oceanographic and Limnological Research Foundation. By the end of 1993 she had agreed to take on the challenging problems of the New York City YWCA as its volunteer president.

Jean Schoonover's career is a classic American success story. Born in rural upstate New York, she early began a lifelong love affair with the Big Apple. She got there by landing a job selling railroad tickets in Pennsylvania Station, but she and her sister Barbara soon found work in public relations.

Neither Jean nor Barbara considered herself a feminist. They were good at publicizing food products because they identified easily with other happily married women raising families. But they did so well that their accounts became the mainstay of Dudley Anderson Yutzy, the firm that employed them. They got past the glass ceiling by buying their bosses out and secured themselves financially by selling the firm to an international advertising agency in exchange for stock.

Jean has now moved out of commercial work. "I think of myself as a problem solver," she says, "and every field has problems. Volunteering in a position where I can use my management and public relations experience gives me a chance to explore new worlds and meet different kinds of people."

Pro bono work can be more fun and more liberating than the work for which a retired professional woman used to get paid. Anita Dore has always been interested in children's literature, but she had to consider more than her own preferences when she was director of English for the New York City schools. Now that she's retired, she can follow her own instincts on the Child Study Children's Book Committee of the privately funded Bank Street College of Education.

Since her retirement from a lifetime of civil service work, Mary Burke Nicholas has served as chairman of the Civilian Complaint Board of the New York City Police Department, which is charged with reviewing complaints against the police. She's completely independent of the police department, and she's valuable because she understands the problems of government bureaucracies.

Representing the public on government boards is a natural role for older women, and it can be fascinating work. Thousands of federal, state, and local boards advise on government policies or review touchy matters such as complaints. Most states have members of the public on the boards that oversee the licensing of professionals, to insure that the professionals are held accountable to the people who use their services. Licensing boards are only one of the many kinds of boards that recruit volunteer members.

There are volunteer opportunities in every profession. It's not just credentialed scientists with the money to travel, like Vilma Kohn, who volunteer their services at archeological digs. Accountants volunteer with the IRS or the American Association of Retired Persons (AARP) to help answer the questions of taxpayers. Teachers volunteer with literacy programs, often to train the volunteers who do the actual tutoring.

After a short training period, college-educated women help paid staffers deal with the public as tour guides or docents in national parks, historical sites, museums, and arboretums. For libraries, they run book sales, read to children, deliver books to shut-ins, or check out books. Dealing one-on-one with the public eats into the time of paid staffers, but it is just the kind of personal helping that many older women enjoy.

There are interesting volunteer opportunities in every organization that serves the public. In some communities, older women have been trained to visit nursing homes and act as ombudsmen for patients. Under a variety of programs, and often through their churches or synagogues, they help out in shelters, hospices, and food pantries, staff telephones for hotlines, or visit homes where child abuse is suspected.

Volunteer work especially designed for older people is available through federally financed programs such as Foster Grandparents, an organization that matches older people — most often women — with children who need special attention. Other programs are designed to enlist volunteers to help other older people by making telephone checkups and working at senior citizen centers. Churches and the Office for the Aging, listed in the blue pages of your phone book, can tell you what's available near you.

The most interesting volunteer jobs are the ones women create or find for themselves. Maggie McQuarrie was looking for a change when she retired as the principal of a Los Angeles high school, so she bought a house in Los Osos, a little town in a beautiful, sparsely settled part of California's Central Valley. When the local fire department learned that it had a teacher in town, it begged her to head the Smokey Bear educational program for getting children to be careful not to start fires. She was tired of educating children, so she declined, but she pricked up her ears when she discovered that the department was also looking for fire inspectors to patrol some of the wilder areas. The job usually went to men, but after the fire captains got to know Maggie, they decided that she could handle a badge.

The job was scary, but not the way running a Los Angeles high school is scary. Alone in a truck, Maggie checked all the structures in a given area for violations of the fire code. She never knew where a dirt road down a canyon would lead, or what kind of reception she would get when she had to knock on a door, give whoever answered a copy of the fire code, and explain what had to be done about the tree branches overhanging a chimney or the dry brush growing too close to the house. As a mere volunteer, she had no legal authority. If a homeowner didn't like what she was saying, all she could do was report the violation.

"The fire department needed people who could meet the public," she says. "And I figured that in a pinch, I could run faster than a man who didn't like what I was telling him." She liked the job so much that she has been doing it for five years. She has also volunteered in the surveillance of arson suspects. In her own, unmarked car, she drives past the house of the person being watched and writes down the license numbers of all the cars parked around it. "It's really not dangerous," she says, a bit regretfully. "They just need a lot of different people to keep track of who goes in and out of a house without arousing suspicion." She enjoys the excitement, but now that she's pushing seventy, she takes a woman friend of her own age along to keep her company on the drives.

Even the classic work of women volunteers doesn't have to be a dead end. When they have the time in their later years, some women use what they've learned about people in trouble to start projects that mend the social safety net, or work for fundamental changes that would prevent the wounds they've been binding up. And they are particularly creative in finding ways to help other women through problems they've faced themselves.

Angela Martinez had always been handy with tools. After her divorce, she taught other volunteers at the Tampa Women's Center how to repair houses that were so dilapidated that professional construction workers wouldn't touch them, even if their owners could afford to pay. With the help of modest grants, her Senior Home Improvement Program (SHIP) has saved the homes of thousands of low-income seniors. And all her "ladies in red" are displaced homemakers or single mothers who are using the work to build their own self-esteem.

Cecelia O'Meara knew what it meant to be tied to the care of an ailing husband. In her husband's last illness, he encouraged her to go out, even if it meant leaving him alone. "You may come back and find me dead," he would say to her. "But I would rather be alone than have some goddamned woman hovering over me."

After he died, she started an adult day-care center with a friend who had served her time as a caregiver, too. Women bring their charges in the morning and pick them up after lunch for a fee of two dollars, which includes lunch. Cecelia and three other women donate their time, a church gives them space in its basement, and local groups like the Rotarians give them money for groceries. Cecelia and her daughters cleared old costume jewelry out of their drawers to provide prizes for an after-lunch bingo game. The out-of-pocket cost of the whole thing runs to $75 a week.

Like their counterparts in the for-profit sector who start companies in their garages, these enterprisers in doing good relish their independence. Cecelia and her partner don't operate in the local senior center, although they are on good terms with the people who run it. If they were part of a government-funded operation, they would have to follow elaborate rules and guidelines. They'd rather stay small and decide for themselves which clients to accept.

Ruth Brinker feels the same way. When Project Open Hand, her program for feeding AIDS patients, grew so big that it was serving more than two thousand people a day, she turned it over to others and devoted herself to a new and more ambitious program. Fresh Start undertakes to teach homeless people how to grow organic vegetables and support themselves on the land. In the fall of 1993, participants were growing organic crops on a quarter-acre plot in downtown San Francisco, and Ruth had commitments from some of the city's famous restaurants to buy the produce.

From the very beginning of America, women have banded together to improve their communities and help one another as well as people who can't help themselves. For generations, doing good was the only role a decent woman was allowed to play outside her home. And because men respected this, ambitious women were able to build a parallel power structure that influenced the political mainstream.

According to historian Ann Scott, the "municipal housekeeping" promoted by women's clubs at the beginning of this century pioneered tax-supported amenities we now take for granted. In many places, women started street cleaning, tree planting, playgrounds, well-baby clinics, libraries, museums, even information on housing and factory conditions.

WORKING FOR CHANGE

Avis-Ann Strong Parke is a thirteenth-generation New Englander and the former wife of a Unitarian minister. In 1982, she greeted a reporter from *Ms.* magazine in trousers outgrown by one teenage son, shoes worn out by another, and thermal underwear she shares with another of her six children. "We don't have any heat," she explained with a smile.

After her husband left her for a younger woman, Avis-Ann and her three youngest children found winter shelter in a Victorian summer cottage on Cape Cod. The reporter had sought her out because she had been appointed to represent welfare mothers on the board of directors of the Massachusetts Commission on the Status of Women.

Far from being embarrassed by her situation, Avis-Ann not only volunteered to talk about how she made out on a tenuous combination of welfare and child support, but she rounded up five other mothers who were willing to tell the world about how they had ended up on welfare. All of them were willing to sacrifice their privacy to the cause of promoting the rights of displaced homemakers. Avis-Ann told her story all over again to the millions who watch *The Phil Donahue Show.*

Avis-Ann wasn't always a rebel. A virgin at her big church wedding, she spent years having babies and doing everything else a proper minister's wife is supposed to do. In addition to taking on the usual social duties, she shouldered the scutwork of the community services her husband was promoting. She served on a tenants' housing council, worked for hospital reform, started a nursery school in the church, and helped her husband start a community college program in space the local high school wasn't using.

That was when she was doing her Christian duty by the needy. Her own divorce and the women's movement convinced her that the disasters she had been mopping up weren't individual accidents that could be relieved one by one. She now saw them as manifestations of the systematic oppression of women by the mainstream culture she was part of, and she set out to do her best to change it.

She brought to the cause all she had learned as a minister's wife. She helped to organize the Cape Cod Women's Liberation Center, joined protest movements, and took advantage of obscure opportunities to promote her cause. When she discovered that local cable TV stations were required by the terms of their licenses to offer training in public access television production, she was one of the first to take the course. Then, with a camcorder provided by the small, woman-oriented Thanks Be To Grandmother Winifred Foundation, she produced a Cape Cod television series on local women and their problems.

Hers is a hand-to-mouth existence. She makes out because she knows how to mend old clothes, stretch food, swap rides to save gas, barter, and sell handpainted sweatshirts for cash. And she's happier than she has ever been, because she feels she's doing something to make the world a better place.

Working for social change is an absorbing role for women who no longer have family responsibilities. Are women specially fitted for it? A uniquely qualified scholar who thinks so is Richard Graham, a pioneer feminist and director of the Lawrence Kohlberg Center for Moral Development at Harvard. He's calling for a "third women's movement" for "human rights for children, women, and men throughout the world." (The first women's movement was for the vote; the second was the one Betty Friedan launched for equal opportunity.)

Not all feminists are comfortable with the notion that women are morally superior because they have been biologically programmed to be more compassionate and nurturing than men. It sounds too much like the nineteenth-century thinking that regarded women as too good for the wicked world of men and put them on a pedestal that effectively removed them from the exercise of real power. But whatever the reason, the fact remains that women are overrepresented in movements working to make our mainstream culture more compassionate. Especially when they are older and on their own, women make major contributions to the causes of peace, the environment, civil liberties, animal welfare, the disabled, the poor, the old, the young, and of course women themselves.

Virginia Vollmer, a widow and a former member of the nursing faculty at the University of Arkansas, is worried about unwanted pregnancy and sexually transmitted diseases, but she's attacking these prickly subjects in a way that respects conservative sensibilities. She readily agrees with conservatives that parents are the best people to tell their children about sex, but she finds that even Bible Belt parents admit that they don't know how to do it and are often unsure of the biological facts themselves. To address this problem, she began Parents as Sex Educators (PASE), a program in which parents share their own wisdom and expertise in how to teach human sexuality to their children. In Arkansas churches and Head Start centers, PASE offers small groups of parents structured discussion guides. Since the parents are their own "experts," they become comfortable and find that they can talk more easily with their kids. The program is now offered to parents in Arkansas Head Start programs and is being considered in other states.

Not all the change makers are innovators or media stars. There's something to be said for the cumulative influence of the many older women who are willing to stick up for an unpopular cause simply because they think it is right. Many of these women pay their own way to protests at Godforsaken sites where nuclear missiles are being tested, or to Washington, D.C., where their protests can be televised. They look into situations the media is ignoring and report conditions to people who can do something about it.

A good example of these influential quieter voices is Mary Agnes Hess. Since we were in graduate school together more than fifty years ago, Mary had always worried about the world and felt that she should be doing something to make it better, but for decades she was tethered at home with a husband and a remarkable father who lived to be 101. After both died, she told me how she felt by sending me May Sarton's poem "Now I Become Myself."

So what did she do? She indulged what she deprecatingly calls her "missionary streak." She went to El Salvador to see for herself and carefully record in a diary what life was like in a Third World country. When she came back to Connecticut, she set up a committee in the Congregational church to watch over Latin American affairs and insure that the plight of the people she had met would not be forgotten.

Mary isn't the only older woman who uses her newfound freedom to go off the beaten travel track and report what is not being reported to folks at home who don't want to listen. Ellen Paullin's husband was a historian who took her along on trips to Communist countries during the cold war. There she learned first-hand that people have a lot in common in spite of ideological differences.

When Ellen's husband died, she decided to visit all the forbidden places. "I guess I'm just spunky enough to not want my government to tell me where I can't go. When Ted and I were in China and the USSR, the one thing our guides wanted most was to be able to travel anywhere in the world. At that time, U.S. citizens couldn't go to Albania, Cuba, or North Korea."

When she was seventy-eight, Ellen went to Cuba, a country regarded as off-limits by our State Department. Back home, she wrote and created — with the help of a Kinko Copy Center Book-letmaker, which could reproduce color photos as well as text — a report she called "Pictures from Cuba: Positives and Negatives." She hopes it will help end the embargo against Cuba, which "punishes a whole country because it doesn't perform the way we think it should."

Albania is now open. Ellen has been to Cuba, "so I guess the next stop is North Korea, which will be more difficult."

Policymakers have to cope with the willingness of supposedly timid older women to speak their minds in public. Older Women's League member Nancy Moldenhauer had never testified in public before, but she volunteered to appear before a committee of the Missouri state legislature that was considering a change of rules to make it easier for women fifty-five to sixty-five to keep health insurance after the end of a marriage. "My heart began to beat rapidly, but my mind did not go blank," she wrote about it afterward. "I spoke about the undue psychological stress that widowed, separated, and especially divorced women have to go through. It was a unique and exciting experience." And successful. In spite of insurance company opposition, Missouri adopted the change that women wanted.

Word power is a female talent that declines very slowly, if at all, with age. Hazel Wolf is a Puget Sound activist who at ninety-six flies around the country speaking out for the environment, the rights of native people, and the impact of pollution on poor people who have to live near landfills. She especially enjoys talking to school classes. In the small, clear voice of an active nonagenarian, she gives straightforward answers to any and all questions youngsters put to her.

A seventh-grader in Decatur, Alabama, asked a question that gave her a chance to strike a blow against ageism: "Do you feel sorry you can't run and play as you did when you were a child?"

"No, I don't," Hazel told him. "When I was your age, I wanted to run and play and go on hikes in the mountains, but I didn't want to make speeches. That would have been very, very scary. Now I don't want to run and play. I would much sooner read in my spare time. And I certainly do really like to make speeches, especially to students. So at different times a person likes different activities. The only time I feel sorry for myself is when I get sick, which is not very often. Don't you feel sorry for yourself when you are sick?"

Widowed a half-century ago, Hazel supported her daughter by working as a legal secretary in civil liberties organizations. She loved the outdoors and always worked for community causes but didn't start to worry about the environment until a hiking companion took her on an Audubon Society field trip when she was in her sixties. Once recruited, she organized twenty of the twenty-six Audubon chapters in Washington by the simple process of looking up subscribers to the Audubon magazine in every locality and arranging to get them together, and she has been talking, petitioning, and lobbying to save the environment ever since.

The expansion of nuclear power in the United States was defeated by ordinary citizens rising to defend their homes and families. Among the many women who were especially aroused by the threat to generations unborn, none was more heroic than an Oklahoma farm wife, mother, and nurse.

Soft-spoken Carrie Barefoot Dickerson (whose maiden name is Irish, not Native American, and who calls her women friends "darlin' ") spent nine years of her life and $125,000 of her own money fighting the construction of a nuclear power plant near her farm outside Tulsa, Oklahoma. She mortgaged the farm and its equipment, sold the small nursing home on which she relied for income, and, although she herself is an RN, hired another to take care of her dying husband so that she could devote all her time to the cause. Carrie's husband didn't live to see her win, and he didn't think she could do it, but he knew he couldn't stop her, so he urged her to leave his bedside to keep up the fight. She was sixty-five when the utility company gave up trying to build the plant.

Carrie didn't know anything about atomic energy when she read about the plant in the local newspaper, but she was interested in health. She had been a home economics teacher and sold health foods before she had the nursing home, and the Dickersons had never used chemicals to grow their produce. She sent for everything she could find to read about atomic energy, and the more she read, the more she worried. Most of her neighbors saw only the jobs the company said the plant would create, but a few joined her in trying to stop it.

She discovered that her group would have to hire lawyers to represent the community at hearings and that these lawyers would expect to be paid in money. She soon found herself sitting for endless hours in public meetings, worrying about how to pay them. When the Dickersons were dangerously low on funds, she woke up one morning after dreaming of a beautiful sunburst quilt. She hadn't quilted since her childhood, but she decided to make that quilt while sitting in the meetings and sell chances on it to other women for a dollar apiece. The first quilt brought $3,000 to the cause and inspired other women to make and raffle quilts of their own.

At seventy-seven, Carrie is still trying to pay off her debts and still worrying about the threat of atomic energy. When she's through writing a book about the fight, she's going to devote the rest of her life to promoting renewable solar and wind sources of energy.

We think of the women's movement of the 1970s as a protest of young women denied access to power, but women's rights have always been achieved through the efforts of women old enough to experience how the mainstream culture shortchanges them. And while relatively young women have been effective spokespersons in the media, older women with experience in groups like the League of Women Voters have built their protests into a national movement.

The woman who got the influential NOW Legal Defense and Education Fund off the ground was a corporate wife whose name never became a household word. In the 1960s, Mary Jean Tully was just waiting for the message of Betty Friedan. Energetic and resourceful, she had always led an active life while managing "the hotel that was our home" wherever the big corporations sent her workaholic husband. As his career blossomed, she enjoyed such benefits as flying across the Atlantic while sleeping in a real bed and running a household in England with traditional servants. But all the time she was waiting for the children to grow up so that she could get out of the home and "join the real world."

She didn't like what the corporations that were always promoting her husband were doing to her. "They sent my husband off to Germany three weeks before my fourth child was due," she recalls. "I managed to keep him home by hemorrhaging — he hadn't even gotten to the office the day he was leaving before I started hemorrhaging. But a year later I was having a fifth child, and they were going to do the same damn thing."

There she was, watching the world from a front-line seat, learning the rules of the political game and getting a chance to practice some of them in the League of Women Voters, but never being allowed to play in the big world of affairs where policies were made. Many women would have accepted the tradeoff, but Mary

Jean was an army brat descended from pioneer Texans, and she didn't like being kept out of the rooms where public decisions were being made.

When she read *The Feminine Mystique*, she saw in writing what she had been feeling all along. "The book spoke to me," she says. "It spoke to me." And as she got into the movement, she saw that there was a unique role for her in it. She saw that the revolution was going to take money, and unlike the young women who were so good at rhetoric, she wasn't afraid of money or the powerful men who had it to give away. By then her husband was chief financial officer of the Celanese Corporation, so she knew how these men thought and how to get to them.

It was hard for corporate officers to donate money directly to NOW, even if they were inclined to do it. NOW was a political organization, so gifts to it were not tax-deductible. But NOW had set up a Legal Defense and Education Fund for specific projects that weren't regarded as political by the Internal Revenue Service, so Mary Jean undertook to raise corporate money for the fund. To start her campaign, she had something better than a shoestring: access to the lavish hotel suites, with unlimited phone and room service, that Celanese maintained for its officers in New York City.

The rest is history. Tully broke the ice with the Ford Foundation and Avon, a male-dominated corporation that was especially vulnerable because it depended on the good will of women customers and salespersons. As a point of pride, she never solicited corporate executives she had met through her husband, but she barred no holds in exacting reparations for women from others. She organized a fifth column, using contacts with people inside the corporations to help her achieve her goals from within.

"I was happy to rip them off with the hotel suites, happy to make these corporation executives squirm and wiggle and sweat," she recalls with glee. "I kept what I call my 'disarmament wardrobe' in the closet. I'd go to work in pants, but in the closet I had dresses and high heels and perfume." At a moment's notice she could turn up for an appointment with corporate executives looking very much like their own wives.

She enjoyed every minute of the fight to get the movement funded. "It was so heady, so exciting. I never wanted to go to bed at night. I wanted to jump out of bed and go on and do, do, do. The only thing I can compare it to is being in love. It was like people, I guess, who have a religious vocation."

Historically, women have always banded together to defend slaves, the poor, the insane, the sick, widows, children, animals, and others unable to fend for themselves. The insane asylum, the underground railroad (first named in Harriet Beecher Stowe's 1852 book *Uncle Tom's Cabin*), and the settlement house are only a few of the institutions they've devised to rescue the helpless.

SHARING WEALTH

Women give because it makes them feel good. They like to be able to reach out on impulse to someone they see needs help. They may not have that luxury if they have to justify what they spend to a husband, but some of them make a whole new life out of sharing whatever wealth they have when it's all their own.

Maddie Glazer is a good example. The money was all hers, really, because it came from her father, but her husband decided whom to give "our" money to, even though she had volunteered and raised money for Iowa philanthropies all her adult life. Soft-spoken, conservative, and as straightforward as Iowa corn, Maddie never doubted that whatever its problems, her marriage would last as long as they both should live.

After forty-four years, it came apart in a thunderclap. Her husband waited until she came home from a hip replacement operation to tell her he wanted a divorce so that he could marry a woman younger than their daughter. Stunned and depressed, she was about to retire in shame from every public commitment when

Drake University asked her to head a $115 million fund-raising drive.

It was a canny challenge. The Drake board members knew that Maddie had some money of her own, that she had always liked Drake, and that her father had given money to the university. But they also knew that they were trying to obtain more money than anyone thought they could possibly get. If Maddie accepted, it would be the largest fund-raising project ever headed anywhere in the country by a woman.

She accepted. Throwing herself into the work, she traveled from coast to coast to visit Drake alumni and solicit them personally. Refusing any pay, she told the board of directors and the trustees that if they could raise $26 million, she would add $2 million of her own. Four years later, Drake had raised $120 million, more than the "impossible" five-year goal of $115 million.

The campaign was just as successful for Maddie Glazer. It restored her self-respect and gave her a new home and family. Now that she's her own woman, she's having the time of her life. From a permanent office at Drake, she maintains the network of alumni she created, and now that she controls her own money, she is spending some of it to help other women do the same. She has made a seed grant of $100,000 to staff an office and newsletter for the newly formed National Network on Women as Philanthropists.

Maddie Glazer is one of a growing number of older women who are finding a niche in the world of doing good. This niche is defined by the Internal Revenue Service as any organization worthy of tax exemption because it is working for the good of the public rather than for private profit; hence the name "nonprofit." It includes almost all nongovernmental health, education, and welfare enterprises: charities such as the United Jewish Appeal and foundations endowed by men with names like Rockefeller and Ford; private colleges, religious organizations, hospitals, museums, and symphonies; and organizations that promote special interests, such as the American Cancer Society. Some of the organizations that have tax-exempt status are as big as the

AARP, which serves 33 million Americans over fifty, while others are as small as the little foundation that administers Ruth Hayre's scholarships for black children in Philadelphia schools.

The nonprofit world is untidy, diverse, increasingly specialized, big, and getting bigger. In addition to the value of the time volunteers donate, individual taxpayers give these groups more than $120 billion a year in cold cash.

The most fun, of course, is to give time as well as money to a nonprofit enterprise of your own creation. It doesn't have to take a lot of money. Some women find a new role for themselves running an animal shelter from home or a neighborhood help project that requires small sums of cash, like Olga Bloom's Bargemusic or Cecelia O'Meara's adult day-care center. And some benefactors are almost as poor as the people they help.

Ruth Hardwick is a retired practical nurse. The year before she turned seventy, she kept dreaming about a long line of hungry people standing outside the door of her home in Perth Amboy, New Jersey. Deeply religious, she began sharing her meager Social Security check with hungry and homeless neighbors. By the time she was seventy-three, she had begged and borrowed enough resources to set up a storefront place called the Charity Restaurant, and when her only daughter died, she used the insurance money to expand the Charity. We know about her because the Giraffe Project found her and gave her an award, but sharing is so common in the black community that there's no reason to believe that she's unique in sharing her Social Security check.

Dreams of sharing are wild and various, but if you are widowed or divorced, there's nobody around to stop you from investing yourself and your resources in a dream that is uniquely your own. Beth Verssen, Toby Ansin, and Genevieve Vaughan are as different from each other as women can be, but that's exactly what each of them did.

As a child, Beth Verssen dreamed of becoming a missionary in India. In a Sunday School play, she even played the role of a woman doctor who founded a hospital there. But then, like so many other girls, she married and had a family instead. Beth's husband objected to her Christian faith and activities, and after the children were grown and gone the couple finally divorced.

Now that she's in her sixties, with marriage and children behind her, Beth is living out her dream in a way she couldn't have expected. She lives in Trivandrum, in southern India, in a beautiful house big enough to accommodate some of the thirty trainees, employees, and fellowship and scholarship holders who work with her on the two charitable trusts she funds. One trains gospel workers. The other helps the handicapped.

Beth is not rich by American standards. If she had stayed on Long Island after her divorce, she would have had just enough income to keep up her house. But after selling the house, she has enough to be a real presence in charitable work in Trivandrum. She now visits the United States to persuade other older people to join her in work where their skills are desperately needed and their retirement income stretches further than anywhere in the United States.

Toby Lerner Ansin grew up planning to become a ballet dancer. She put on her first ballet slippers at five, after a doctor suggested ballet lessons to correct her turned-in feet. But when she was a teenager, she looked in the mirror one day and decided that she didn't have the talent or the technique to be a ballerina. She refocused her energies on achieving a Wellesley education. After college she married and spent the next few decades as a traditional housewife and mother of three children in Miami, a city that had no ballet company of its own. All she could do was to serve on the arts committees of local organizations.

Shortly after her midlife divorce, a chance encounter made ballet the center of her life. Edward Villella, a former principal dancer for the New York City Ballet, came to Miami to present a dance program. Toby was so impressed with him that she decided then and there that he was the one to create the professional ballet company that South Florida needed to round out its cultural life. At her invitation, he came back and outlined a ten-year plan.

Toby put up $1,000 herself, got six friends to match the gift, and threw herself into the daunting task of launching a professional ballet from scratch. Although she had never held a paying job of any kind, her enthusiasm made up for her lack of business experience. She bought a computer and learned how to use it to set up lists, stuffed envelopes, organized benefits, flew to Europe to woo celebrities for attention-getting galas in Miami, and insured local press attention by distributing homemade cookies in newsrooms.

And it worked. Her inspired efforts have put Miami on the ballet map of the world. In the past few years, Miami City Ballet has performed to acclaim in England, France, Israel, South America, Central America, at the Edinburgh Festival, and in thirty-five American states, and its debut at the Kennedy Center in Washington, D.C., was set for the 1994 season. Recently Toby organized three gala performances that raised $750,000 for the ballet, an unusual achievement in support for the arts.

Over the years, Toby did just about everything for the ballet except dance herself. The closest she came was to visit company classes in a tutu. In 1993 she commissioned *Tobiniana*, a classic ballet in the romantic style she prefers — and cried unashamedly all through its debut performance, "because that's the way I would have looked if I could dance."

Genevieve Vaughan inherited money from her family's investments in oil. She has always had everything she could possibly want for herself, but she believes that the system that provided her privileges is inherently flawed. During the middle part of her life she began to struggle with impulses to give money away, not to the standard, male-oriented charities but directly to individuals who needed it. She eventually came to the conclusion that the present system of philanthropy coopts wealthy women into exploiting their sisters against their will, that no one is free who is consciously or unconsciously constrained to exploit other people, and that as beneficiaries of the patriarchy, many of us are its unwitting enablers.

Genevieve's beliefs aren't just theory. Since her midlife divorce from an Italian philosopher, she has been spending her time and money on projects to promote peace, justice, alternative healing, native rights, and other feminist values. In 1987 she set up the Foundation for a Compassionate Society to coordinate them.

Genevieve chose the word "compassionate" to contrast with what she regards as patriarchal cruelty. The foundation supports compassionate values through media projects, such as a two-hour daily program on a shortwave radio station out of Costa Rica called FIRE (the Feminist International Radio Endeavor), WINGS (the Women's International News Gathering Service), *Let the People Speak,* a weekly program on Austin Access TV, and WATER (Women's Access to Technological Resources), a facility for training women in radio, video, and computer skills.

In 1994 Genevieve was writing a book on a women's alternative to the male economic paradigm of giving only for the sake of what you can get in return, which she calls "the gift-giving economy." She believes that women give because they are socialized to be nurturers, while men give for the sake of what they can get back for themselves — *do ut des,* Latin for "I give so that you will give." She feels that most of the evils of the world are caused by the exchange or money economy of men, and she is working to replace it by the freely giving, other-oriented "gift economy" of women.

Now in her fifties, Vaughan is happier with her life than she has ever been before. As a protest against the "rape of Mother Earth," she and her three daughters bought twenty-two acres of land near a nuclear test site in Nevada and gave it back to the Western Shoshone people, to whom all the land in that area originally belonged. In 1993, with the help of a group of like-minded young women, she was having a temple built to the Egyptian goddess Sekhmet, in fulfillment of a promise she made to the goddess when she was in Egypt twenty-eight years ago, trying to get pregnant with her first child. Designed and constructed by women of ecologically appropriate straw bales and stucco, the temple is rising not in Egypt but in Nevada.

Many of the "alternative" causes women like to fund bring new issues to the public attention that become the mainstream of tomorrow's world. Because these women's names aren't on buildings, we tend to forget what we owe to them. For instance, consider two rich widows who spent their money on causes that must have set their husbands whirling in their graves. Without Alva Belmont, women might not have won the vote in 1919. Without Olivia Sage, we might be making welfare policy without the benefit of disinterested research into the true causes of poverty. Both women were content to stay in the background, so they've been ignored.

Alva Belmont was a southern girl who acquired her fortune by two strategic marriages, the first to a Vanderbilt, whom she divorced to the tune of a princely settlement, and the second to the son of a New York banker. When her second husband died, in 1908, she threw her money and a talent for publicity that shocked New York society into the cause of woman suffrage. Although her methods are routine now, she invented stunts that kept her cause visible. She brought the militant Englishwoman Christabel Pankhurst to the States for a lecture tour, collaborated with Elsa Maxwell on a suffragist opera, and financed a national press bureau to publicize the progress women were making. Most of all, her deep pockets funded the movement, down to a bitter fight in the corrupt legislature of her native Tennessee, whose approval made the Nineteenth Amendment part of the Constitution.

Olivia Sage was temperamentally the opposite of Alva Belmont. She was the model of a modest, nineteenth-century Presbyterian schoolteacher who believed that women were morally superior to men. At forty-one, she married Russell B. Sage, a fifty-three-year-old robber baron devoted to money and horses. They had no children, and he did not share her interest in causes and charities, ranging from campaigns against liquor and vice to the support of schools and hospitals.

Philanthropy attributed to Russell Sage began at his death, in 1906, when his widow got her hands on the $63 million he left her and decided to give it all away for the betterment of humanity before she died. It was a daunting task, but she seems to have enjoyed every minute of it.

"I am nearly eighty years old, and I feel I've just begun to live," she remarked at the first meeting of the board of trustees of the Russell Sage Foundation, which she set up for "the improvement of social and living conditions." Although she herself blamed poverty on poor people's lack of character, the research she funded laid the foundation for the dispassionate study of poverty and for social work as it is presently practiced.

Until her death, at ninety, Olivia funded hundreds of educational, religious, charitable, and civic causes. She gave at such a frenetic pace that her total gifts have been compared with those of Andrew Carnegie, John D. Rockefeller, and J. P. Morgan, men who had none of her inhibitions about claiming credit for their benefactions. And though most of her gifts featured the name of her husband, including Russell Sage College for women, her biographer, Ruth Crocker, notes that she put the names of her grandmother and mother-in-law on some of the buildings she gave for the education of women. An Emma Willard graduate, Olivia supported women's colleges, scholarships for women, and training that would give women a chance to have a paying career other than teaching.

Both Sage and Belmont illustrate not only Margaret Mead's cryptic contention that a rich widow is the best thing to be in America, but the cynical observation that there is no end to what you can achieve if you don't want money or credit for it.

BREADWINNING

Reva Buck got to be fifty years old without knowing anything much about earning or spending money. The first of her six children was born when she was twenty, so she was always too busy at home to have a serious paying job. It didn't seem to matter much at the time, because her husband was just as traditional. A professor of veterinary medicine, he was the sort of old-fashioned head of the household who doled out money for groceries and took charge even of the pin money Reva occasionally earned by taking care of other people's children. Then, when all the children were grown and some had started families of their own, he left her for one of his students.

After the divorce, Reva was so glad to have a credit card of her own that she acquired thirteen of them. She ran up an $11,653 bill before Consumer Credit Counseling persuaded her to cut up eleven of them and work out a repayment scheme. The same thing happened with taxes. She didn't know that she was supposed to pay quarterly income taxes on the $1,200 a month alimony she received, so when the IRS caught up with her, it worked out a plan that will keep her paying off back taxes for years.

Down, yes. But not out. "Reva's basically an upbeat person," a friend says of her. "Give her scraps, and she'll make a quilt." When she took stock of her situation, this is the quilt she made of it: She was open-minded about sex, but she didn't want ever again to depend on a man. She didn't want a house, and she didn't want to live with any of her children, but she wanted to keep up with all of them, and they were scattered over several states. She knew she had to earn money. All she really knew how to do was to take care of other people, but since caregivers are always needed, she thought she could always be sure of finding a job that would cover her food and cheap lodging.

Reva's real home is her Ford station wagon, in which she neatly stacks all her clothes, files, pictures, and other indispensable personal possessions. She travels from child to child. As soon as she arrives in town, she registers for a job in day care, home care, or a nursing home. She has a track record with chains such as Kindercare, Beverly Nursing Homes, Interim, and Home Health Plus, and though titles vary from state to state, she has taken enough short training to qualify as a nursing assistant registered (NAR) and a certified nursing assistant (CNA). She may rent a room in the home of a friend or a distant relative for five dollars a night or live with a patient for whom she is caring, and she spends her days off with her children and grandchildren.

Unless she's needed to help with a family baby — she has been present or nearly there for the births of six of her eleven grandchildren — Reva moves with the seasons. From March to November she lives with a friend near two of her children in St. Paul, a union town where a nursing assistant registered can earn ten dollars an hour, with time and a half for overtime. Then, when the Minnesota snows begin, she heads for Missouri to be near two other children.

No, she isn't tired of traveling around. When she is in Missouri, she sees a man she remet at her high school reunion, but she's not ready to settle down with him. From here on out, she's paying her own way, helping when she can but making all of her own decisions. Bored? Never!

Reva Buck is an authentic displaced homemaker, a woman who signed on for the job of traditional wife and mother when she was young and lost it in midlife when she lost her husband. Tish Sommers coined the term in 1974, when millions of American women were in this anomalous situation. With Laurie Shields, another displaced homemaker, she organized the Older Women's League to give such women a voice in national policies, and she left much of her estate to OWL when she died of cancer, in 1985. Since then, OWL has continued to analyze and represent the special interests of all older women in taxes, pensions, housing, health, education, and welfare.

Unfortunately, the campaign to help older women has unwittingly reinforced the stereotypical image of the poor, helpless little old widow who never expected to have to cope with the world on her own. Some displaced homemakers fit the stereotype. But some don't.

Norma Glad used to be Norma Papish. Glad is her mother's family name, and after two bitter marriages she had a party to celebrate going back to it. Norma had three children when she was widowed at thirty, and her second husband was a psychiatrist who had two of his own younger than hers. All five children were severely injured in an automobile accident, and the youngest died. Then Norma lost a kidney to cancer. When the remaining four children were grown, her husband started talking in vague psychiatric jargon about mutual change to improve their relationship. Norma noticed that somehow she was the one who was doing all the changing, and she had the courage to leave.

Divorced at fifty-two, with no marketable skills, Norma supported herself in retailing for a few years, learned typing in the hope of making more money, and landed a job with a psychologist who counseled cancer patients, which capitalized on her own recovery from cancer. Then her eyesight began to go. She couldn't work full-time or read without strain, and eventually she lost her job with the psychologist.

What could she do to earn a living without using her eyes? Massage! In her sixties, Norma developed a practice in massage therapy, which used the empathy and compassion she had learned the hard way.

Displaced homemakers often have powerful inner resources. Laura Jean Masters was a displaced homemaker who didn't think anyone would hire a sixty-year-old who was newly divorced from a physician. She had met him while she was studying dietetics, and she had practiced while he was interning, back when dietitians didn't have to be registered. But after World War II, she had settled down to raising six children and doing the volunteer work expected of a physician's wife.

Laura Jean was lucky. At the time of her divorce, the Federal Women's, Infants, and Children's (WIC) program for supplementing the diet of low-income families was starting up in her area of Michigan, and she was the only person in town who came close to meeting the qualifications for becoming the director for her area. It wasn't easy to supervise men with newly minted degrees who were half her age. To match their education, she earned a master of public health degree through an independent study program she could pursue while on the job. But at the outset, one young man in particular was openly hostile. When Laura Jean sat down next to him and his friends in the lunchroom, they would pointedly get up and move away. But now he's gone — and she's still there.

At seventy-five, she drove two thousand miles a month through the bitter Michigan winter of 1994 to cover the operations in the six counties she supervises, and she was beginning to be consulted on policy at the national level. Because she is a government employee, she can't be retired against her will, but she was smart enough to ask her boss if he thought she should retire. He said no (it might have been illegal for him to say anything else), and he then asked her to give him a year's notice if she did decide to quit.

What would induce her to do that? Bad health, of course — "or falling head over heels in love with a rich man who wants to marry me, and I know this isn't going to happen."

Money isn't always the only reason that displaced homemakers work for pay. A great many cherish the prestige of breadwinning, which they feel they were denied earlier in life. If you walked into Caroline Miller's office at the United Jewish Appeal–Federation of Jewish Philanthropies, you'd never believe that this briskly professional tax expert quit college at nineteen to marry a young dentist and didn't collect a paycheck until she was almost fifty. Or that she was so comfortable with the traditions of Old World Jewry that when her uncle, in his eighties, lost his wife, she arranged for him to marry her husband's newly widowed aunt, in her sixties.

Caroline was the only child of one of the many immigrant couples who lived in Queens, New York, when she was growing up. Her father was a bookish dreamer, so her mother paid the bills by working as a bookkeeper and impressed on her the importance of carefully managing the family finances so that she would never have to work outside the home.

Caroline took after her mother rather than her father. Efficient, practical, and ambitious, she became the picture-perfect model of the wife of a successful professional man. And when her well-run home and well-adjusted sons weren't enough, she found an acceptable outlet for her energy by taking on increasing responsibility in volunteer work. She directed the resettlement of sixty Russian Jews a year in the Albany area. One of her jobs was serving as a citizen volunteer on the New York State board overseeing the ethics of psychologists. Through this work she was invited to join the American Psychological Association and was assigned to its ethics committee.

The disasters came after the boys were grown. An automobile accident permanently disabled one of Caroline's legs so that she could barely walk. Three years later, cardiac arrest leading to an irreversible brain injury left her husband facing twenty to thirty years of life at the six-year-old mental level. Insurance, including catastrophic medical insurance, kept Caroline financially secure, but she couldn't take care of her husband at home because of her own disability. She called in her chits among psychologists to get the best possible care for him, and when she found that no one had looked into long-term care for the brain injured, she got a grant to set up standards, which are now used by the New York State Health Department.

When Caroline's husband died, three years after his heart attack, she had enough money to get along, but she was ready for a radically different life. The Peace Corps sounded exciting, but she was tired of being a volunteer. "I wanted to get up in the morning and go to an office and produce a paycheck at the end of the week. I wanted to keep interacting with people. I wanted to make it on my own. I didn't want to be emotionally or financially dependent on my children." It took a lot of networking and searching, but her present job is a perfect fit.

Good jobs go to people who have worked their way up over years, so a woman who doesn't get on the lower rungs of the ladder when she is young is going to have to find some unconventional way to get onto it. Caroline Miller did it by making the tricky transfer from volunteer to paid professional fund-raiser in a nonprofit enterprise.

It's an almost ideal life. She lives in a co-op she bought in New York City, and her salary adds enough income to make city life rewarding and comfortable. Best of all, she is a respected professional who deals every day with wealthy families and the shrewd accountants and lawyers who advise them on the tax consequences of philanthropic gifts.

Another side door is the Peace Corps. Gloria Ross had had an exciting two-year career as an advertising director while she was married, and she did similar work in the Peace Corps. She had never graduated from college, so she didn't have the credentials for a career in a field such as journalism or teaching, but in the Peace Corps, ability to do what's needed is more important than credentials. In Tonga, Gloria was able to do public relations work for local businesses, and when a credentialed teacher failed to show up, she got to teach English in the local high school. On her return, she wrote articles for the local paper about her experiences, and that led to a regular job as an editor with the AARP.

Cynthia Coupe went back to college while she was still married, and got her degree the same year she got her divorce. She needed to work, but she wanted more than an entry-level job. "Since I was coming out of a divorce, there were many things going on in my life," she says, "and I just didn't think that the kind of job I could get would satisfy me." She wanted a challenging job that would help others, and she found it in the Peace Corps.

For two years she developed health education programs in a rural pueblo twelve hours by bus from Asunción, Paraguay, where cotton was the main crop and source of income. When she returned, she still wasn't willing to take "just any job," so she went back to college to get a master's degree in English, with a concentration in English as a second language. She has now taught students from all over the world, not just a new language but also the important lesson that learning another language will not threaten their native culture.

Rather than settling for less, the most able and enterprising displaced homemakers create work for themselves. Remember Barbara Kelley, the woman who characterized her divorce as "a plunge into a cold mountain lake"? Barbara quickly discovered that there were no jobs in Westport, Connecticut, that would keep a displaced matron in the style to which she had been accustomed, let alone for a woman who hadn't worked for pay in decades. But that didn't stop her.

Her first step was to request an interview with the director of the hospital where she had been volunteering. "I've worked here as a volunteer for five years," she told her. "Now my situation has changed. I'd like to stay on with you, but I need a paid position. I know the hospital, I know the community. I've worked on a newspaper. What can I do for you?" She walked out with a job as a public relations consultant.

Barbara admits that she finds it more fun to start things than to administer them once they're off the ground, so she has found it easier to talk herself into jobs than to keep them. When the hospital job ran aground, she worked for the Retired Senior Volunteer Program (RSVP), a federally funded project for older people. After being fired from that job, she convinced a Norwalk community group that the city needed an adult day-care center for the frail elderly and got herself the job of planning the facility and writing the grant request. The group got the grant, but a few years later Barbara was fired from that job, too. In line with what she deplores as the tendency to "medicalize" the care of the elderly, the director who was chosen to run the center was "a short nurse — who told me I was too tall, too loud, and too articulate."

Discouraged with employers, Barbara tried working for herself. With no experience except in cooking, she undertook to open a restaurant with a friend. When the friend opted out, Barbara racked her brains to think of something she could do with the location they had found and decided to open a consignment shop. Soon she was brokering expensive antiques, a good business in a wannabe Norman Rockwell community. All went well for twelve years, until the landlord found a tenant who could pay more rent than Barbara could afford.

Undaunted, she went into another business that's always needed in a community of houses with extensive grounds. She became what she herself deprecatingly calls a "lady landscaper" specializing in planning and tending perennial gardens. The work depends so much on the weather that she doesn't dare hire regular help, so she takes on only as much work as she can handle herself. Now in her sixties, she boasts that she's "the healthiest old broad in Fairfield County," and she has never been happier.

Women who come into a little capital in their later years have more options. Rental property is a reasonably safe investment for a woman who has the time to manage it, especially if she knows something about keeping it up because she has been a householder herself. After her husband died, Effi Testi went traveling to all the places they had planned to visit together, but when she came home she wanted something to do, so she started buying property.

"I now own six different properties, and I take care of all of them," she wrote me in 1992. "Sometimes I even clean them. I do all the renting and all my own book work. I am now eighty-two years old and I just can't sit around and do nothing or I would go crazy . . . I try to keep everything brought up to date so if anything happens to me, my kids won't be left with a lot of problems."

But even the gamblers who invest a divorce settlement or inheritance in a restaurant or a franchised business, or who turn the big house they inherit into a bed-and-breakfast inn for tourists, don't expect to make a killing. Women who start a business of their own in their later years usually hope only to make a little money or, if necessary, a modest living doing something they enjoy. They start a service they think is needed or enjoy providing, or find a way to make a small business out of a hobby or a talent they would be pursuing anyway.

Grace Graves is a widow who made her hobby pay not only in money but in a stimulating new life that is making her friends all over the world. She became hooked on Haviland china when she inherited an incomplete set from her grandmother, but collecting it didn't become a hobby until she quit working as a secretary and devoted herself to her children and the vintage ten-room house she and her husband, Bill, bought on a shoestring when Bill joined a law firm in Milwaukee. At the estate sales Grace haunted to furnish the house, there were always a few pieces of Haviland, so she completed her own set and started collecting odd pieces, which often went for a song because they were valuable only to those who had a set of that particular pattern. As she soon discovered, completing a Haviland set isn't easy. During the nineteenth century the company shipped 60,000 different patterns to America, some of them only slight variations of others. All of them are now discontinued, but the brand was so popular that the attic of every old house is likely to harbor a leftover piece or two. Cataloguing and identifying them has become a specialty in its own right.

So began a hobby that sometimes filled Grace's big dining room table as well as her basement with thousands of pieces she couldn't resist. She studied the patterns and began exhibiting at antique shows and sharing her knowledge with local antiques study groups. And as people came to her with sets to complete, she was often able to sell the odd pieces she had collected at a substantial profit. She never thought of what she was doing as a business, but to keep the trickle of money out of the household budget, her husband helped her incorporate the Grace Graves Haviland Matching Service, Ltd.

Then, in 1990, Bill died suddenly in his office of a heart attack. Bill's partners and their many friends surrounded Grace with loving attention, and the phone rang constantly with solicitous offers of help and condolence. Although numb and stunned, she found it a relief to pick up the phone and take a cheerful call from a collector in Texas, California, or New York who wanted to talk only about china. Soon she was devoting more and more of her time to what was rapidly becoming a business. In 1992, she celebrated the hundred and fiftieth anniversary of Haviland by bringing to Milwaukee a show of museum-quality pieces lent by collectors, and by visiting Limoges, France, where the china is still made, as the guest of the company.

The Grace Graves Haviland Matching Service, Ltd. isn't making Grace rich, but it pays the expenses of her travel all over the world. "And it keeps me in balance," she adds. "When something bad happens in my personal life, something marvelous always seems to be happening to the business."

The displaced homemakers Tish Sommers identified in the 1970s are victims of history. They married when women expected to be supported all their lives at home, and then, when what used to be called their "best days" were over, they found that the rules had changed. Even when their husbands turned them in for a younger model, they were expected to earn at least part of the money they needed to achieve anything like their married standard of living.

But their numbers are dwindling. Every year, more of the women turning fifty have been to college and worked before they started having children, and younger women often don't quit their jobs when they have babies. The expectations of both sexes have changed. Young women no longer expect to be homemakers. Young men are learning that they can't expect to have steady jobs with pay that rises predictably with the expenses of a growing family. Security requires two paychecks.

Both men and women are learning to plan for change in their work over the course of their lives. And when they look around to see how it's done, the best role models they can find are displaced homemakers who have exploited the soft spots in a supposedly rigid job market. They are the unsung pioneers of the new way of working for people of all ages in the twenty-first century.

PRACTICING A PROFESSION

Louise Ulrich thinks of herself as tough, strong, resilient, good-natured, enthusiastic, decent, honest, caring, responsible — and sometimes zany. When she was fresh out of Vassar, she got her mother to dye her hair green for Christmas, and the two of them had a ball stopping traffic in Macy's. "I'm generous with my time," she wrote of herself, "and tight with my money, although I've tried to contribute over 10 percent of my gross income to 'causes.'"

The causes are liberal. A "card-carrying member of the American Civil Liberties Union," Louise believes, among many other things, that one should not make decisions for others, that the rights of all other forms of life are equal to our own, that the Book of Genesis is biased against women, and that "our very being requires that we touch and nurture one another." A religious humanist, she respects the existence of mysteries and miracles.

This was the way she described herself in her application to theological schools when she decided to retire early from the post office to become a Unitarian Universalist minister. Meadville/ Lombard Theological School in Chicago accepted her for its four-year course when she was fifty-six, so if she can manage it financially, she could be ordained at fifty-nine, or "in her fifties," as she plans to say when she gets her master's in divinity and starts the process of finding a congregation that wants her for its minister.

What decided Louise was a sermon her own minister preached on "Why I Am Still in the Ministry." As he talked about his love for reading, reflecting, and being involved in people's lives, she thought to herself, "That's me! That's what *I* want to do!" It sounded unlikely for a woman who had quit social work for a dull job in the post office because it paid enough to support her and her three teenage children without any help from their father. But twelve years later, after she had put all the children through college, she found a way to do it.

It took sacrifices, of course. She spent a precious year trying to get grants. When none of them came through, she tried to sell her house, but by then the real estate market was so bad in Binghamton, New York, that she had to rent it to meet the mortgage payments and lay out cash when the furnace had to be replaced. But she did it. She moved from a ten-room house in a community where she had been active for twenty-six years into a single room with a shared bath and kitchen on the South Side of Chicago, where she lives on what she can earn working part-time at $6.50 an hour.

More than half of Louise's fifty fellow seminarians are over forty, two thirds are women, and all of them are warmly supportive of one another. Ahead is a lot of moving around for unpaid clinical pastoral work in prisons or hospitals and interning in a church, but when Louise gets her M.Div., she hopes to find a congregation where she can promote the causes dear to her heart and use the experience in counseling she acquired in social work.

The ministry professionalizes the nurturing instincts and verbal talents of older women, and the same can be said for law, medicine, nursing, teaching, psychotherapy, social work, and other professions that require special graduate training and licensing or some other form of public regulation.

Age is no problem for *practicing* one of these professions. On the contrary, maturity is an advantage, and even the appearance of maturity can help. But *getting into* them is another matter. Professional schools and licensing bodies discourage older, or as they put it, "nontraditional," applicants, in part at least to maintain fees by limiting the competition, but also because the training takes so long that older applicants don't have enough years of practice ahead to repay the costs of their education. This is an effective bar for the many women who would love to be doctors, but every year a few persistent older women jump the high hurdle and get into one of the other learned professions.

In the 1990s, older women aren't as rare in law school as they were when Ruth Kinnard got her law degree from Vanderbilt University in 1970. Women over forty are now so common on college campuses that they no longer attract attention. When Barbara Morris was divorced at fifty, she went back to college to get certified so that she could work in New Mexico public schools as a library science teacher. She worried because she was the oldest student in her class, but her professors told her that their best students were the older ones.

Some "returning" women are studying for the profession they should have entered earlier. Marguerite Hibbard-Taylor's real vocation was nursing, but she didn't discover it until she was fifty-eight. To please her parents, she had gone to the Juilliard School of Music and practiced three or four hours a day. Her heart wasn't in being a concert pianist, but for forty years she thought of music as her vocation, and when she left the husband she had married at twenty, she was able to support their four children by teaching and playing the piano as a professional musician. It wasn't until arthritis made playing painful and her youngest son quit college to go into the army and marry that she felt she needed a new challenge.

But what would she enjoy? The answer came as she was pushing her vacuum cleaner. Newborn babies! She wasn't at all sure she could learn to be a nurse. "I needed to understand people better, I needed to be able to stand on my own two feet, and my body needed to get strong enough to take eight hours of physical activity," she wrote me. "So before applying to nursing school, I took courses in psychology, public speaking, golf, and tennis."

It worked. She found nursing school a joy, especially the clinical work with babies. After three semesters, she became a licensed vocational nurse (LVN). Submitting to the discipline of head nurses in a hospital was hard, but "I buckled down and found that time helps in adjusting to changes." At eighty-four, she was still taking a shift or two a week in the newborn nursery at Cottage Hospital in Santa Barbara and still loving every minute of it.

"To me, there is nothing in this world that compares with the feel of a new baby just born, and the miracle of birth never leaves me," she wrote me. "Physically, mentally, and in every other way this taking on of a new life has been the most wonderful action I could have taken for the real me. It has kept me young, kept me challenged, kept my body active and my spirits high. I feel needed and wanted."

Marguerite is unusual in claiming that her age wasn't held against her in starting her new profession. Most older women get around age discrimination and long training by finding a way in through a side door. You can't be a doctor, perhaps, but shorter training will get you into licensed medical specialties such as physical therapy, speech pathology, nutrition, practical nursing, and massage therapy. (Massage therapy sounds strenuous, but older women who do it say that it takes more skill than strength.) These and many other medical specialties require a few years of graduate training and supervised practice, leading to licensing by the state or certification by a professional association.

Similar opportunities have attracted older women into specialties in the helping professions of social work, special education, and psychotherapy. Some of them have made professional use of their own life experience by qualifying as counselors in substance abuse, study habits, sexual hangups, marital problems, or vocational guidance.

Joan Blumenfeld is a successful psychotherapeutic specialist who was attracted to her career by her personal experience. She went to a psychotherapist for help with problems in her marriage of thirty years. The therapy didn't save her marriage, but it proved so fascinating an experience that she became a therapist herself.

Capable, courageous, outgoing, and intensely verbal, Joan married in her sophomore year at Sarah Lawrence, stayed on to get her degree in early childhood education, and quit her job as a preschool teacher when her first child was born. Then, five years later, she bore a son who turned out to be both deaf and aphasic. Some experts thought that he ought to be put into custodial care, but Joan wouldn't take institutionalization for an answer. Instead, she hired an exceptionally creative speech therapist and made a full-time career out of caring for him herself. She took training in special education, learned how to interpret for the deaf, took chances with radical new ways of getting around his difficulties. And, against all the odds, she succeeded. At thirty-five, her son has a job as an inventory control specialist for a phone company in Minnesota, a wife, who is also deaf, and two children with normal hearing.

It was when the boy left home that Joan's marriage fell apart. Her husband was the one who wanted out, and when she reluctantly agreed, she knew that she'd have to find a way to earn money. But what could she do? She could interpret for the deaf or become a special education teacher, but neither paid enough to maintain her in the style her stockbroker husband had provided. Even more important, she was ready for a change.

A career in therapy sounded like just what she needed, so soon after her husband moved out of the house, she started taking courses leading to a master's degree in counseling at the nearby University of Bridgeport, Connecticut. During the three years it took her to get the degree, she worked during the day as an interpreter for a deaf girl attending a private school and went to the university in the evening. Her parents picked up most of the education bills, bought out her husband's share of the house, and helped her convert the family playroom into a large professional office suitable for groups as well as individual therapy.

Although it seemed to Joan that almost everybody in her town was seeing a therapist, she had a hard time finding a place for herself in the psychotherapeutic community. At the top were the medically trained psychiatrists, who could prescribe drugs and get up to $200 for the famous fifty-minute hour. Just below them were the Ph.D. psychologists, licensed to do psychological testing, who charged $120. And below them, charging much less, came counselors like Joan, with master's degrees in counseling, mental health, social work, or education.

Finding clients wasn't easy. At first, Joan tried a broadside. She compiled a mailing list, starting with everyone she knew and acquaintances she spotted by scanning names in the phone book, and sent out six hundred announcements. Nothing happened. Next she tried a rifle shot. Capitalizing on her own experience, she teamed with a speech pathologist to set up a workshop for the parents of deaf children. The workshop was a success, but it didn't produce clients. Undaunted, Joan attended nearly every meeting in Connecticut for the disabled and concluded that so many free and low-cost services were available to people coping with disabilities that they didn't have to pay for private counseling.

Workshops on problems in the news proved more fruitful. The breakthrough came when a woman who had had a history of unhappy relationships with men called to tell her she had just been moved by the book *Women Who Love Too Much* and asked her to lead a group of women who would like to discuss it. The seminar was so successful that Joan repeated it again and again, each time drawing some women who were willing to pay for individual counseling on how to stand up to men who were mistreating them. When Joan discovered that many of her clients had been victims of sexual abuse in childhood, she organized workshops and seminars on that problem, which set off another chain of referrals. The problems of adult children of alcoholics started still another chain.

Now in her sixties, Joan has created a niche that fits her. She was too impatient to take long doctoral training and too old to be interested in starting a salaried career with a social agency, so she has built a practice around problems with which a sizable group in the community can identify.

To maintain this practice, she networks with other professionals, runs therapy and support groups, lectures, holds workshops, mails out a newsletter, and does a great deal of pro bono community work. In 1994, for instance, she accepted the invitation of a rabbi to speak to a Jewish men's group on "Parenting Our Parents," a special problem that might lead to individual counseling. Her patient load fluctuates, and since insurance companies generally won't pay for therapists who aren't licensed by the state, everyone who comes to her has to pay her fee of $80 for a sixty-minute hour, although she accepts lesser amounts from people she thinks she can help who simply can't afford that much.

Joan isn't shy about why she has succeeded where so many others have failed. "I'm good at my work," she says. "I don't give up. I stuck with it because I really had to earn my living." She agrees that counseling on specific personal problems is one of the few occupations for which older women have a natural advantage. Not only are they perceived as having more experience in coping than younger people, but both men and women find it easier to talk about their troubles to an older woman than to a man.

Although Joan was reluctant to divorce, she likes her new life. She likes spending her own money and marvels at how she once accepted living on a cash allowance from her husband "as if I were a child." She likes the idea that she isn't financially accountable to anyone. Her boyfriend, an older man, didn't want to go to Nepal with her, but that didn't stop her from undertaking the adventure of serious trekking in primitive places.

Licensing restrictions may make it hard for older women to take Joan's professional path, but there are other ways into the professions. Women who have learned the ropes through years of administrative or volunteer work can usually upgrade to professional status by getting the required schooling. And as insiders, they know what to expect and where to look.

Maria McNamee Walp was a music major at Pomona College, but she fell in love with the law while working as legal secretary, office manager, and process server for a small law firm. At fifty-six she went to law school, and she later found a job as an associate attorney doing research, drafting, briefs, legal documents, and court appearances.

Kay Main worked for twelve years as an office manager for a Presbyterian church before quitting to study for the ministry. After she was ordained, she was able to work as a hospital chaplain.

Elizabeth Bingaman had trouble finding even a clerical job when she separated from her husband. "You've stayed at home too long," prospective employers told her. But she remembered that when she was in the fifth grade her mother went back to college, and subsequently was elected to Phi Beta Kappa and became a teacher. By passing a civil service test, Elizabeth landed a clerical job in the Minneapolis Public Library, and she worked her way up while getting her master's in library science. On the ground and qualified, she was able to upgrade to the job of librarian, with professional pay and retirement benefits.

Instead of getting into an established profession by getting around age limitations, a few lucky and talented women have found ways to create a professional role for themselves out of their own life experience and talents. Rice Lyons had spent most of her adult life on the Princeton campus, twenty years of it in the prestigious Office of Population Research. She was going on sixty, facing divorce and retirement, and looking for something new to do with her life when it all came together in a flash that woke her up at four in the morning. She had always been able to make people laugh — it was one of the secret weapons she used as an administrator — so why not use that ability to show other people how to relax, dance, exercise, and have fun?

LAFF, Life After Forty-Five, is a workshop that offers relaxation, massage, the gentle exercises Rice has done since serious back surgery, the folk dancing she taught as a hobby for decades, and techniques she learned from her training in Gestalt psychology, all put together with her own irrepressible brand of bubbly humor. "I have three daughters," she tells her classes. "All of them grew up to be outstanding women, taller, wiser, and older than myself." She laughingly admits that this sort of nonsense softens even the dourest bureaucrat.

Rice had another asset. Her administrative experience helped her launch a professional service. She talked the Physical Education Department at Princeton into letting her start a pilot class in LAFF once a week in the lunch hour. Academics, therapists, and nurses wrote rave reviews, and she went on to offer the workshop in a rehabilitation center, the local Y, retirement communities, conference centers, and "wherever laughter belongs."

Joan Schine is an innovator who used a stormy career as a volunteer to crash her way into the supposedly impenetrable groves of academe. Although she now bears the formidable title of director, National Center for Service Learning in Early Adolescence, Center for Advanced Study in Education (CASE), the Graduate School and University Center, City University of New York, she thinks of herself as a citizen activist.

She started when her four children were in school and she

was worried that they weren't getting as good an education in the public schools as she had enjoyed at Horace Mann, New York City's elite private high school. Like many other socially conscious suburban mothers, she served on the school board. She wasn't universally loved when she came out for busing inner-city kids into the community of Westport, a rich, conservative suburb of New York. In the uproar that followed, her enemies got her recalled from the school board under a local statute, which the superior court later declared invalid. Joan served through her second elected term and decided that if she was going to work day and night to improve education, she ought to get paid for it. But she didn't think of herself as a likely candidate for any job she would like to do.

She explained the dilemma to Parker Lansdale, an academic at the University of Bridgeport whom she had met when he was involved in a study of urban-suburban collaboration in education. "When I present myself to a potential employer and say, 'I have a twenty-five-year-old B.A. and a lot of experience in community conflict,' I wouldn't expect them to grab me," she said to him.

"Wrong," replied Parker. "We need you here." And he got her started on Interarts, an innovative program in which talented high school students were brought into Bridgeport from neighboring school districts to work with practicing artists. One experimental program in education led to others. Joan's Early Adolescent Helper Program, funded by the New York Foundation, enlists middle-school kids from the inner city to work in child care, tutoring, neighborhood improvement, and other tasks in an effort to get them to see themselves as agents for change.

Politics is a career with very few prerequisites. It is open to just about anyone who can win and hold the trust of her neighbors. Age is an asset, not a liability, and so is freedom for an unpredictable schedule. Emily Anne Staples is a good example of how politics fits into the independent life that older women can enjoy when they are on their own.

Emily Anne was always interested in politics. Her father had served as secretary and public relations consultant for the mayor of Minneapolis. She and her husband, a successful commercial real estate broker, led an active social and political life while rearing their four children. When the children were older and needed her less, Emily Anne served a term in the Minnesota state senate, but she was defeated for reelection by a Republican who heavily outspent her. She later earned a master's degree in public administration from Harvard, but as long as her husband was alive, she confined herself mostly to volunteer work on public and private boards and commissions.

Then, when she was one year short of sixty, a double catastrophe knocked the bottom out of her life. With absolutely no warning, her husband was stricken with a heart attack. On the way to the hospital, the ambulance was involved in an accident that knocked Emily Anne unconscious. When she came to in the hospital, she was told that she had a broken collarbone and her husband was dead. A week later, she found herself involved in a time-consuming lawsuit with the bank over her husband's estate.

There was never a question of being lonely. Emily Anne had so many friends that she doesn't remember eating a single dinner at home for the next year and a half. Her friends couldn't understand why she did it, but in 1990 she ran for lieutenant governor in the Democratic primary. She lost. Undaunted, in 1992 she ran for commissioner of Hennepin County, coterminous with Minneapolis and the biggest county in the state. She won.

Emily Anne brings to the commission the understanding of health care and social problems she gained in volunteer work, and she is spending all of her time working on the commission. She is free to sit with judges in the courts to check on sentencing guidelines, to visit jails, and to spend time in the community listening to problems. She finds overseeing the billion-dollar budget of the county more interesting than the work she did in the state legislature.

Volunteer work is the ideal preparation for politics, and women are more apt to serve this apprenticeship than men. Until recently this splendid experience has gone to waste. Even if politics ran in the family, concerned and experienced women could only cheer from the sidelines, stuff envelopes, study public issues in the League of Women Voters, or protest. Barbara Bush is said to be a better pol than her husband, but like a traditional woman, she practiced behind the scenes.

In the 1990s, many of these closet politicians have been running and winning in their own right. Some of them, outraged by the treatment of Anita Hill by an all-male congressional committee, were moved to run or, just as important, to give money to female candidates. The election of 1992 was called "the year of the woman" because it was the first in which female candidates were able to raise as much money as their male opponents. And except for those in the diehard right wing, most Americans had become accustomed to independent women.

A nasty divorce didn't keep Ann Richards from winning the governorship of Texas in 1990. Voters may have more confidence in candidates who are married, but a personable husband is not as helpful in getting elected as a personable wife. The husbands of Britain's Margaret Thatcher and New Jersey Governor Christine Todd Whitman have contributed largely by keeping discreetly out of the way.

Most women — and some men — postpone their political ambitions until their children are grown or at least old enough to cope with the spotlight of round-the-clock public attention. Massachusetts state senator Lucile Hicks thinks that many high-profile women in politics are single because "their former husbands or potential partners chose not to subject themselves to the incessant glare of the media and loss of privacy of a political spouse. For many men, their egos are not secure enough to tolerate a public perception of holding a secondary or lesser position in the marriage relationship."

Older women alone are an ideal resource for public service. They have more to give and less to lose. And they have been a breath of fresh air for constituencies disenchanted with old-style male politicians. In my home town, Poughkeepsie, New York, two widows ran for mayor against an unpopular male Republican incumbent in 1993. The winner was Sheila Newman, a fifty-four-year-old consultant on computer systems and former school board member who says she would never have accepted the nomination of the Democratic party if her husband, a well-known local physician, had not recently died.

Ann Brady Rupsis, an eighty-eight-year-old gadfly of city government, ran as an independent. Some people in Poughkeepsie took her candidacy as a joke. All through her eighties, she attended every open meeting of the city council as a self-appointed watchdog, and she didn't mind asking embarrassing questions. If no one applauded, she let it "just roll off me," pointing out that her husband, John, had "led me to believe I was perfect, and I never doubted his good judgment."

Ann was appointed to Poughkeepsie's Urban Renewal Agency before John died, and she went to a meeting a few days after she buried him, because "I didn't dare take my hat and coat off."

She decided to run for mayor because she felt that "Poughkeepsie needs some good old-fashioned discipline in government." Despairing of the nomination from the Democrats, with whom she had long been affiliated, she got on the ballot through her own People's Equity Party (PEP). In her campaign, she used her advanced age as an asset, referring to her political opponents as "young men I pushed when they were in baby carriages." Although she lost, she insists she is going to run again in 1995, when she will be ninety.

Professional status is especially important to women in midlife who haven't had the recognition they deserve, but the real payoff comes when they are in their sixties and seventies. For professionals, retirement doesn't mean a forced termination of work at a specified age. Self-employed doctors, lawyers, therapists, and accountants can continue working as long as they please, and even those who have always worked on salary for a school, hospital, library, social agency, or law firm can cut down on their hours or shed chores they don't like in order to undertake projects that especially interest them.

Retired ministers can lead tours to the Holy Land. Retired teachers and social workers can serve on the board of a church, hospital, college, or other local nonprofit organization. College professors can continue in their field by writing a book or maintain a presence on campus by teaching a favorite course or doing academic jobs that particularly appeal to them. And many women find it even more rewarding to use the political capital of their professional credentials to demand reforms they've learned are needed, like so many women who have created new lives for themselves in social change.

CREATING ART

Isabella Threlkeld can't remember when she wasn't drawing, painting, designing, or producing some kind of graphic art. It's always been how she knows what's going on inside.

At fifty-one, when her husband died suddenly of a cerebral hemorrhage, she discovered that her art was becoming freer. She started painting bigger, brighter canvases in the colors she remembered from Morocco, where she and her husband had been the year before, on their last trip together. But she also noticed something else that was new: when she didn't like what she painted, she found herself destroying the whole thing in a fit of anger. Alerted, she caught herself giving short answers even to friends and realized that her husband's death had made her angry as well as sad.

Like many artists, Isabella had fitted art into whatever deal life handed her. Born in Omaha, she went to Wellesley during World War II, worked and studied art in Washington, and married a commander in the navy. They had no children, so she continued to travel with him after the war, when he practiced as an international lawyer, and she became acquainted with museums and artists during extended stays in Seattle and Rome. Home base was a rented duplex in Omaha, so Isabella was able to keep up with the growing interest in art in her native city.

The first two years of her widowhood in Omaha were dark and hard. Her landlord was a Sicilian of the old school who tried to get her out so he could raise the rent. "A woman alone!" he scoffed. "Without a man, you are nothing!" She told him he had no right to talk to her or anyone else that way, but relations were strained, and as her art production picked up, she began to need more room for her new, bigger canvases.

She and a woman photographer bought a house big enough for the two of them and their work. Producing art often doesn't pay for itself, so like most artists, Isabella supported her work with teaching and other art-related activities. With space to spare, her house became a freewheeling center for international students. "It was like an academy where artists, piano teachers, and even language teachers could give private lessons, hold small classes, and meet each other. If an artist got a commission to go to Spain, I'd find someone who could teach him what he needed to know of the language."

Eventually Isabella made a business out of all the things that she found herself facilitating. She incorporated Threlkeld Art Industries as an umbrella organization, not only for selling her own art but for curating, appraising art for estates, brokering sales of existing works, and finding artists to do portraits of corporate officers and murals for corporate offices, restaurants, and banks.

"Wellesley didn't teach me anything about business," she says. "But I watched my father and my husband, and I learned how to do it." In the 1980s, Omaha became what she calls a "pocket of prosperity," and interest in art and artists was growing. By 1993 she was making more money, at least in absolute dollars, than her husband had ever been able to earn as an international lawyer. But most important, she had built a life for herself that combined service to the community with the opportunity to continue growing as an artist. At seventy-two, she was learning more about three-dimensional art, an area in which she thought she was weak, and was planning yet another exhibition of her work.

It's safe to say that millions of older women would like to be in her shoes.

All of us are born with the urge to express ourselves in the arts. As little children we all draw, model, tell stories, pretend to be someone else, dance, sing, and even make up tunes. For everyone but the occasional child who is good enough, persistent enough, or lucky enough to become an artist, growing up means giving up the urge and even forgetting that we ever had it. But late in life, the urge that we suppressed in the heat of the day can come out like the stars at night.

The number of older people who are making art has surprised even those best placed to observe it. When *Modern Maturity* magazine sponsored a competition for graphic artists fifty years or older in 1985, more than ten thousand sent colored slides of their work. "We knew a lot of older people were interested in art, but we had no idea that we'd have that many," says Linda Hubbard, the editor who ran the contest. "Most were working artists — not big-time, but people who painted regularly and showed their work in local or regional shows."

Even the performing arts offer opportunities. A reader in Wyoming wrote to *Modern Maturity*'s Malcolm Boyd about what the piano had done for her after the breakup of her thirty-six-year marriage. "I discovered I could communicate my deepest feelings by composing music and playing it on the piano. My rage and sorrow poured out, were fully expressed. I feel healed now. Also I am communicating in new ways: I am making new friends, starting a new relationship, decorating my apartment — and playing the piano for people in a retirement home." Church also provides a place for the music that many older women have made for their own enjoyment.

Show biz is a jungle, but some older newcomers relish competing in it. Women who always wanted to be actresses realize their dream by appearing in television commercials or as models in ads aimed at the growing market of older people.

When Shirl Rendlen was fifty-five, her natural white hair attracted the attention of a photographer looking for a grandmother to put on a cereal box. Newly divorced, she figured she had nothing to lose by trying. It wasn't as easy as she had thought. "They wanted a plumper grandmother," she says, "so to get that special look, they stuffed my jacket with tissue paper. For two and a half hours I sat on a rocking chair under hot lights, holding a child who must have kissed me about two hundred times before it was a wrap." From there she went on to television shows, mail-order catalogues, and advising other older women on how to get into modeling. Although she is much publicized, she lays out more money in wardrobe, makeup, and promotion than she earns.

Fay Porter, of Medina, Ohio, is proving something to her former husband. She started modeling after he divorced her to marry a woman twenty-six years his junior. She herself was in her late fifties, an age she describes as "twenty-six going on twenty-five." According to the material she sends to talent scouts, she is blond, blue-eyed, five feet five inches tall, and 155 pounds, and presumably needs no tissue-paper stuffing to achieve the normal appearance of the mature women she models. A teacher with thirty-five years of experience, her "special abilities" include playing the organ, jujitsu (she has a green belt), and speaking in a German or Swedish accent. Her credits include ads for retirement communities, hospitals, medical centers, banks, and insurance companies.

Relatively few older women have the looks, physical coordination, stamina, and desire to express themselves in one of the performing arts. The graphic arts take materials and space as well as talent. Whatever the reason, many more older women choose to express themselves in words than in any other of the other arts. But as Virginia Woolf so eloquently prescribed in *A Room of One's Own*, a creative writer needs uninterrupted blocs of time and emotional space, and it's hard for a woman to get this space while she's living with a husband.

Nancy Means Wright, Vassar '48, wrote poems in her twenties and even had a few published, but she was soon too busy raising four children and teaching to think of poetry. When she and her husband bought an old house in Vermont and ran a craft shop in the barn, she found enough time to publish four books, two of them novels; to work for local newspapers; and to write fiction for women's magazines. But her husband disparaged poetry writing as "artistic." If she were to lock herself up in her room for three hours on end, he thought, she ought to be producing something that would make money. So she concentrated on commercial fiction and again stopped writing poems. She thinks she just lost confidence in herself.

When she was sixty-one, she moved out and went to live in the house of a bachelor in another town. He wanted to marry her, but for two years she insisted on separate quarters. She needed that room of her own, that space to herself, and in it she began again to write poems, one of which ends with the line "There's juice in the old girl yet." Her chapbook, entitled *Split Nipples: Poems Suggested by the Life of Mary Wollstonecraft*, was printed in 1992 by New Spirit Press. Unlike the husband she has now divorced, her housemate admired her poetry, and after two years they were married.

Mildred Miller worked at the Library of Congress until her first child was born. Her husband was in politics, so everywhere she went she became known as his wife and the mother of their four children. After his death, she started writing poetry "as a compulsion," and when she sold some, she began thinking of herself as a writer. In order to establish herself in her own right, she stopped using her husband's name and became known in the Minneapolis community for her volunteer work and contributions to the local newspaper.

Women are the verbal sex. Most of us have written poems at some time in our lives, if only for ourselves or to tuck into letters to friends. And if large numbers of us hadn't kept diaries as girls, it wouldn't have been profitable to manufacture the ones you used to be able to buy with a lock and key, presumably to safeguard your secrets from your mother.

It's hard to imagine men doing either. Very few males express their deepest feelings in words, write poems unless they aspire to become poets, or take the trouble to write expressive letters even to their beloveds. Nor is it pure sex discrimination that relegates the writing chores of organizations to women. Most of us like writing minutes, press releases, notices, and newsletters. We are often right in thinking that all the words we have been writing in the ordinary course of our lives are as worthy of print as those we've been reading. What's more, we get so much practice talking and writing that we keep getting better at it.

You're never too old to write. Theresa Meyerowitz and her husband, William, were both painters, and after William died, Theresa started writing his biography. When she was ninety she sent the first four chapters to an editor she had met at a party, who found her style "gripping" but added that he "didn't think that at your age you will ever write a book." Lydia Brontë, who tells the story in her book *The Longevity Factor*, reports that Theresa went on to write six books, including two books of poetry and a book of the elaborate stories she had made up to entertain children when she was painting their portraits.

When we have that room of our own, some of us plunge into the mainstream literary marketplace and write for what the trade calls "the general reader." A few displaced homemakers have made money writing steamy commercial novels based on their own experiences or, more often, their sexual fantasies. But anyone who has lived long and perceptively has stories to tell. *And Ladies of the Club*, a bestseller of 1982, was a first novel written by an eighty-eight-year-old retired professor of English in a nursing home. It chronicled the life of women in a small American town from 1868, when they formed a club, to 1932, when the last charter member died.

Some older women get interested in a corner of history or the lore of a region and break into writing as specialists. After she left her husband, Lila Line moved from metropolitan Washington to a cottage on Chesapeake Bay and got to know the hardy women who make a living fishing, crabbing, and oystering in its waters. She was fifty-seven when *Waterwomen*, her book profiling five of those women, won a $5,000 prize offered by the Queen

Anne Press, a foundation-supported project for collecting stories about the Eastern Shore of Maryland.

Lila had always loved both writing and the water, but during her marriage she never got enough of either. After her third son was born, she found herself bored with the role of suburban housewife, so she started taking courses in writing at the University of Maryland and found a job as an associate editor with a federal agency. The move to the bay gave her a chance to write about hardy outdoor women whose independence and courage attracted her.

The success of *Waterwomen* set her up to speak and write books and articles about the region; for instance, in 1991 she taught Chesapeake Bay lore on an Elderhostel schooner while it cruised on the bay for a week. While these activities do not add up to a reliable income, Lila's earnings from teaching classes in writing at a nearby college, leading workshops, and lecturing at schools and libraries add enough to a small Social Security check to allow her to live comfortably.

"It would have been far easier to stay in a financially secure marriage," she writes, "but I would never have experienced the joy and contentment of having made it on my own, being paid for what I love to do, and being recognized and admired by the people in the area I now call home."

More and more nonfiction writing is being done by specialists in the subject rather than professional journalists or writers, so older people can often capitalize on what they've learned in life by writing about it. Joan Ellis always wanted to write, but she married too young to have any adult time to herself and spent decades raising children and helping her husband develop a lucrative business in electronic counting equipment. They parted company when he wanted to retire and travel and she was ready for an enterprise of her own.

She had always loved movies, so why not write about them? Her share of the family business left her without money problems, so she redid the house in New Jersey to make a workshop and started writing and syndicating movie reviews. Since she knows how to run a business, she hopes to distribute the reviews through a 900 number that would give subscribers a rundown on movies showing in the vicinity. Until she can work that out, she's syndicating her reviews for newspapers and writing for local publications.

Beginners are always told that the best way to start writing is to write about themselves, and that's just the kind of writing that many older women are eager to do. The formula worked perfectly for Frances Weaver. I met her when I was researching this book at a "Senior Expo" supported by merchants in Minneapolis. She was speaking to promote *The Girls with the Grandmother Faces*, a book of advice to women "singled and sixty," which she wrote and published herself.

Her book tells her story. A medical technologist by education, she married a medical student and brought up their four children in Pueblo, Colorado. Her husband was rigid, reserved, and busy, but she was always telling jokes, and soon found herself chairing every good cause in town. Two years before his sudden death, a magazine published a light-hearted account of how Frances and other similarly situated wives enjoyed flying kites because it gave them time away from home to talk freely about their feelings.

After her husband died, Frances tried being a travel agent. She promoted tours by writing clever brochures and letters to her friends, but the writing part was more attractive than the business, so she decided to concentrate on writing. She went to writers' conferences in the East, studied writing at Adirondack Community College in New York, looked at magazines such as *Writer's Digest* and *The Writer* to find markets, and started keeping a journal of her thoughts every day. After she finished her book, promoting it at meetings made her a polished standup comic.

In Minneapolis, her standing-room-only audience of seniors roared at ageist jokes they would never have accepted from a young person — or read in politically correct mainstream publications. "Better get a new outlook," she advised her gray-haired fans. "Everything else has fallen off, fallen out, or leaked." She got a laugh over the grandchild who said that "someone has let the air out of your arms." A widow who complained that "it has been seventeen years since I lost Ted" was told, "That was careless of you." But Frances's moral was always upbeat: get out and make a new life for yourself.

Frances Weaver enjoys herself as much as her audiences enjoy her. She likes meeting new people, speaking her mind, making people laugh. She doesn't have to make money at it, but she breaks even and can deduct the expenses of the traveling, writing, and publishing she would do anyway from her taxable income.

Older women find platforms for writing and speaking in conferences, workshops, short courses, newsletters, and specialized publications, not only those for women but those for seniors and writers. When I started looking for salty old women, everyone directed me to two who were making a career of writing and speaking to other old women from all of these platforms. Both Ruth Jacobs and Jane Porcino have one foot in academic sociology, but unlike sociologists who write for policymakers, they speak directly to older women as older women themselves.

Ruth Jacobs is a feisty Quaker who earned her Ph.D. in sociology when she was forty-five. Her first book, *Life After Youth: Female, Forty — What Next?*, was a relatively sedate sociological treatise on the growing problems of ageism and sexism. Since retiring from her academic post at Wellesley in 1987, she has taken to the road to advise, encourage, and exhort victims of these problems to help themselves. A tireless promoter, she brings copies of her book *Be an Outrageous Older Woman — A RASP: Remarkable Aging Smart Person* to sell when she speaks at workshops, conferences, women's groups, senior citizens' associations, and Elderhostels, and she distributes big buttons saying "I'm an Outrageous Older Woman," provided by her publisher.

Like Ruth Jacobs, Jane Porcino is an advocate. A suburban housewife, mother of seven children, and community volunteer, she cured herself of a midlife depression by going back to graduate school. Hooked on learning, she received a master's degree in social work at fifty-two, and continued on to earn a Ph.D. in gerontology at fifty-seven. Her first book, *Growing Older, Getting*

Better: A Handbook for Women in the Second Half of Life, was a pioneering effort, concentrating on the problems and potential of midlife and older women. Her next book, *Living Longer, Living Better: Adventures in Community Housing for Those in the Second Half of Life,* suggests creative forms of community living, including cohousing. A persistent networker, Jane founded the National Action Forum for Midlife and Older Women (NAFOW), which issues a quarterly newsletter of information about the current physical, emotional, and social concerns of aging women. *Hot Flash,* now in its thirteenth year, is written and edited by volunteers and supported solely by member contributions to NAFOW. Jane Porcino teaches at New York University and lectures around the world.

Most older women aren't writing as advocates. Like Mildred Miller and Nancy Wright, they have taken to writing in order to explain and express themselves. Women were two thirds of the six thousand people who entered the Legacies writing contest, which invited people sixty and over to submit a brief story about their accomplishments or something that happened to them "that you would want your grandchildren to know."

All over the country, older women are passing what they have written around to one another in workshops, clubs, poetry readings, and conferences. They are taking and teaching courses in writing, not just writing in general but the kind of writing they are trying to do: keeping a journal, writing an autobiography, or researching a family tree. Two examples illustrate how very specific these workshops can be. One of the winning entries in the Legacies contest was written by an eighty-year-old member of a writing group composed entirely of widows. Esther Nelson, another winner, was collaborating with her writing teacher on a book about the special art of teaching writing to the elderly.

Low-cost desktop publishing makes it easy for women to share what they have written. *Broomstick* is a nonprofit publication in San Francisco that describes itself as "a national feminist reader participation quarterly by, for, and about women over forty." It aims to be "a network . . . not a platform from which experts tell women over forty how to live." Every issue features poems, letters, memoirs, and stories contributed by women over forty. According to the editors, *Broomstick* stands for "skills: homemaking and paid jobs; change: the new broom sweeps clean; power: the witch flies on the broom; healing: witches were the ancient healers; confrontation: compelling society to look at the lives of women over forty."

I learned about *Encore*, "a bi-monthly magazine celebrating the return of the crone," when Joyce Cupps, the editor, wrote to ask if she could reprint my salty old woman piece from *Ms.* "We'd be willing to give you a free copy of the magazine, plus advertising space, as an exchange. 'We' is just me right now, doing what I can to celebrate older women, so I can't afford to pay you." The issue that carried my reprint also had an interview with Ruth Jacobs.

Encore celebrates the return of the crone "after centuries of abuse, ridicule, and rejection by a society afraid of her power and wisdom. And she is You — the midlife or older woman, with youth and childbearing behind, in your third fulfilling phase of life." Croning ceremonies, held by women to welcome a woman's menopause with song, dance, and candles, have become popular on the West Coast (*Encore* is published in Galt, California), but in 1993 Joyce assured me that the movement was spreading to the East and that a book of croning ceremonies was on the way in Maine.

These are only two of what may be hundreds or even thousands of small publications written by, for, and about older women. Started by a few friends in a burst of missionary zeal, they appear for as long as the enthusiasm or the limited resources of the founders last. No one knows how many older women are writing about themselves, but the production of literature by, for, and about older women may be growing faster than the mainstream press which ignores it.

Sandra Martz stumbled into this well of creative output by accident. By 1994, her anthology *When I Am an Old Woman I Shall Wear Purple* had sold one million copies. She wasn't burdened by the conventional wisdom of publishing. Compiling and printing anthologies was a hobby she took up while holding down a "real" job as a manager at TRW, a California defense contractor. In 1986 she put an ad in *Poet and Writer* magazine soliciting poems, stories, and photographs about old women — no pay offered — and was flooded with almost seven hundred replies. Much of this material would have languished unread in the slush pile of a mainstream publisher, but Sandra was moved by the way in which these women were pouring their hearts out and read each one.

Choosing what to use was a labor of love. For nearly a year, Sandra rushed home from work to sort the submissions into piles on her living room floor. The title poem is one of the few pieces in the anthology that had been previously published. Someone sent her a photocopy of it without the author's name, and she liked it so much she decided she would have to have it, if she could find the author. A friend found it printed in a women's magazine, which named the author and the publisher, so she was able to get permission to use it from Jenny Josephs, the British poet who wrote it.

In 1987, Sandra printed up three thousand copies of the book, packed a load of them into her car, and spent her vacation dropping them off on consignment at every bookstore between Los Angeles and Seattle. Everywhere older women loved it, because it told them what they needed to hear but weren't being told: you don't have to act and look younger, you're fine just the way you are. Distributed in gift stores, the book was just what people wanted to tell their mothers. And it came just when older women were rebelling against the message of eternal youth beamed at them by the cosmetic and fashion industries.

Reorders poured in so fast that Sandra had to quit her regular job to take care of them, but the first payday that passed without a check threw her into such a panic that she took a part-time job stocking grocery shelves to have $75 coming in every week for sure. She is a natural-born publisher, a reader rather than a writer, with an ear for what real people feel and say. Her Papier Mache

Press is named for "the art of using common everyday materials to create articles of great strength and beauty" and issues a few books every year that appeal to her.

As of 1994, there was no mention of Sandra Martz or the bestselling book she had published in the index to the *New York Times*. The success of the book illustrates, but does not explain, why so many older women take to writing about themselves with such stunning impact.

As a professional writer who has made a living putting one word after another for half a century, I've had a hard time identifying with this torrent. I've always known, of course, that there are many reasons for writing — more, perhaps, than for any of the other arts — but I thought at first that I ought to be able to distinguish between those who write for the sake of the product and its impact on other people, or even the money it can bring in the market, and those who write for the effect of the process on themselves.

But the more I thought about it, the blurrier this distinction became. Even a dyed-in-the wool journalist like myself draws on her own experience; hopes to influence others to her own point of view, like Carrie Dickerson and Ellen Paullin, who wrote to promote their causes; enjoys being recognized by strangers, like Joan Ellis; and gets a healthy rush of self-confidence from the process that is good for whatever ails her. And sometimes, as has happened just now for me, she gets to learn something important about herself.

In this new climate, even established writers take to writing about themselves in their later years, and sometimes with as much, if not more, success than when they wrote about general topics in their youth. May Sarton became a cult figure and a bestselling writer when she brought her poet's ear to her feelings about growing old. Doris Grumbach, the novelist and former National Public Radio book reviewer, earned some of her most enthusiastic reviews and substantial sales from *Coming into the End Zone* and *Extra Innings,* her candid memoirs of her later years. "I have not retired," she wrote me in response to my query. "Does a writer ever 'retire'? I doubt it." A few weeks after I received this note, I read a glowing review of her new book, *Fifty Days of Solitude*.

Experienced writers often turn to writing about themselves when they think they have learned something that can help other people. Now that she's retired and divorced, a veteran New York book editor and author is tackling the story of a schizophrenic son who left the dinner table, ostensibly to buy cigarettes, and jumped to his death from the roof of her thirteen-story apartment building. She hopes some good can come from a chronicle of the years she spent trying to prevent his suicide under the guidance of social workers, psychiatrists, and psychiatric services, and what the failed attempt did to her and her family.

Okay. So it's mixed motives for everyone at every age. That still doesn't explain why older women seem especially attracted to writing about themselves. Two themes emerged from my talks with various women about it. First, writing about what hurt them has made them feel better, even if no one else has read it. Second, if anybody else has read what they have written about themselves, they have been recognized as a person by people who don't know them personally. Both therapy and recognition can be very important for an older woman who is reorganizing her life to live it alone.

First, therapy: all art can purge unpleasant feelings, but words have always done it best. Like the published poet May Sarton, the Legacies winner Esther Nelson is among the many women who say they write poetry when they are ill or depressed. The therapeutic value of expressing your emotions, of "letting it all hang out" where you can see it, is the cure behind most psychotherapy.

In the past few decades, "life review" has become the preferred treatment for the mental illnesses of older people. The idea is that people can feel better about their past mistakes if they find a more charitable way of looking at them. It works for both groups and individuals, and especially well for the guilt-prone, who remember what they did wrong and forget about what they did right. Older people who are drawn to writing seem to understand this intuitively.

Contributors to the book *Legacies*, which contained the winning entries in the contest, were eloquent in explaining just what writing their stories had done for them. A woman devastated by the death of a daughter said that writing about it had helped her "to put the past behind and take hold of myself and my tomorrows." Widows told how their contributions had helped them cope with grief. One woman wrote that she had been able "to truly, finally mourn the loss of my husband." Anne Browner had always liked writing, so when she kept dreaming that her late husband was telling her how much he hated to leave her, she wrote about her memories of him; the piece was published in the *Legacies* book under the title "I'm Not Alone, Jack," and Anne went on to write "The Story of Annie," about her own childhood, for the sheer fun of writing for her children.

A more sophisticated writing-out of the trauma of separation was the book Jane Poulton put together when she discovered that her husband had kept all the letters they had written to each other while he was away in World War II. She was able to edit them into a personal record that helped her work out her grief and that was later published as a historical record by the University Press of Virginia. Seeing it all in print was "a thrilling experience."

Recognition can be just as important a reward as therapy. Marge Kalina, of Omaha, thinks older women of this generation become writers because "traditional marriages forced them to be silent about their feelings" but moving away from a traditional lifestyle adds emotional wounds that can be healed by writing about them. Both figure in her plans to write when she retires.

Marge went to college in her late thirties for an experience she had missed — "defining myself in my own terms." By the time she had four children, her husband was disabled, which left her to support the whole family both financially and emotionally. At first the dream of college seemed selfish and pointless, but later she came to think of it as part of a larger design.

The broadening horizon she gained from her job in a resource center and study toward a degree in counseling shook Marge's traditional Catholic faith, and when her husband died, "a part of the person I used to be died with him." Therapy had prepared her for relief and guilt, but not for two disturbing dreams that occurred a few months later. In the first, her dead husband appeared to her looking peaceful, healthy, happy, and cared for. In the second, he looked the same but was moving away from her toward a bright light. She thinks the second dream may have been influenced by what she had read about near-death experiences, but in both dreams she felt "washed in bright light, peace, and wholeness." She had always doubted life after death, but the dreams led her to believe more strongly in that possibility.

Helen Crosswait had an even rougher transition to personal independence. After her divorce, she laid out part of her life savings to print her memoir, *Reflections of a Paleface from Rosebud*, but she can't think of a better use of the money. She says that the outlay would have been worth it even if only three or four friends read it and said they understood, but she has sold five hundred copies on her own.

Helen was born on the Rosebud Indian reservation in South Dakota, the blue-eyed child of white parents. They were down on their luck. Her father, an expatriate Britisher, had homesteaded in South Dakota and, when he couldn't make a living at it, was lucky enough to land a job as a letter carrier. Helen married a school administrator and didn't think of college as a possibility until she visited her grown daughter in Lincoln, Nebraska, and took courses in women's studies at the university there.

The brief experience with college made her feel so much better that she wanted more. Her husband had a Ph.D. himself but was against it and told her she would have to choose between college and him. After a stormy year, she was divorced. At fifty-four, she earned her bachelor's degree in university studies, with a major in women's studies. But she discovered that the jobs for which this degree prepared her were in teaching and required a master's degree.

Unemployed, she sat down and wrote a poem about getting

a parking ticket, another about the death of her brother, and then others about growing up on a reservation. In 1993 she learned to play the guitar, in hopes of getting billed as a singer of songs and storyteller at conventions. She was also hoping to get funded for a master's degree in women's studies and to write her autobiography as a thesis.

Recognition as an individual is rewarding for women who have spent most of their lives as traditional wives, even if their marriages have been happy. Alice Blackstone always wrote poems. Before her husband died, she felt modest about admitting that she loved an audience, "but now I think it's all right to toot your own horn." Her poem "At 80" describes her own journey, the stories she has to "tell and retell" and the "stockpile of skins I have outgrown."

Maybe it's just human to create art. Esther Nelson doesn't think there is any mystery in why women turn to writing in their later years: "Our real entitlements are time, leisure, and society's permission."

Maybe my problem was that I asked the wrong question. Instead of wondering why people take up art in their later years, I should have been asking why they don't do it earlier.

SWITCHING ROLES

New roles are hard to classify, because there are so many ways you can think about them. Some of the most successful women have invented roles that could never apply to anyone else because they are made up of an individual's unique life experience, like Rice Lyon's LAFF. Others have tried so many roles that you can't put them in any one place. I call them role switchers.

Role switchers thrive on changing roles. They enjoy coping with new situations and transferring skills learned in one to another, and they are always on the lookout for new fields to conquer. The adrenaline rush of a new challenge can be addictive.

Vilma Kohn started out as a medical technologist. When her husband was alive, she taught biology, then became a lawyer. Since her husband's death, she has roamed the world as an archeologist. She thinks she learned the patience for archeology in the "mundane tasks" of her longest job, as a court administrator.

Some women seem to be born to cope. Jeanne Kretschmer, the round-the-world sailor and Peace Corps volunteer, adapts almost effortlessly to any situation. Arthritis didn't stop her from living in a Fijian hut without a chair; she just carried a pillow around with her. Once when I asked her how the world looked to her these days, she said, "Especially bright now that I've had my second cataract operation." She's been a business manager, enterpriser, world traveler, consultant, coach, and teacher.

Some women seem to get the hang of switching from role to role, gathering strength as they go like a snowball. That is the image that comes to mind when I think about the career of Ruth Humphrey, wife, mother, student, social worker, breadwinner, community caregiver, chef, advocate, and all-purpose problem solver.

I met Ruth over the problem of Clancy, a Siamese cat with a nasty disposition who had been spoiled rotten by my friend Leslie Koempel, a retired professor of sociology. When Leslie was eighty-five, she was invited to close up her house and go live with a nephew. Her own welcome was clear, but nobody knew whether the nephew's animals were willing to put up with Clancy. We were going around on this when I recalled that in the course of defending Clancy, Leslie had once mentioned that a former colleague by the name of Ruth Humphrey had admired him when he was a kitten. It was a long shot, but sure enough, we found Ruth Humphrey in the phone book, and yes, she remembered Clancy, and what could she do for Leslie?

None of Leslie's other concerned friends knew Ruth, but she proved she too was a friend. Not only did she agree to provide a home for Clancy, but she spent a week helping Leslie decide what to keep, what to take, and how to get rid of the rest of her stuff. And on the sad last day, when there was nothing in Leslie's little house but labeled boxes, she brought in a tasty hot supper for the score or more of well-wishers who had turned up to see Leslie off. No trouble at all, said Ruth. She had everything she needed.

No trouble at all? It was only when we were cleaning up afterward that I discovered that Ruth is permanently disabled, with a leg brace from floor to hip. She manages to cook for friends by using a dazzling array of little tricks she has invented. The hardest part is getting the heavy boxes of food and equipment from car to house, so she contrives to arrive early, preferably when nobody is around to see her. And she paces herself. After a job she goes straight home to bed and stays there for two days. Pain? It's always there, but she has taught herself how to live with it. So much for the "sick role" ascribed to women in her condition.

Ruth Humphrey has packed a lot of living into her fifty-five years. Bad things have happened to her, but she has survived by making them work for her. Abused as a child, she dropped out of school at sixteen, married an alcoholic who abused her, and, as so often happens, left him to marry a similar man, who gave her two children before she had to leave him too. With young children to support and no high school diploma, she passed the high school equivalency test and landed a full four-year scholarship to Bard College, a small liberal arts school in the Hudson Valley.

Friends wanted her to put her children in foster care and live in the dormitory, but Ruth refused to abandon her boys. Working at low-paying jobs, she lived with them off-campus while carrying a full academic load. For her senior thesis, she chose the topic of child abuse, and after her graduation she started the Task Force for Child Protection, an organization that has since become a permanent institution with a paid director.

The next decade was smoother sailing. Ruth married a prosperous chiropractor and developed her talent for gourmet cooking. But the good times weren't to last. First she had a heart attack, and then, a year later, her husband died. The boys were grown, so she was once again on her own, but disabled now and living alone in a big house. Ignoring medical advice, she started to cook for a living at clubs and restaurants. She had worked her way up to chief pastry cook at the historic Beekman Arms in Rhinebeck, New York, when she slipped on a melon peel, which landed her in the leg brace.

Women like Ruth think of their new roles as ways around problems. When one door closes, they look around for another to open. Joan Rowland thinks that adversity brought out the best in her. "Every time disaster struck, I tried something new, and when it worked, I gained confidence in myself." She doesn't think she started out with much self-esteem. Precocious in music, she was forced as a child to practice six hours a day. A shy teenager, she studied all the performing arts, married in her early twenties, and didn't even try to have children until she was in her thirties.

Then, when she tried, she ran into one problem after another. Two pregnancies ended in miscarriage, two of her babies died in infancy, and when she turned to adoption, she found herself responsible for two children who turned out to be neurologically impaired. But since each disaster directed her toward something new in her work, she acquired professional experience in theater, dance, jazz, and classical music.

The final disaster was her marriage. By her forties, Joan had acquired enough self-confidence to divorce her husband, who had established himself as a public relations consultant. She was now on her own in the very worst of circumstances. No longer young and responsible for three children under twelve, two of whom were adopted and too disturbed to stay with anyone else for more than an hour or two, she didn't even try to date. To care for the children, she taught from her home in Manhattan during the day and sang and played in hotels and restaurants at night, when she could leave them with babysitters. After a year of this, she had a bright idea that put all her experience together, and she put it into practice with the help of the publicity skills she had learned from her husband.

She established One Touch of Whimsy, an art gallery on Manhattan's Upper East Side that attracted customers and attention by offering live music, theater, dance, and an art school on the premises. For three years it prospered. When Joan lost her lease, she survived by selling art wholesale to out-of-town galleries and organizing ventures such as trips to China for prep-school children.

On her sixtieth birthday, Joan had an attack of angina and was ordered to exercise regularly. She found the New York air bad and had a dim memory of a brochure she had filed, for want of a better place, in a folder she labeled "Peculiar Things." It turned out to be a notice for a race-walking clinic open to the public in Central Park. Intending only to get some fresh air and exercise, she went to the clinic one Saturday morning and absorbed the basics of race walking (helped, of course, by her experience as a dancer). She entered a race on Sunday and came away with the gold medal. It was the start of a new career as an athlete.

In 1993, Joan Rowland was world champion of the U.S. National Senior Sports Classic in race walking for the 65–69 age category. At sixty-seven, her children are grown and she is living the life of a celebrity. She does TV commercials, gives race-walking clinics, and competes in track-and-field events all over the United States and at World Veterans Association meets abroad. "Every time I do a race," she tells reporters, "I know I'm adding days, weeks, and months to my life." Musician, teacher, art dealer, impresario, travel agent, athlete — these are only some of the roles of Joan Rowland.

Sue Mathias, a divorced mother of five grown children, has always had the chutzpah to find a dramatic way around bad luck. Although she hesitates to advertise her age, in her late sixties she is blissfully working at an occupation she chose, among other reasons, because she could do it "from a rocking chair at a hundred and five." As a handwriting expert, Sue is consulted by employers for personnel screening and by individuals wondering whether they will be compatible marriage or business partners. Her firm, Insight/Impact, grew out of a lifelong interest in handwriting analysis, and she promotes the endless possibilities of her field by writing newspaper articles and three monthly columns.

Sue learned to fly both helicopters and airplanes while in her forties. At that time she also began her career outside the home, because her husband had bought a St. Louis sightseeing tour called the Riverfront Trolley and expected her to manage it. When she was divorced at fifty-two and needed a job, she asked the head of KMOX-CBS, a powerful radio station, for a job as their first female on-air traffic reporter. Although she had no broadcast experience, she got it. Known all over town as "Sue in 'Copter Two," she later moved into news reporting for the station and racked up a row of "first woman" credits.

Fabulously successful women have the knack of seeing all the possibilities that can grow out of what they are doing and pursuing the ones that attract them. Phyllis Diller, whom most of us know as a comedian, was trained as a concert pianist. In her fifties she went back to playing with symphony orchestras, until she could no longer afford to take the time to practice. Then, for her seventieth birthday, she gave herself an art studio and started to paint, with such success that six years later she was setting up her fourth one-woman show in Chicago and finding time to practice the piano again. Pianist, writer, entertainer, comedian, painter — all these roles are comfortable for her.

When Joan Rivers was fifty-five, she characterized her career as "hard, hurting, little steps." At the time she was hosting the five-day-a-week *Joan Rivers Show,* awaiting publication of the second part of her autobiography, *Still Talking,* and launching the Joan Rivers Classics Collection, a line of jewelry. Actress, author, screenwriter, businesswoman, TV emcee, comedian, and later a playwright, she is as forthright about her age as Phyllis Diller.

Some women always see the next step to anything they are currently doing. Margo Miller started out in early childhood education in California, tried running a play program for toddlers and their parents after she was divorced, and went on to sell ads for a positive parenting magazine. "Now, instead of teaching in a classroom, I teach people about advertising their businesses, and all the people I see are doing something for children or parents," she notes in "My Second Childhood," a piece she wrote about herself when she was sixty-five. "I went to a modeling school to see if they would advertise for child models in our paper. I left with the ad and with the seed planted in my mind that I could be a model myself . . . For many years, my identity was that of wife, mother, and teacher," she concludes. "Now, when someone asks me what I do, I tell them I wear many hats. 'I sell advertising,' I say, or 'I do modeling,' or — and this is the most exciting thing in my life right now — 'I'm writing a children's picture book.'"

There's a lot of evidence that switching roles is good for you. As I pointed out before, Phyllis Moen's Cornell study found that the healthiest and longest-lived homemakers were those who had played the most roles outside the home when their children were young. Doctors, lawyers, policymakers, and artists seem to live longer than people who spend years doing the same thing in the same way every day. These professions force people to deal with the complicated situations of real life that don't yield to routine solutions. To act at all, they have to search creatively for analogies with similar situations and learn to live with uncertainty.

Margo Miller's title, "My Second Childhood," may be an apt description of what switching roles is doing for her. Older women who plunge into a new role shatter the crust of habit that eventually inhibits everyone's possibilities and set off a new round of the kind of personal growth that makes childhood and youth exciting.

5

PATHWAYS TO
NEW LIVES

AS I TALKED with women, I asked them how they had found the new roles that were giving them what so many spontaneously insisted were the best years of their lives. Many of these women remembered how disoriented they had felt when they were first alone. The ultimate questions put aside at the end of adolescence come flooding back in the empty space left by the end of a marriage: What's it all about, anyway? Who am I? Where am I going? This feeling of being lost is nowhere better described than in the opening lines of Dante's *Divine Comedy:* "Midway upon the journey of our life I found myself in a dark wood . . ." If anyone had told these women when they felt that way that they were now free to do what they pleased, they would have thought that person was making a joke in bad taste.

So how did they get from there to here? Somehow, they found a new way of thinking about themselves, a way to take a role on a bigger stage than the one from which they had been so unceremoniously thrust. Established religious faith didn't seem to provide a well-charted path out of the dark wood, though some stepped up the work they had been doing for their church. Those I talked with were more likely to look for answers to the ultimate questions by undergoing psychotherapy, talking about their feelings in support groups, or writing about them in poems or autobiographies.

When I looked for patterns, I found that the smoothest transitions were made by the few who planned what they were going to do while they were still married. When Gail Deaver realized she was going to divorce her husband, she went back to college, did all but the dissertation required for a doctorate in education, and started a twenty-eight-year career of teaching mass communications at the college level. Later she married a dashing airline captain and enjoyed thirteen happy years traveling around the world as his wife. Before his retirement because of ill health, she often went along, sitting in first class and chatting with the passengers while he piloted the plane. When he had to retire, she was already established as a teacher.

Another who planned ahead was Evelyn Stefansson Nef, one of the women with long careers mentioned in Lydia Brontë's book *The Longevity Factor*. In her early sixties, she unexpectedly fell in love with a man so much older that she knew she would outlive him. (She knew what to expect because her second husband, the explorer Vilhjalmur Stefansson, was thirty-three years her senior.) Despite her age, she was able to persuade the director of the Institute for the Study of Psychotherapy in New York to admit her as a student. By the time John Nef died, she was practicing her new profession in Washington. She feels she is a better psychotherapist than she would have been if she had trained and entered the profession at the conventional age.

Role finding seems to be a skill that improves with practice. Jacqueline Thea, a nurse who had become a health educator between marriages, started a new business as a conservator for older people who can't manage in their own homes without outside help. Looking a few years ahead to when she herself would be without a partner, she began acquiring land in Oregon to set up a community home for a dozen older women.

Louise Ulrich had the same idea. While still in divinity school, with her career as a Unitarian Universalist minister ahead of her, she was planning to open a group home for a half-dozen older women with independent and unconventional views. Describing herself as a "lusty old woman," she hoped to find housemates who would join her in viewing X-rated movies!

When I started collecting new roles, I looked first for radical changes of direction. I counted myself out, because after all, I've worked steadily as a nonfiction writer for more than fifty years. But when I pressed myself with the questions I would have asked someone else, I had to admit that I now do it in a different way. I write many more books than articles, almost always now on subjects of my own choosing. I get Robin Walsh or Lauren Muffs to go to the library for me (they're reference librarians, so they are better at it, as well, of course, as at bending and stretching in the stacks and clambering up and down the spiral staircases). And yes, I'm writing about the situation of other old women (no editor would dare to think I'm too old to write about *that!*).

Some women I interviewed were put off by the very idea that they had a new role. "New role?" they'd say. "Not me. I'm just doing what I've always done." Some of the transitions were so natural that the women hardly noticed them. Grace Graves had always been interested in Haviland china, and that interest developed naturally into a business when she had the time and attention to devote to it. A woman who always had a lot of friends made a career of fund-raising, politics, or selling. A woman who liked to ski and got to be good at it created a role for herself as a volunteer coach.

New roles hardly ever start from scratch. Even a startlingly new life turns out to come from a disregarded talent or interest that sprouts when the time is right, as naturally as a daffodil pushes up through a springtime snow. Grandma Moses may have started to paint at seventy-eight, when her fingers were too stiff for embroidery, but when she was a little girl she had drawn pictures in grape juice on the newsprint her father brought home. After her mother told her to spend her time more usefully, she switched to expressing herself graphically in handicrafts like embroidery.

We all have to make ourselves up as we go along, developing skills and storing them away for future use when they're no longer immediately needed. Grandma Moses was unusual only in reaching so far back in her life for a way to do what she wanted to do.

So what we should do is take an inventory of what's been wrapped up for ages in those little parcels in the back of the freezer. Or, to change the metaphor, we should shift the spotlight from one part of ourself to another. One door closes, another opens.

BACK TO A GIRLHOOD DREAM

While I was writing this book, a friend thought I should know about a fragile old woman who had been seen wheeling a battered bike away from the Salvation Army, where it had been marked down because it didn't work. She said she didn't mind, because she wasn't strong enough to ride it, but she had always wanted a bike and never been able to afford one before. Once she got it home, she thought she could find a way to put her feet on the pedals.

People who never stop dreaming are very likely to find some way to make that dream come true. Carole Woolley had always wanted a horse. She couldn't afford to buy one when she was widowed at fifty, but her time was her own, so she took a job caring for horses at a local stable. There she met Chuck Ferguson, a carpenter down on his luck who was working there because he was trying to stay sober. Pitching hay together in the predawn cold, they fell in love. With Carole's support, Chuck succeeded in reversing what may have been a hereditary tendency to drink. He's been off the stuff for the seven years they've been living happily together. Chuck has no children, but he's a favorite with Carole's grandchildren, and since he's been working steadily he and Carole have acquired two horses of their own.

Dreams seldom come true exactly the way you dream them. Sometimes the reality is better. Toby Ansin didn't get to be a ballerina, but in her wildest dreams she never expected to have a whole ballet company to her credit and a classic ballet named after her. Beth Verssen dreamed of serving as a missionary when she was a girl, but the service she is rendering her faith in a hospital in India is richer and broader than she ever imagined.

Even when the reality is disappointing, it can be enlightening. One of the women I talked to, one of the few blacks in an Irish Catholic neighborhood in Steeltown, Pennsylvania, wanted to be a nun, but her parents wouldn't let her. She married young and was widowed when the youngest of her six children was only two. For the next few years, she worked the night shift at a post office and studied sociology at Temple University by day. The post office didn't hold her race or sex against her, but she had always led a deep and active spiritual life, and she yearned for a more religious setting. So when she was forty-two she left the post office to become a caseworker, and eventually to work for the Archdiocese of Philadelphia.

Somewhat to her surprise, she found that she still wanted to be a nun. Her age and even her race were formidable barriers. Entering a religious community is not like getting a job. You have to have a genuine call for it. Usually the call comes early in life, but so few young women now enter these communities that they are overloaded with aging sisters and have had to become even more wary of accepting older women. And while the church admits no color bar, it's no secret that blacks have not always been welcome in close-knit religious communities.

At one point, she considered getting around age discrimination by founding a new community expressly designed for older women, but she had to give it up, because "starting a religious community is not like starting a hat shop." So she persisted in trying to get into an existing order.

"It's not enough for a woman to find the lifestyle appealing," she says. "You have to show that you have genuine spiritual reasons." Through the archdiocese, she had the advantage of good spiritual guidance. For years she met once a month with a sister who helped her examine her motives, and every year she went on an eight-day spiritual retreat that gave her time and peace to reflect. After eight years, her spiritual director steered her to the Handmaids of the Sacred Heart of Jesus, a small international order dedicated to teaching, social work, and retreats, which has only forty-five members in the United States.

She edged into the Handmaids slowly. She spent weekends living in the community for a year before she resigned her job at the archdiocese to become a postulant, beginning a period of training and trial during which she lived with fourteen other sisters. After ten months, she took her first vows as a novice and was sent to work in North Carolina as a pastoral associate. That's where she began to have doubts about whether she was really ready to become what she calls "a corporate person."

Although she loyally denies having any problems with the other sisters, she began to chafe at what seemed like senseless limitations on her personal freedom and at being confined with women who did not share — and may have resented — her broader life experience. Part of the problem, she thinks, was that the order was not designed for American culture. She couldn't help contrasting it unfavorably with what a friend told her about the Mercy Sisters of America, a thoroughly American order whose members were allowed to live outside the cloister when their mission required it. And she freely admits that another aspect of the problem was that she was too low in the pecking order to influence policy.

She didn't take her final vows. Her spiritual adviser helped her to realize that her calling was primarily to her work, and the spiritual life she had coveted was actually distracting her from it. She's now back working in the social ministry of her archdiocese and living happily by herself in an apartment near five of her children. She can be accountable or not to anyone she chooses to be accountable to, pray when she feels like it, and pursue her spiritual growth on her own terms.

Sometimes the dream leads to the discovery of a role that makes sense now. Women who have given up trying to become a doctor or a lawyer sometimes go back to college and become speech therapists or paralegals. One of the many women who wanted to be an actress as a girl wound up helping mental patients act out their anxieties in a psychodrama program. Others, as we have seen, become models for print or television ads. And some of the women who dreamed of traveling when they were tied down at home get to do it in the Peace Corps.

College is the dream of many older women who missed it. Today every college awards diplomas to women in their fifties, sixties, and seventies. Professors like them because they are eager to learn for the sake of learning. "You know, Mom, if you and I were in class together, I have an idea you'd be one of those people I would hate," the daughter of one woman confessed. "You'd always have your hand in the air, always want to talk. You'd be sitting in the front row and would drive the rest of us students nuts."

For traditional homemakers who married early, college represents the years of adult independence they see young women enjoying before they have children or pursue a career. A mother of nine who eventually divorced her abusive husband and went back to college remembers "the feel of a new book and the smell of newly sharpened pencils from as long ago as grade school."

Shirley McKittrick had a similar experience. She had always wanted to become a teacher, but instead of going to college, she entered the workforce. At twenty-three, while working at General Dynamics, the company that makes submarines for the navy in Groton, Connecticut, she met and married. She returned to work after her first child was born, but opted to stay at home after the birth of her second child. For eleven years she worked at various part-time jobs, such as house cleaning, taking in sewing, and ironing. Meanwhile, her husband, who was an alcoholic, continued to drink and go from one job to another. Eventually he lost his job at the post office and was jailed for stealing from the mails. Shirley divorced him and returned to General Dynamics, and with the company's tuition assistance she attended college. She graduated with a B.S. in business thirty-five years after graduating from high school.

During the women's movement of the 1970s, traditional homemakers sometimes looked to college as the pathway to personal liberation but encountered opposition from husbands who saw their ambition as a threat, if not a preparation for divorce. "I was troubled because my husband didn't support my dream," Marge Kalina wrote in an essay on the theme of independence for the Bicentennial. "I realize now he was anxious and afraid that I might change and want to do something different with my life if I became a 'liberated' college woman. I really wanted his approval, but my dream was so strong that I was determined to live it out. Many people questioned my dream. 'Why go to all that trouble at your age.' 'Your husband supports you well. Why work so hard?' 'What if your marriage fails because you insist on doing your own thing?' 'You should be home for your children.' These ideas may sound very quaint to those of you born after 1960, but they were burning issues for me and many of my friends then."

As it turned out, Kalina's degree enabled her to get a job that supported the family when her husband developed brain cancer, but she resisted the temptation to ascribe her persistence to divine providence. "It should have been obvious to me that I would need a college education to support myself after Rich died," she wrote. "It wasn't the obvious that kept me going, though. I had a need to see my goal through to the end — to realize my dream."

If you can't think of any girlhood dreams, you've probably forgotten them, the way most of us forget the dreams of the night by the time we've brushed our teeth. But that doesn't mean that they are worthless or gone forever. Traditional wives and purposeful people have learned to suppress yearnings that don't make sense at the time, but dredging them up is a good way to get back in touch with yourself when you have to change direction, and there are all sorts of ways to do it.

A simple way is to shop for courses that sound interesting in the catalogue of the local community college. A riskier but potentially more rewarding route is to look up a girlhood chum and reminisce with her about what you were both interested in when you were ten-year-olds. Her memories won't match yours, but they can remind you of parts of yourself that you've been neglecting. You can also get in touch with your past by using various techniques for meditating and encouraging your thoughts to wander. In *Revolution from Within,* Gloria Steinem describes how a psychotherapist helped her discover her "inner child" with self-hypnosis.

DEVELOP SOMETHING YOU'VE ALWAYS ENJOYED

"The best thing to be in America is a rich widow." Margaret Mead was a feminist, so her famous declaration may have been no more than an elliptical way of complaining that married women had no control over money. But I prefer to think that she was also saying something positive about widowhood: if you no longer have a husband, tradition no longer stops you from pleasing yourself. In Mead's day, rich widows were the only women who had both the money and the freedom to do that.

The best example of what I think she meant is the widowhood of two southern sisters. Their married lives were as alike as two peas in a pod, but when they were widowed they invested the energy released from the relationship in ways they wouldn't have imagined as little girls.

Before they were widowed, Madeline Blue of Romney, West Virginia, and Ruth Kinnard of Franklin, Tennessee, could have stepped out of an old *Saturday Evening Post* cover by Norman Rockwell. Born in 1915 and 1919, they grew up as proper southern young ladies on the big plantation their father owned in rural Alabama. Madeline took a two-year course that qualified her for a job teaching the deaf in a special school in Romney and married John Blue, who ran the general store there. They had three children, John, Julia, and David. Ruth graduated from college, married Claiborn Kinnard, and bore Judy, their first child, while he was serving overseas as an officer in the Eighth Air Force. After the war, the Kinnards settled on his parents' farm in Franklin,

Tennessee, and Clai started what turned out to be a successful business making concrete building blocks. Their two sons, Clai and John, live in Franklin still.

Both Madeline and Ruth married men with roots in the rural South and lived most of their married lives in ancestral homesteads. Both reared two sons and a daughter in households supported by loyal black servants who regarded themselves as part of the family. Both were devoted to their husbands and children and were deeply religious members of local Protestant churches.

As luck would have it, disaster struck them at about the same time. In 1964, John died suddenly of a heart attack. When Madeline called her sister to tell her about it, she found that Ruth was bringing Clai home from an operation to remove a malignant brain tumor, from which he never recovered. By this time, the two older children of each household were away at college, so both Ruth and Madeline were left with a teenage son in a big old house haunted by happy memories.

Both sisters were crushed. For Madeline, a born-again Presbyterian, the worst part of the early emptiness was the feeling that God had deserted her. "I was angry at God. I asked him why he hadn't taken me instead." Ruth was physically drained from Clai's illness. "I had been a wife and mother for twenty-seven years. Now I didn't feel like a person anymore. I was a zombie."

Both women credit their sons with snapping them out of their depression. Madeline's healing began when the Holy Spirit visited her to tell her that she should be taking care of her boy. From that day on, she has never lived in the past. Ruth's son made the suggestion himself. "Ma, I know that Clai died," he said one night at dinner. "But I'm still here."

That's where the sisters' paths began to diverge. Madeline, who had been a sociable little girl, reached out to the people around her to continue as best she could the life she had led with her husband. She resigned from her teaching job and took over running her husband's store. According to her, all she had to do was say yes when the superintendent of schools asked her to run for the school board. It was a natural outgrowth of her teaching, and one that her husband would have approved of. After that, everything just followed. Work on the board led to statewide involvement with education and health, which earned Madeline enough political clout in the state capital to bring a projected center for the developmentally handicapped to Romney.

Ruth, in contrast, opted at once for a radical change. "I couldn't see trying to continue my old life without Clai — doing volunteer work and going to parties with a couple picking me up and taking me back home." But what to do? Interest and aptitude tests pointed to the law, a subject in which she had never before been interested. Law school was rough, and finding a job at fifty-one even rougher. Before going into private practice, she worked in the trust department of a bank and served a term as a bankruptcy judge.

Sometimes the door to a new life is concealed in the paneling and yields unexpectedly when we are thrashing about. We've seen where an interest in local history led California Quint and how a perfectly normal interest in cooking and eating led Ruth Humphrey to a career as a high-powered chef. After her divorce and retirement from her job as a librarian, Dana Hull made a satisfying second career out of her hobby of restoring organs.

In her eighties, Fay Smith is reaping the rewards of an enthusiasm for Spanish colonial history which she caught from a dedicated professor she encountered as a freshman in college. After her marriage, she saw to it that her children were bilingual, visited Spanish-speaking countries with her husband, and learned Portuguese when her husband started shipping used cars to Brazil after World War II. Since his death thirty years ago, she has been free to track down documents of the colonial period in Mexico City and elsewhere. At eighty-one, she was translating documents on microfilm from the University of Arizona and the Archdiocese of Mexico; one of her translations had been published and another was at the press.

Most married women don't get a lot of practice thinking about what they would do if they could do as they please, so the first reaction after losing a husband is often to think, "Oh, there's nothing I really want to do!" But think again. Try making a list of all the things you've wanted to do but never got around to and asking yourself, Why not now?

After my husband died, my list included reading Homer in Greek, learning musical theory, going to the Grand Canyon, looking up the Bird genealogy, taking a course in the history of art, and swimming three times a week. Since I drew up the list, I've managed to squeeze in most of these. Such activities don't make a new life, but they ring a bell in your head about the existence of a whole new world you might like to live in. Would I like to spend the rest of my life as a classical scholar or a genealogist? Probably not, but at the time reading Homer and learning family history kept me focused on the infinity of future possibilities that lies ahead.

TAKE OFF FROM WHAT YOU'VE DONE ON A JOB

Resourceful women build a new nest for themselves out of the debris of their old ones. Women who don't need a lot of money when they retire specialize in some part of the work they have done in the past that they have particularly liked. A good example is Clarice Strasser. She had learned a lot about kids by running the camp associated with the private school her family owned. When she was widowed, she developed a counseling specialty in helping teenagers choose schools and colleges.

If you like the field in which you have worked, you can often find something to do that you enjoy more than your old job. When my college classmate Marie R. Haug retired at age seventy as professor of sociology at Case Western Reserve University, she kept two offices in the university. In one she advises junior faculty on research and conducts seminars on securing research funding. In the other she continues research with colleagues from medicine and nursing, under a MERIT (Method to Extend Research in Time) award, which is granted for a ten-year period to senior investigators by the National Institute on Aging.

Women with a track record in business, law, medicine, fashion, academia, or the arts find roles for themselves as consultants, teachers, mentors, policymakers, advisers, publicists, advocates, or historians. Martha Graham became a choreographer. First an opera singer, then managing director of the New York City Opera, Beverly Sills has become a nationally known advocate for the arts in general. A retired librarian at Vassar College has volunteered to edit the papers of Matthew Vassar. And if you know any field well, you may be able to teach at your local community college.

Marion Bryant retired from the business service she built, but she has kept her notary public commission "for sentimental reasons," still does the taxes of former customers she regards as friends, and has worked as a temporary at a local savings and loan. At eighty-four, she lives alone and drives her Toyota wherever she needs or wishes to go. "You do not grow old," she says. "You become old by not growing."

Marion now devotes most of her time to her church and to the many organizations in which she holds office. A self-styled "joiner," she began her business career working for a black insurance company in the days of racial segregation, and she has been extensively honored recently for her service to the African American community. She is quick to admit that black women are more influential in their communities than white women are in theirs.

Teaching is the ideal skill for moving from one arena to another. We've seen how Margo Miller, the role switcher, started teaching children, then taught mothers how to play with children, and wound up teaching advertisers how to reach educators. Jeanne Kretschmer, the round-the-world sailor, started out by running a business school, became interested in the sea when she helped her son teach marine navigation, taught business to Fiji Islanders in the Peace Corps when she wanted a change of scenery, and eventually taught Peace Corps volunteers how to teach in alien cultures.

TURN A PERSONAL PROBLEM INTO A VOCATION

Joleen Bachman built a new life out of the meaning of the experience of college to women like herself. For twenty-seven years she led the life of a hard-working farm wife with nine children. Her divorce left her with five teenage sons, but she had the courage to quit her clerical job and go to college. Eleven years later she earned her Ph.D. in adult development and higher education administration, a field that allowed her to write her dissertation about what college had done for her and seven other midlife returnees. Her conclusion: they had all gained "newly-found identities leading to a concept of intimacy-with-self, a strong element of risk-taking, and a zest for living."

Now close to sixty, Joleen is back in the Iowa countryside, not as a farm wife but as a professor of developmental psychology at the local community college. She also organized The Woods, a country retreat center for transition and career counseling, massage therapy, stress management, and other health and healing activities.

If you've faced and overcome a personal problem, chances are that there are others who need help with it. Remember Irene Stambler, the woman who cried after her divorce because she couldn't fill her supermarket cart? When employers snubbed her because she had been "just a housewife," she started a temporary help service that grew into a multimillion-dollar business.

Remember Barbara Kelley, the homemaker who managed to survive alone in Westport, Connecticut, a suburb full of upscale couples? One of the many things she did was to help start a Unitarian program for singles. And when Caroline Miller, the professional volunteer, couldn't find residential care for her brain-damaged husband, she organized a board, which set standards that provide guidance for others facing the same problem.

Joan Blumenfeld isn't the only woman who became a psychotherapist as a result of the dissolution of her own marriage. Jean Remke was a traditional homemaker who, she now says, had "no self-esteem." She went to graduate school when she was forty-eight, divorced at fifty-one with moral support from a minister who had trained as a psychologist, and moved her five children from Illinois to Minnesota, where she found a job as a counselor. A watershed on her road to independence was deciding to paint the house she had bought a different color without asking anyone's permission.

Remke is now a psychotherapist associated with a mental health clinic in St. Paul, and she feels she is especially helpful to women experiencing a separation in later life. "I know you will find this hard to believe," she tells them, "but now is going to be the best part of your life. You will miss your husband, but you will find that it is the best thing that ever happened to you."

Divorce is a growth industry that engages lawyers, psychotherapists, social workers, and teachers, and women who have survived it are especially credible providers of these services to others. Harriet Newman Cohen went to law school when her own marriage was sputtering and her four daughters were in their teens, and her first case was her own divorce. Nineteen years later, she had made $1 million as a top-notch divorce lawyer in New York. "I sort of became a full service to people in distress," she told a reporter. "And I was really awfully good at this specialty."

There's plenty of room for improving the legal services available to divorcing women. Audrey Tegethoff learned firsthand how insensitive lawyers and courts can be to women who are inexperienced in dealing with them. It took her three years and three different lawyers to get a decree that insured her a tiny but reliable income from her affluent husband. At the suggestion of the Older

Women's League of St. Louis, she wrote to the *St. Louis Post-Dispatch*, and when it printed her letter, eighty women called OWL. With this base, Audrey set up a support group for women undergoing divorce, who can exchange their experiences and get impartial advice from experts on how to deal with their legal problems. Since then, more than one hundred women have called her personally.

"We hear of pretrial hearings taking place without the knowledge of the client, of lawyers not showing up at the appointed time, of documents misplaced, of information not gathered, of questions that will be asked and then aren't, of lawyers who prefer to go to trial rather than negotiate, and of bills being $15,000 or more," Audrey wrote. "Why does this happen? One reason is that women are too trusting."

Audrey feels much better about her life now that she is doing something constructive with what happened to her. As chairwoman of OWL's Divorce Advocacy Committee, she is mounting a campaign to show other women "how to select lawyers; how to interview them; what questions they should ask; what information they should expect to receive; what are appropriate retainers and appropriate hourly costs." In 1994 she was campaigning for a Missouri state law that would reform the divorce process, and in 1995 she hopes to work on an ethics bill that will regulate divorce lawyers.

Working to change the attitudes that have penalized you is a healthy response. Divorce makes feminists of even the most traditional women, and stars like Avis-Ann Parke, Frances Lear, and Genevieve Vaughan have made brilliant use of the experience to help other women.

Lydia Bragger is one of the few who have openly advocated a better public image for older women. After a devastating divorce in her late sixties, she joined the Gray Panthers. She founded the group's New York chapter in 1972 and began monitoring the depiction of older women on television. At ninety she was continuing the fight as the host of a radio talk show that deals with issues of aging. A recent BBC documentary introduced her as "the oldest talk-show host in America."   ·

CAPITALIZE ON YOUR AGE

Jean Benear is one of the lucky people whose genes work with her. At sixty-eight, she hasn't a gray hair on her head, and her figure is so marvelous that she has been asked to provide proof of her age when requesting a senior discount. She reads without glasses (and so did her father when he was ninety-two). She was the first woman to study engineering at the University of Oklahoma, so she was able to run her husband's engineering company when he died, but she also has a degree in radio and television and has won 750 senior sports trophies, including one for a race walk she ran in a neck brace.

Jean's real metier is promotion. Since qualifying for Social Security, she has made herself a role model for seniors, showing the vigor they can expect if they exercise, eat right, and learn to enjoy competition as much as she does. When she wrote, in a large round hand, the essay required of applicants for a team of ten adults over fifty-five who exemplify healthy aging and the athletic achievements of seniors, she began, "I *want* to be your 1993 U.S. National Senior Sports Organization Spokesperson. And I'm *sure* I am well qualified . . . This qualifying year, I won eleven gold medals. Since I always wear U.S. flag attire, I have been photographed by the *New York Times* and appear on television . . . A great gift of gab and enthusiasm make me an excellent motivator . . . Praises have come from so many who have now learned to eat correctly, exercise regularly, and learn to *enjoy competition* . . . Since I'm past sixty-five, the plane fares are very inexpensive . . . I compete at least once every weekend and have for years . . . On all occasions, I try to make my appearance memorable . . . I have modeled in many shows . . . I do like myself and try very hard to make others like me too. My enthusiasm is contagious!"

The judges agreed. In 1993 Jean toured the country, making speeches, appearing on television, and taking care to be photographed in stars and stripes with everyone from Snoopy to Ross Perot, for whom she had collected signatures during his campaign for the presidency.

But there are other ways to make your age work for you. As we've seen, even extra flesh around the middle becomes an asset if you're a mature model. The theater favors youth, but the most challenging roles for a serious actress are portrayals of older women. Most people remember Jean Stapleton for her television series *All in the Family*, but her finest role was as Eleanor Roosevelt, and at seventy, she was playing the tragicomic part of the nurse in Shakespeare's *Romeo and Juliet*. The ultimate female role is Medea, the wronged wife who revenged her husband's infidelity by killing their children, and it's not a part for an ingenue. At fifty-five, Diana Rigg continued a long and diversified career as an actress by playing Medea to rave reviews in London and New York. Jessica Tandy won her Academy Award for *Driving Miss Daisy* when she was eighty, only five years before her death in 1994.

The career of Phyllis Sanders illustrates how a smart woman used first her sex and then her age to make a role for herself in broadcasting. Women were rarities in radio news and features when she broke into radio by starting a program on women's issues on WNYC in New York. Although *The Changing World of Women* was addressed to women, the station head was nervous about how it would be received. "My dear," he warned her, "people don't like to hear a woman's voice for more than five minutes!" The program ran for eight years.

When Phyllis was fifty-seven, she began to capitalize on her age by appearing on New York City's first television series on aging, *The Prime of Your Life*. After she moved to Philadelphia, she appeared regularly on WCAU-TV with a seniors report and a half-hour show called *Over 50*. She used her age to promote the show and made no attempt to conceal a difficulty in walking shared by many of her viewers. When she began to use a folding cane to get around the labyrinthine hallways of the studio, the station bought her an electric scooter and warned all hands against the hazard of getting in the way of "Phyllis's Ferrari."

Capitalizing on your age works in many other professions, too. A retired ballet dancer now coaches other older women on the exercises she has devised to keep herself limber. Physicians, psychotherapists, sociologists, and social workers become especially credible specialists in the geriatric applications of their professions as they get older themselves. Retired college professors are ideal teachers of their subjects to other people their age in Elderhostels and the growing number of cultural programs for seniors.

Among the single older women with whom I talked, a nurse, a physical therapist, a health educator, and a minister are planning third careers serving other old people. Some aspire to become geriatric managers, helping fragile old people stay in their homes. Others are organizing a group home for themselves and a few chosen age mates.

As we develop more of our potential, our alternatives grow and become less like anyone else's. If we live to be very old, we defy all generalizations and may wind up doing something really new under the sun.

6

SECOND

THOUGHTS

THE FIRST PART of an investigative book is the honeymoon. I had a wonderful time talking with the pioneers. They were all smart, open, upbeat, and enthusiastic about their new lives.

Drawing conclusions about what you've found is always much harder. What does the experience of these women have to say to others who want to follow in their footsteps? What can I say about them as a group?

For starters, they have a higher income and more schooling and better jobs than their counterparts in the general population. Maybe this was to be expected. Pioneers who take the risks that blaze trails for the rest of us are usually above average. And while privilege makes for the self-confidence that goes with pioneering, it doesn't seem to be essential. When I sorted my database by income, I found that three of our most innovative pioneers were living in poverty, and one of these was also a high school dropout. And we all know rich, well-educated women who are models of convention.

I can't forget the casual way a Vassar alumna once referred to the departed "active part of my life." Although she had lived all her life on a comfortable Du Pont trust fund, she was as re-signed to a role on the sidelines in her later years as a traditional chimney-corner grandmother. It was years before I thought of writing this book, but my shock at her tone of voice stayed with me. No, privilege does not in itself a pioneer make.

I started thinking over the women I talked to, one by one, for clues I had disregarded at the time of our open-ended conversations. Several of them had mentioned mothers who had been forced to take control over their lives when widowed or divorced. Quite a few had spontaneously told me that they had been rebels or tomboys as girls, and even more had volunteered information about some way in which they or their experiences were exceptional.

As I mulled these things over, a warning bell started ringing in my head. If these women were all that exceptional, was it fair to use them as role models for other women? And what were they exceptions from?

Maybe I had been asking the wrong question. Instead of "Why do some older women succeed?" I should be asking, "What does their success tell us about what's holding most women back?" Maybe I'd been making the mistake of thinking of the universe in terms of the stars you can see instead of the dark matter that astronomers say really defines it.

What bothered me was that many of these women sounded like the famous successful career women of the 1950s that I called "loophole women" in 1968, because they had wriggled through or around the barriers I was reporting in my book *Born Female*. My life-stage pioneers proved that age alone doesn't keep a woman from building a new life for herself, just as the loophole women of *Born Female* proved that sex was not an inherent barrier to success in business. But once I got them all together and looked at them as a group, I realized that like the pioneer successes in business, they were the exceptions that proved the rule.

When I asked myself what really enabled each of these women to build a new life on her own, I found that most of them had found some way through or around the stereotypes that keep the normal, average, everyday older woman in limbo. Some were simply lucky. Others made a place for themselves through extraordinary talent, experience, or simply being "twice as good and working twice as hard" as colleagues of the acceptable age and gender.

Another warning signal was the miscellany of roles these successes had found. Most of the breadwinners were in temporary, one-of-a-kind, free-lance work, and most of those who weren't getting paid — the artists, advocates, and volunteers — had found roles outside the mainstream.

Finding a new job later in life seemed to require the knack of finding a niche so specialized that age and sex are at worst no handicap and at best an actual advantage. Many women cheerfully agreed that they couldn't live on what they earned, but they "weren't really in it for the money." Like the women who were doing something they liked for no pay, they had enough other income to survive. Those who didn't have enough were forced to scrounge. And as we have seen, rich old women were kept out of the mainstream in more subtle ways.

I began to notice and worry about the large number of pioneers who were making new lives in the age-segregated world of other old women. It began to dawn on me that capitalizing on your age was very much like capitalizing on your sex. Were these "older women's women" like the "women's women" who achieved real careers in the 1950s by going into fields "where it helps to be a woman"?

Finally, I was struck by the casual way in which so many women fell into their new roles, and how surprised they were to discover how much fun they were having.

Like it or not, I was going to have to dig into the obstacles that keep most older women down.

PART III

The Invisible Women

A visitor from a village in China might well wonder what Americans do to their women. Wherever he goes there are plenty of old men, but the women all seem to be younger.

He finds few visibly older women in the factories and offices he visits or at the parties he is invited to attend. There are occasionally a few on the streets, but none in store windows, on the covers of magazines in the newsstands, or in the television shows and mail-order catalogues he's advised to study for what they can tell him about American culture.

Do American women die young? No, he's told. Actually it's the other way around. In 1995 there are 31 million women over fifty-five but only 24 million men. After that the men start dying off so fast that beyond the age of eighty-five there are only thirty-nine men for every hundred women. What's more, nearly half of the men who survive beyond eighty-five have live-in wives to tend them, but more than 90 percent of the women this age have to make it without the help of a husband.

But where are they? Gently, the visitor is told that women are treated so well in America that they never grow old. You can't tell a woman's age by looking at her. Some of them have their faces lifted or their wrinkles removed, and most of them have been coloring their hair since long before it turned gray. Unlike women in China, American women stay young.

Our Chinese visitor is like the innocent child who said out loud what everyone else was tactfully concealing: American women do grow old, but no one is willing to admit it. Older women exist in America, but it's hard to find us. We are seldom seen at parties, at work, on television, or in the halls of power. We are forgotten by marketers, segregated by social programs, disregarded by our doctors, and systematically excluded from the good jobs for which some of us are the best qualified candidates.

Especially when we're on our own, we're invisible. You'd never know there are millions of us, that our ranks are growing, and that almost all younger women can expect one day to join us.

7

INVISIBLE
IN EVERYDAY LIFE

THE VERY EXISTENCE of an old woman is so embarrassing that we don't look at her. Or we look right through her as if she were thin air, to the point where it causes accidents.

I first learned about this from Pat Moore, a product designer. When she was researching the environment of older people, she disguised herself as an old woman to feel her way into their world. In *Disguised*, the book she wrote about this experience, she reports that people were so unwilling to look at her that they literally ran into her on the street — and without the murmured apology she was used to getting when she wasn't in drag. She also noticed that people were more apt to push ahead of her in supermarket lines, again without comment or apology, as if she were an inanimate obstruction.

This sounded far-fetched until several of the women I interviewed reported that the same thing had happened to them. The incident came to mind only when I asked them whether they had ever been badly treated because of their age.

People simply don't like to be near old people. One experiment found that children — even children as young as four — "sat farther from an elderly target than from a middle-aged target, looked at the elderly target less, spoke less, initiated conversations less, and asked fewer questions." Children are just acting out the feelings of adults.

Newly single older women are avoided. Widows have to contend with the embarrassment of becoming an object of pity. They report that people they've known for years cross the street to avoid them and the effort of the insincere sympathy they are expected to express. Acquaintances nervously tell them how well they look, and for the first time, the clergy may come to call. Divorced women are a social problem to friends, who worry about seeming to "take sides." According to one woman, the good part of divorce is finding out who your real friends are: "You discover the hard way where you've been invited for yourself and where only as the wife of your husband." Divorce still stigmatizes women more than men, and widowhood carries the additional stigma of death.

Evelyn Nef recalls how isolated she felt in the Dartmouth community after the death of her second husband, the famous Arctic explorer Vilhjalmar Stefansson. "Widows were not invited out the way couples were," she told Lydia Brontë, "and without the famous husband, life was a little more restricted."

Givers of dinner parties in traditional communities don't know what to do with "leftover" women. ("Relict," the old-fashioned word for a widow, is derived from the Latin verb meaning "to leave behind" and has nothing to do with "relic," which implies veneration.) Leftover women are an embarrassment to hostesses who plan a dinner table in terms of couples. After her divorce, a New Jersey woman who had built a business with her husband was invited to a dinner party that grew to the odd number of fifteen and found herself seated away from the other guests at a card table with the host and the host's single young daughter. Headwaiters in good restaurants discriminate against single older women as a matter of policy. Many of the women I spoke to told stories about being seated next to the kitchen, or in one case next to the ladies' room.

Private clubs have defended what they regard as their legal right to drop these "leftover" women. In the past, many golf clubs were men's clubs that extended privileges to the wives of members at reduced dues and never recognized them as full members. Rules varied. In my home town, Poughkeepsie, for instance, a lawyer married to a doctor was excluded from the "networking table" of the Amrita Club, even though every lawyer in her firm was on it and she had privileges at the club as the wife of a member. The exclusion not only affected her professionally but irked her so much that after her divorce she refused to join when full membership was extended to single women.

All-male private clubs are being pressured or legally forced to accept women as members, but most of them have always had arrangements by which the wives of members could use club facilities at designated times and places. The clubs contend that they have never accepted single women as members, so that wives have no status after they've been divorced. But it's more humiliating for a woman to be forced to leave a club where she has been known and accepted than to be denied membership in the first place.

Finally, single older women are regarded — and all too often regard themselves — as sexually invisible. This doesn't bother women who are interested primarily in making the scene. One older widow who went on a cruise after her husband died was delighted to get to all the nightspots at the ports where the ship stopped as the "date" of a bachelor her son's age, because he wanted to check out the girls without pursuing any one of them. But not all older women are content to chaperone parties or sit on the sidelines.

Sexual invisibility is hardest to bear for women who have staked their identity on attracting men. Helen Gurley Brown, the editor of *Cosmopolitan*, was devastated when a Broadway producer ambled up while she was chatting with a pretty young singer and then addressed himself exclusively to the younger woman. Helen Gurley Brown is not used to being ignored. She considered burning the new red Oscar de la Renta dress she was wearing and decided instead to consult a shrink for advice on how to cope with the new situation.

It's much worse, of course, if you don't have a man of your own. Traditional hostesses are so intent on balancing the table that they will dig up an extra (and usually unprepossessing) man to escort you to the party, or even ask you to find and bring someone yourself. Your real friends who are married won't drop you, but they'll take to inviting you out for lunch, and you'll find yourself reciprocating the same way. Gradually your social life dwindles to events set up during the day for women.

Single *young* women aren't as limited. Now that clothes, hairdressers, jobs, sports, college dormitories, and even dance steps have become unisex, they think nothing of sharing an apartment with young men who are not their sexual partners or ducking into the men's room if it looks as if no one's in there. Young women and men go everywhere as singles, but older women were brought up to feel out of place in public without a man, so they cling together for support.

The imbalance hurts wherever older people go. Salespeople for retirement communities point out the men in their dining rooms. When too many single old women sign up for a cruise, the director may quietly hand out free tickets to a few presentable older men, preferably retired army officers. Royal Viking Cruise Lines provides older male "hosts."

You don't see single older women in everyday life because they are segregated in housing, travel, recreation, and even social programs designed for them alone.

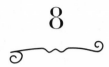

8

INVISIBLE

IN THE WORKPLACE

I HAD JUST TOLD *CNN Morning News* that continuing to work after sixty-five was the best investment I had ever made. "Now that I'm seventy-seven, my Social Security check is much bigger, and because I'm over seventy I can keep all of it."

I shouldn't have said it.

"You look fabulous!" gushed the anchor, wasting valuable TV seconds on the obligatory ritual of fake surprise. But what followed was even worse.

"I'm ninety-five and a half and I've gone back to work," a young-sounding voice called in. "I got a job in fast foods but lost it after three weeks because I set the french-fry machine on fire."

During the 1980s, fast-food chains recruited retirees because they couldn't find enough youngsters, but by the spring of 1992 we were hearing complaints that the older people were taking jobs that the young people needed. Was the caller pretending to be old in order to suggest that older people shouldn't work? I could have told him that workers over sixty have fewer accidents than teenagers, but it wouldn't have helped. The objection is really, of course, about turf.

Americans generally believe that the old should retire and give their jobs to the young. The notion goes back to the Depression of the thirties, when Social Security was promoted as a way to cut unemployment. The premise is false. Economists know that there isn't a fixed number of jobs to dole out, so that young people gain the jobs that old people lose. Jobs grow or decline with changes in the economy. But the notion persists that older people should be willing to step aside.

Preferring the young is so natural in America that employment interviewers have a hard time remembering that it's illegal. They have been known to inquire about an older woman's health ("What about arthritis? Do you have stamina?"), ask her whether she can "work with younger people," and describe the firm as "youth oriented."

Polling data tell us that 80 percent of people think that employers discriminate against older applicants and 61 percent of employers say they do. And employment specialists take it as a given that the older you are, the longer it takes to find a new job and the more likely you are to wind up earning less or give up hunting altogether.

Younger is cheaper, so the quickest way to cut costs is to get rid of people who have grown old working themselves up to higher salaries and replace them with newcomers who cost less in wages and benefits. Ever since the 1970s, big organizations have been investing money not in retraining older workers but in "preparing" and persuading them to retire. This is the real reason that bureaucracies have consistently ignored or damned with faint lip service the increasing evidence that older workers perform just as well as or even better than cheaper young ones.

Well-heeled, highly visible enterprises like IBM can afford to pay their older people to retire "early," but most people work for smaller businesses, which have to rely on attrition. If highly paid older workers quit of their own accord or are fired for cause, the company can save on pension costs and premiums for health and unemployment insurance as well as on the wages of their replacements. And when business is slow, it's tempting to nudge these employees into going.

There are hardheaded reasons that women who have worked their way up to a good salary are more attractive targets than men. Their health insurance costs their employer more. The behind-the-scenes, nonpolicymaking work they often do looks easy enough for a replacement to do. And managers believe it is easier to persuade them to leave. Although women live longer than men, they used to be allowed to retire earlier and are still required to do so in Britain. The idea is that they want to retire when their husbands do, and their husbands are usually older. Which isn't, of course, much help to the growing number of older women who no longer have husbands.

Gentle persuasion often comes first. A solicitous boss can think of all sorts of reasons that an older woman should want to retire, warning her of changes ahead she may not like, or making the suggestion in the course of sympathizing with her about a personal problem. After one woman returned from a family funeral, her boss told her that she had better retire, because she "would never be the same." When she refused, he demoted her twice and "lost" the employment file that recorded the years of good work she had done before her misfortune.

While a sixty-four-year-old editorial assistant was in the hospital, her forty-year-old male boss hired a sexy young woman as a temporary replacement. When she returned, the personnel director tried to persuade her that she really didn't want her old job. "We know how hard it is to come back to work when you're sick," the personnel director sympathized. "Your work is fine, but you might want to consider taking an easier job in another department." But as both of them knew, there simply weren't any other jobs.

Older women are supposed to be so timid and touchy and worried about what people think of them that if the boss hints that they're no longer wanted, he or she may be able to get them to go quietly. That's the sexist scenario, and when it works, the victim isn't likely to talk about her humiliation. "It was time to go," a specialist at a big-city board of education told a college classmate. "A new young supervisor wanted me to start programs I didn't like," she added, implying that the disagreement had been over principle. Maybe it was, but maybe it wasn't. Most older women with a long and distinguished record prefer to think of their departure as voluntary.

We don't know how often senior women really leave of their own accord, but most people with extensive work experience can think of times when an employer forced a woman out by tactics that can only be described as downright nasty. Verbal harassment, sexist slurs, nitpicking criticism, demotion, hardship assignments, no assignments, and campaigns of shunning are seldom reported in the media. Since tattling is bad for careers, fellow employees may hesitate to talk about these incidents. And the victims themselves would usually rather keep quiet.

These are the stories women don't like to tell about themselves. It's one thing to complain about losing out to a less qualified man or a person of a different race. But it's a personal humiliation for a woman to admit that she's "too old" and is losing out to someone younger. The very idea is so devastating that many women refuse to admit it, even to themselves. When they are driven to seek legal redress, they prefer to sue on the basis of sex, race, or disability.

The result is that while "everyone knows" that older women are badly treated in the workplace, there's an uncanny silence about how they are forced out of their jobs. The most effective ploys are subtle and hard to prove. It often boils down to his word against hers, and even other women discount what a woman says, especially when she feels she has been victimized. Even if a reporter thinks she has concrete evidence, her editor may hesitate to tangle with an employer who has a stable of high-priced lawyers ready to challenge any smudge on the company's reputation.

Fortunately, however, these practices can be documented from the libel-proof pleadings of court cases available to anyone willing to dig them out of the law library. Men who think that sexual attractiveness is essential for women in office jobs have sometimes been caught saying so, in clear violation of the Age Discrimination in Employment Act. "I like to have young women around," one man was quoted as saying. "They lift my spirits."

Preference for attractive young women is so accepted in secretarial work that some men don't mind saying so to women who are no longer young themselves. Bettie Crane, an experienced secretary at the Catholic Health Association, was only fifty when her sixty-year-old boss retired. In an unsuccessful lawsuit against the association, Crane alleged that her new young boss told her, "I want someone with a more youthful appearance. Do you mind working for a younger man? How old are you? Are you going to quit?" When she didn't, he succeeded in replacing her, Crane says, with a young model, typing skills unknown, who had tried out for a beauty pageant. The Catholic Health Association denied Crane's allegations.

The double standard also persists in television. An anchorman can be any age, but an anchorwoman had better look young, or else. Christine Craft says she was fired as a news anchor for the ABC affiliate in Kansas City in 1981 because she was "too old, too unattractive, and not deferential enough to men." Ten years later, Diane Allen alleged in a lawsuit that she was unceremoniously ousted as coanchor of the prestigious eleven o'clock news of WCAU-TV in Philadelphia when she was forty-three, not because she wasn't good at her job but because management decided that it "wanted youth" on the show. Diane says that she was to stay on doing other work at a big cut in salary, but the younger woman who replaced her on the show was given no raise for the promotion to coanchor.

Managers bent on reducing their payroll costs can sometimes get a woman's coworkers to do their dirty work for them. And both men and younger women colleagues are often all too willing to cooperate. "Don't bother the boss, she's menopausal" is an apocryphal workplace remark that could come from a younger woman as well as a man. (Does anyone ever say, "Don't bother the boss, he's going through a virility crisis?")

Fault-finding is a sexist tactic that is supposed to unnerve older women until they can be legitimately faulted for not doing their work. "Look, you didn't write on the line!" That's what the young editor of a newspaper in Massachusetts said while inspecting the way a veteran female reporter was filling out a routine form of instructions for a photographer. Hired when the paper was trying to cut costs, she took to looking over the shoulders of all the older women reporters, whom the paper was trying to force out.

One of the easiest ways to get an older woman to quit is to persuade her that she's not as competent as she thought she was. A steady drumfire of disapproval is particularly devastating for professional workers whose performance depends on self-confidence and can't be measured objectively. The campaign begins with a withdrawal of praise and may culminate in the disappearance of former favorable job appraisals or even the disappearance of the old file altogether. According to Crane, her new young boss started keeping a "Bettie book" of minor infractions, including behavior that he interpreted as "piercing my armor."

Ignoring the barbs may lead only to worse behavior. A new boss who failed to rattle an older secretary was forced to spell it out for her. "You know my former secretary? I used to harass her so that she'd go to the ladies' room and throw up." Later he had her prepare a statement of her own dismissal on grounds of incompetence, which she refused to sign. The story is told in *Forced Out,* a 1987 book by Juliet F. Brudney and Hilda Scott of Boston.

Verbal harassment can even lead to blows. J. C. Penney would like to keep it quiet, but here's what happened a few years ago in the shoe department of its store in Fort Smith, Arkansas. Euna Fay Blake, then fifty-six, was the top producer of sales among the commission-paid "shoe sales specialists," but the runner-up, twenty-five-year-old Daniel Hubbard, was determined to outsell her. Daniel appeared to be a model young man who worked part-time as a preacher, but he was also a ruthless competitor. He would hog customers by trying to serve more than one at a time, even though other clerks were idle. And while he talked nicely, especially to women customers and superiors, he was capable of surprisingly insulting language. When Euna made a big sale, he would call her a "crazy old woman" or a "senile woman" to her face.

Euna complained, but to no avail. She says that everyone knew what was going on. The store was trying to get rid of older, more expensive employees, often by demoting them to awkward shifts and entry-level work. Euna was being required to stock more than twice as much of the merchandise as the younger clerks. Euna told me that the human resources director, a woman older than Euna, saw Daniel as just the aggressive kind of young salesman the store should be encouraging.

Daniel stepped up his verbal attacks. When word spread that Euna's pregnant daughter-in-law had a brain tumor and might need help with the baby, he played the family card. "Why don't you go home, you crazy old woman? You don't need to work here!"

Euna requested a transfer, if necessary to the stockroom work she had done seventeen years earlier, but her request was refused. "You've only three more years before retirement," she was told. "You can stand anything for three years!"

The implication was clear. If she couldn't stand it, she'd have to quit before she could retire with her benefits. But the management also knew that she had been diagnosed three years earlier with cancer, and although she seemed to be clear of it, she would never be able to get health insurance on her own.

One day Daniel walked along beside her in the narrow aisle of the stockroom while she was trying to get a pair of shoes for a customer. "Get out of my way, you senile old thing!" he hissed.

Euna had raised two sons without laying so much as a finger on them, but in sheer frustration she turned around and slapped Daniel across the face so hard that it left a visible mark. Two days later, the company fired her for assaulting a colleague and hired three young salespersons.

Demotion is another way of humiliating a woman into quitting before she can collect benefits. In a failed lawsuit against Kelly Temporary Services, Ann Buckingham claimed that a few months short of qualifying for a pension, she was demoted from branch manager to supervisor. After four months, she quit.

Libraries and other hard-pressed small organizations may have benefit plans, but they have long saved payroll pennies by getting work done by temporary or part-time workers. When a woman stays long enough to get raises or comes close to qualifying for a pension, they simply cut back on her hours.

Sadistic bosses can make life on the job unbearable for a woman who objects to the way she's been treated. When fifty-seven-year-old Kathryn Jones complained that the Veterans Administration unfairly passed her over for promotion, she was transferred to the outpatient area of the admissions office of her hospital and forced to work standing at a counter, although coworkers in the area and her successor in the slot were provided with desks and chairs.

Threats to punish are safer for the boss than outright actions, and they may be even more effective in undermining an older woman. "You're not going to like working here," the new chief editor of a technical journal announced to a sixty-one-year-old editor he had inherited. A few weeks later he asked her whether she had thought about what he had said and hinted to others, who could be counted on to talk to her, that his measures would be subtle enough for him to avoid criticism. "I'm not going to kick the old lady downstairs!" he said.

Hardship assignments are regarded as a good way to get rid of older women. Employers haven't hesitated to add physical tasks to the job description of a woman who they know can't perform them. It's hard to believe, but this particularly nasty tactic has been used by hospitals to get rid of older nurses who have health problems of their own. In several reported cases, the victims have had to be admitted to their hospitals as patients. The practices are coming to light because the 1990 Americans with Disabilities Act gives these women grounds for suing for discrimination in employment on the basis of disability as well as age and sex.

In a pending suit against a Texas hospital, a nurse tells a story that sounds incredible. The hospital, which has denied all the charges, is in a very small town on the Gulf coast of Texas, hundreds of miles from the nearest big city. In 1992, the hospital chain that bought it determined to turn a profit. "We have to cut expenses," the plaintiff in the suit says the head nurse told the nursing staff. "My job is on the line. Those who don't like it can get out."

According to the plaintiff, older nurses were the obvious targets. She says that one nurse in intensive care was pushed so hard that she suffered an emotional breakdown and had to be hospitalized, and that another nurse in her mid-sixties, who had headed education for many years, was told to go back to working on the floor or resign. She resigned.

The plaintiff, a licensed vocational nurse who had worked at the hospital for twenty-five years, feels that she looked like an easy mark. According to her, all the other nurses knew she had a heart problem. In 1986 she had had a hysterectomy at the hospital, and she had suffered a heart attack three days later. When she returned to work, she was assigned to the least physically demanding floor, and if she had to push a heavy patient in the thousand-pound hospital bed with heavy equipment attached, another nurse would do it for her, in exchange for a less strenuous but more skilled task, such as starting an IV infusion.

This nurse claims that in order to get her to resign, the new managers pulled her from the job to which she had been assigned after her operation and put her on demanding floors, sometimes switching her two or three times in one eight-hour shift. But she needed her job, and she forced herself to endure the stress. At the end of one shift, her chest pains were so bad that she went straight to the emergency room for treatment. The second time it happened, she was admitted to the hospital for four days of intensive cardiac testing. She complained of her treatment to her superiors, but after she was discharged as a patient, she went right back to her difficult job to prove that she was capable of doing it.

Rougher measures were obviously going to be needed to get her out, and according to her, a nurse manager didn't hesitate to take them. The nurse was called in and scolded for her formal complaint. She claims that she was told she was too old for the job and ought to find an easier one, and that she was falsely accused of breaking hospital rules. She says that in an effort to force her to disobey an order before witnesses, the charge nurse took her out in the hall, where idle nurses were watching, and ordered her to push a patient in his hospital bed for nearly half a mile down winding ramps to the intensive care unit below.

It was high noon. The nurse says that one of the other nurses offered to do the pushing but was told that she would have to do it herself. What none of the spectators knew was that arrangements had already been made to take the patient down in the elevator on a stretcher, and after the nurse had been tongue-lashed for stalling before witnesses, she says, that's how it was done. Two days later, she was fired for "delaying" the transportation of the patient.

"Working to rules" is a weapon that workers in bureaucracies such as the police force have used to shut down an operation without actually striking, but it can work the other way around as well. A communications expert at a midwestern university thinks that her boss deliberately trapped her into a violation, which he used as a pretext for firing her. He agreed verbally to let her borrow a few days of the next year's vacation time to go to Europe, but on the day she was to leave, with her bags packed, her tickets bought, she was handed a memo warning her that she could be fired if she was absent beyond her annual vacation time. She went anyway. When she returned, no one spoke to her. She wasn't invited to meetings, and a column she had always written had been assigned to someone else. She had to eat alone because the secretary with whom she had always lunched was afraid to be seen with her.

Such tactics have been the staples of psychological warfare over the centuries. Shunning isn't an invention of the Amish. It's an age-old device for policing behavior and a recommended way of dealing with rebellious children. It's especially devastating to a single older woman who looks to friends at work for the daily human contact she no longer has at home. She may understand, but she's deeply hurt all the same when colleagues no longer stop by her desk, or a friend of many years explains that she can't have lunch "because the boss might see us."

In one big national company, a department head called in a

woman with years of good job reports to tell her that nobody wanted to work with her. He wouldn't say who had complained, but he advised her to start looking for another job. She felt like bursting into tears and fleeing from the scene, but she resisted when she realized that's just what he wanted. If she quit, she'd lose her pension and badly needed health insurance. The next day she consulted a lawyer, who brought suit against the company for damages and advised her to stay on the job while it was pending. Every day was an ordeal. Fault was found with what little work she was assigned. Fearful of being fired, friends looked the other way when she passed them in the hall, although some of them ventured to smile at her in the parking lot.

Leaving a woman with no work is an especially cruel way to demonstrate that she's no longer needed or wanted. After fifteen years with Morrison's Management Services, Inc., a company that runs cafeterias for institutions such as factories and hospitals, Linda Spanier had worked her way up to assistant cafeteria manager, but when her new twenty-seven-year-old boss said he preferred to work with male managers, she was replaced by a twenty-three-year-old man and put on "unassigned status," because there were "no openings." Finally, after ten months, during which younger men were assigned to five jobs for which she was qualified, she was asked to retire. When she refused, they fired her. The reason? The company needed "younger people that were more qualified."

"Hanging a woman out to dry" is especially effective in the professions, where pride in achievement can be as important as money. Colleges that want to get rid of a professor assign her favorite course to others. In the 1980s, Merced Community College in California tried to get rid of the older woman who was the only female in its art department. The managers assigned a course she had developed that was popular with older women to one of the male art teachers. When she complained, they moved heavy file cabinets into her office, denied her the supplies she needed, and threatened to revoke her parking space.

LEGAL REDRESS

Aren't there laws against this sort of thing? Isn't there anywhere these women can go for legal redress?

There is no lack of laws. Federal, state, and municipal laws exist against discrimination on the basis of race, sex, and disability as well as age, each with slightly different provisions. This means that an older black woman with a heart condition has an embarrassment of remedies and places to go. You often have to apply first to the federal Equal Employment Opportunity Commission, which is so overloaded that it can't respond promptly and is primarily interested in getting rid of complaints that fall outside its jurisdiction.

The catch is that you need a lawyer just to find the best place for your particular complaint and to present it in a way that will insure it will be heard. Lois S. is happy to tell anyone how hard this is. She claims that in 1985, after fourteen years of service, at a time when she was ill and couldn't afford to lose her health insurance, she was fired from her job as a psychiatric counselor at a Florida hospital and replaced by a man who was cheaper and younger. Although she believes she had persuasive and voluminous evidence of discrimination on the basis of age, sex, and disability, she was unable to get any help from the EEOC, the Florida Department of Labor and Unemployment Compensation, the Florida Commission on Human Relations, the Commission on Civil Rights, or the Office for Civil Rights of the Department of Health and Human Services. Sometimes an organization simply lost her file. Sometimes it referred her to another agency, which said it had no jurisdiction or the time limit had run out. Lois complained in vain to the Miami office of the Florida Insurance Commission and the United Nations Commission on Human Rights. In 1993 she sued the United States government for violating due process under the Fourteenth Amendment. A year later, she was advised that her case was still "under consideration," with no time limit.

The cases I dug out of the law books are the tip of an iceberg of unfathomable dimensions. People who have been fired from their jobs may have a good case, but they seldom have the money to hire a lawyer. Theoretically, a woman with a good case can find a lawyer who will gamble his or her services for upward of 30 percent of any monetary damages eventually recovered, but the plaintiff may have to dig up thousands of dollars for out-of-pocket costs, and even if she wins, she won't recoup that sum for the years it takes to get a verdict.

In 1991, Lou Glasse, president of the Older Women's League, urged a congressional committee to amend the Age Discrimination in Employment Act to award damages in addition to lost wages, so that lawyers would have an incentive to represent plaintiffs on a contingency basis. She testified that a lawyer had told her that 80 percent of those who suffer discrimination will not file for it, and "of those who do file, only 2 percent are probably accepted by a lawyer, so the rest would have to represent themselves."

The woman who was fired by the midwestern university by what she regards as a trick is a good example of what happens to most female victims of age discrimination. She protested the infraction of vacation rules through university channels but was turned away because her word went against the written record. She thought of suing, but the only lawyer in town who handled discrimination cases was busy with contingency-fee cases that looked more rewarding. So she resigned a year before she would have been eligible for health insurance and a bigger pension.

The public is especially unlikely to hear anything about the 2 percent who do sue. If a suit has a reasonable chance of success, the company will settle out of court on terms that the plaintiff agrees to keep secret. The figure may be too high for a strapped plaintiff to turn down, but to the company, with superior resources and long-term concerns, a few hundred thousand dollars is cheap insurance against even the very small chance of setting an unfavorable legal precedent that would inspire other employees to sue.

The bottom line is that most cases are settled out of court. That's the only way a woman and her lawyer can be sure of getting any money. Settling is good for the plaintiff and good for the defendant.

The woman who felt like bursting into tears when her manager told her that no one wanted to work with her consulted a lawyer who took her case on a contingency fee and pursued it to a settlement in which she agreed not to reveal how much money she received. She isn't well enough to work, and she is so afraid that the company will sue her for slander that she has asked me to conceal her name, job, employer, and location. If she were sued, she'd have to pay for her defense herself.

Diane Allen, the anchorwoman, settled her suit against WCAU-TV after several years with a clause that silences her about how much money the station paid her. She is now devoting herself full-time to producing television documentaries, some of which she has sold to the station she sued. She believes that her suit slowed management attempts to get rid of other women over forty.

The only women for whom we can be sure of getting the end of the story are the exceptional few who refuse to settle and press on to a court verdict. They take heroic risks, and losing can change their lives forever.

Christine Craft, the anchorwoman who wasn't "deferential enough to men," succeeded in winning verdicts from two juries, but both were eventually set aside. When she found herself "bored to tears" by the local TV jobs that she was able to get, she switched careers and went to law school to learn how to defend other women from illegal discrimination.

Bettie Crane, the secretary displaced by an aspiring beauty queen, lost her case, and the lawyer lost his fee. She had already anted up for the expenses, but after she lost, the employer sued her for *its* expenses in defending the suit, and since there was no hope of recovering money, she had to pay her lawyer to defend her.

Ann Buckingham, the Kelly Services manager who was demoted, was denied a jury trial by the judge. Fourteen years later, after spending her life savings of $19,000 and funds raised by an organization called Friends of Ann Buckingham, she still owes $20,000 in legal fees and is bringing a new trial against Kelly.

The nurse in Texas was awaiting trial in November 1994 on a suit brought by her second lawyer. The first one negotiated a settlement of $10,000, but he wouldn't sue when she refused to take what she called "hush money." She now has no health insurance, her health is deteriorating, her savings are running out, and no one will hire her. "Everywhere I applied, when the prospective employer wrote to the hospital for reference, it sent back to them detrimental reports," she wrote me in July 1994. "My bosses were extremely angry that I turned them in to the EEOC, so they have kept me from getting a job. My lawyer is suing them for slander. No one seems to care. Pray for me."

Some do win. According to one study, women who elect to sue are more apt to win than men who sue. If so, the reason may be that they are after more than money. They seek legal redress to vindicate themselves, because they are furious at the treatment they've received, because they hope to benefit other victims, or some combination of these more or less impractical motives.

Euna Blake was one of the winners. She sued J. C. Penney for age discrimination in order to clear her name of the disgrace of being fired. She and her husband live in a tiny crossroads town on the Arkansas-Oklahoma border, and she did not want to live the rest of her life with a blot on an otherwise unblemished reputation. She's an old-fashioned woman with traditional values. The names she was called are so far out of her normal vocabulary that she refuses to repeat them in discussing what happened to her.

Euna was lucky enough to be well represented by a young woman in the local law firm that had handled her parents' will, but the uphill battle took all of her time and energy for four years. The Equal Opportunity Employment Commission has to respond to a complaint of age discrimination before a victim can sue, but Euna had to get the help of her congressman to force the EEOC to respond before the time limit for filing a suit ran out. The commission's chairman at the time was Clarence Thomas, who was later accused of deliberately delaying age discrimination complaints.

When the suit was filed, J. C. Penney was so alarmed that the manager imported a big-time lawyer from Dallas to defend the case. At the trial, the jury awarded Euna damages, but the judge set aside the verdict, and Euna had to appeal the judge's decision to get it reversed. Four years later, she won $35,000 in damages, her lawyer's fees, back pay for the four years she had been out of work, and reinstatement in her old job. According to the defense lawyer from Dallas, it was the only such case the firm had ever lost.

Euna's story has an even happier ending. In 1993, she was back selling shoes in Penney's and breaking sales records in an entirely new and reformed shoe department. Daniel had left to become the youth minister of a church in Kansas, and the human resources manager who thought he was such a fine young man had retired. Euna gets along with everyone and likes the job so much that she may just stay on after she turns sixty-two and becomes eligible for retirement with the health benefits she couldn't get otherwise.

Legal redress is slow, expensive, and draining. Even those who win are forced to invest so much physical and emotional energy in the fight that their main reward has been getting even with their tormentors. When Euna Blake's husband told her that if she didn't calm down she wouldn't live to see the trial, she retorted that she would be there if she had to go in a wheelchair.

Litigants who persist often get so angry that they devote themselves to warning and helping other women. Ann Buckingham publicizes her experience as a horror story and is active in the Gray Panthers. Bettie Crane directs volunteers at a local women's center. Others became active in the Older Women's League.

The cards are stacked against a woman who sues, because employers have deep pockets and are willing to dig into them to avoid a precedent that could encourage other employees to sue. Smart lawyers — and lawyers defending employers are the smartest money can buy — know how to make a protesting woman sound like the witchy bitch of the stereotype. This can make a victim mad enough to refuse settlement and go for broke.

American Airlines didn't declare Barbara Sogg unpromotable and move her to a job that was then eliminated because of her age, sex, or heart surgery — oh, no. The problem, said company officials, was that she was "inflexible, insensitive, and stubborn." In June 1992 a Manhattan jury found for Sogg to the tune of more than $7 million in various kinds of damages, some of it to be personally paid by officers of the company who had wronged her. American Airlines fought the decision in every legally possible way and succeeded in getting the amount of the damages reduced, but in the end, the company and the executives who had persecuted her were forced to pay her about $3 million.

Ann Hopkins was refused partnership in Price Waterhouse because, the company said, she wasn't womanly enough. Although she had brought more business to the firm than any of the other eighty-seven candidates for partnership in 1982, she was criticized for being "abrasive," "harsh," and "macho" and of "overcompensating for being a woman." She was advised to "walk more femininely, talk more femininely, dress more femininely, wear makeup, have her hair styled, and wear jewelry." But if she did, would she be aggressive enough to be a Price Waterhouse partner? Infuriated, Hopkins carried her suit to the Supreme Court and won. She's now a Price Waterhouse partner by court order.

Plaintiffs have a hard time in court because the basic law of the workplace favors employers. In the United States and Britain, workers have no inherent rights to a job, as they do almost everywhere else in the developed world. The fundamental premise of our common law is that employers have the right to hire and fire at will.

In the past thirty years, court decisions and antidiscrimination laws have chipped away at this premise. Employers can't renege on promises made in employee handbooks. They can't defraud employees. And there is now a confusing tangle of federal, state, and even municipal laws forbidding discrimination in employment on the basis of race, religion, ethnic origin, sex, and age. Lawyers lump all these laws and precedents together in the field of "wrongful discharge."

The law on protection against such discharge is deliberately murky and seeded with escape hatches, and the Reagan and Bush administrations did everything possible to keep it so. Government agencies set up to protect the civil rights of employees have been deliberately discouraged and underfunded, which has allowed the legal talent available to big corporations to defend vigorously any suit that threatened to set an unfavorable precedent.

Older women who try to take advantage of one or more of the protective laws run into maddening roadblocks. You can't collect punitive damages for "emotional pain, suffering . . . mental anguish and loss of enjoyment of life" for age discrimination or harassment under the federal law, but you may be able to get them under your state's law, so most plaintiffs sue in both federal and state courts. You have to prove that your age or sex was one of the reasons why you were fired, which means that you have to be able to defend your job performance as practically faultless.

Laws against age and sex discrimination have inspired efforts to educate the middle managers of big companies, but questionable practices are still widespread. The prospect of wholesale suits for wrongful discharge was a nightmare to big companies when they were pushing older workers to retire in the early 1990s. IBM was so generous in settling such suits that the late Dan Lacey, author of *Your Rights in the Workplace*, figured that it would have cost the company *billions* of dollars to settle all the potential suits at the same rate.

Plaintiffs' lawyers and rights organizations have generally favored confidentiality clauses. The employer gets silence and the victim gets money. But a case can be made that more is at stake than the immediate interests of the parties.

Publicity is just what is needed to force employers to obey the law. And litigation in open court is just what is needed to make the law clear to those who are tempted to violate it. The employment agreement a worker has with a company that employs a huge number of people is not a private bargain between supposedly equal individuals. Whatever its status in law, the employment policy of a major employer works like a public policy affecting the welfare of hundreds of thousands and the economies of entire communities. At the very least, employer compliance with existing laws should not be shielded from the continuing scrutiny of employees, the public, and the courts.

Theoretically, our free press ought to be digging into these cases, but they are hard stories to research and even harder to sell to editors. Good newspapers aren't deterred by the fear of losing a company's advertising, but their own lawyers are disinclined to risk libel suits, which it would be in the interests of the company to bring in defense of its reputation. When a reporter asks the company to comment on the employee's story, the company may warn that the situation is full of legal complexities. Sensing land mines, editors and reporters find something less troublesome to write about.

Untested and piecemeal, employment law remains confusing. In the eyes of the law, for instance, older women aren't a special category. They can sue on the basis of age discrimination and, on a separate count, on the basis of sex discrimination, but these are two separate headings. Women of color have the benefit of laws that recognize their double risk. Because both race and sex are "suspect" classes, in need of special protection, women of color are a double suspect class. But age is not a suspect class, so while old women get the protection of laws against age discrimination and other laws against sex discrimination, the combination does not give them the extra legal protection of a double suspect class.

And in spite of the many laws, there are big holes. There's nothing in the law to protect a woman against the favoritism shown to a younger woman who is having an affair with her boss. In her complaint, Elaine Candelore alleged that her troubles began with the arrival of Ginger, a younger woman who got longer lunch hours, easier work, and new office furniture because, Elaine claimed, she was having an affair with the boss. No luck. The judge threw

Elaine's case out of court before even considering whether what she said was true, because "preferential treatment of paramour by employer, while perhaps unfair, did not state claim for sex or age discrimination in violation of equal protection clause or Age Discrimination in Employment Act."

Older women have no special champions even in the civil rights community. The Women's Bureau collects data on discrimination against minority women but "doesn't have enough money" to pay special attention to older women. The Worker Equity Department of the AARP watches for cases based on age alone, leaving the cases based on sex to the underfunded Women's Bureau and to privately funded women's advocacy groups.

As victims of a double whammy, black women have the support of civil rights and women's groups. But women over fifty-five of every skin color are as vulnerable to double discrimination as black women of every age, and there are more of them. In 1992 the workforce included 6,654,000 women over fifty-five of all races and 6,999,000 black women of all ages. The two groups at risk are just about equal, but old women are not a legally protected class. When Washington attorney Francine Weiss studied the EEOC record for the Older Women's League, she found only 108 decisions on the basis of both age and sex in twenty years.

It certainly looks as if older women have suffered more from age discrimination than older men, but not everyone agrees. Men sometimes say that *men* have been specially targeted because they make more money and their work can so easily be done by lower-paid women.

Whatever the workplace facts, all the civil rights lawyers I talked with agreed that very few cases have been brought on the basis of both age and sex. And they agree that women are much more willing to sue on the basis of sex than age. Women just don't think of themselves as old and don't want to entertain the notion that other people think of them as old, either.

Feminists who are no longer young and who remember the old days of blatant sex discrimination are especially unwilling to believe that older women are at any special disadvantage. In 1992, just before retiring from Catalyst, the organization she founded to persuade companies to promote women, Felice Schwartz exulted that the country was having its "first equal opportunity recession."

Alice Miskimin, a sixtyish partner in a Connecticut law firm, faults younger women for worrying too much about their rights. "I find myself far less sensitive to perceived discrimination, slights, etc., than women thirty years younger than I, who complain incessantly and feel inferior all the time," she writes. "We do plaintiffs' employment cases and EEOC work, but *rarely* is age a factor in the complaints we bring on behalf of women. Older men get laid off or terminated just before retirement, classically — but women get offers of a golden handshake to *avoid* a lawsuit."

She may have a point. Although women bring far fewer suits than men, according to a study made at Syracuse University, they win more of those they do bring. This may mean only that they are more apt to sue in principle or even blind fury, and employers may recognize that a furious woman can be a dangerous adversary.

Generalizations about which sex is temperamentally most apt to fight are a sexist game. You could theorize that a man harassed in such a petty way as some of these women were would be tempted to ball up his fists and hit back, maybe even literally. But that's just what conventionally ladylike Euna Blake did.

Losing a job after fifty is demoralizing to men as well as women, but women have more to lose. An older man thinks he can find another job somewhere else. An older woman who has worked her way up to a high-paying job knows that she has less chance than a man of getting another one anywhere near as good. Look at Clarice Strasser, who was warned that she couldn't get a paying job in counseling work because she hadn't been paid for the professional work she had done in the private school her family owned and she was "overqualified" for any work she could get in the job market.

Even worse, a displaced professional may find that she's overqualified for any job *below* her level, so she can't compete for clerical work with younger women, whose qualifications do not embarrass their bosses. There is also a perception that an over-qualified older woman is more apt than a less qualified younger woman to become bored with a routine job and leave it.

It is no accident that so many of the pioneer women I talked with were working outside the mainstream, in jobs so specialized that age and sex didn't matter. Rice Lyons designed her LAFF workshops around her own personality. Handwriting analysis isn't a big industry, but Sue Mathias avoids competition by specializing in character analysis and personnel selection, applications that are less lucrative and steady than working for courts and lawyers.

The Peace Corps is outside of the mainstream by definition, so it is interesting to see what happens to older women when they have to leave their professional-level work overseas and return to the American job market. Older women who survive the rigorous selection process are as flexible in learning new skills and adapting to new situations as their younger colleagues, but reentry may be harder for them. Most of those I talked with thought their Peace Corps service was more responsible and rewarding than any work they had been able to find at home.

THE GLASS CEILING

Career ladders are shorter for women than for men. Women may climb high enough to see a top job, but they are rarely allowed to touch it. This glass ceiling has kept women down. In the past, women dropped out of the labor force before they were old enough to reach it, but during the 1980s, prosperity and affirmative action promoted a sizable proportion of women to middle-management posts where they could see the next step, which they weren't being allowed to take.

In the 1990s, recession has lowered the glass ceiling. Middle management became a layer of fat ripe for cutting just as women are being promoted into it. As newcomers with relatively little management experience, they have become vulnerable to the personal criticism that thrives when jobs are insecure.

Growing job insecurity may have something to do with the new hostility to career women that Susan Faludi documented in *Backlash*, her carefully researched report on what was happening to women during the 1980s. Many male bosses are having trouble figuring out what tack to take. Young men who have grown up with the concept of equal opportunity have learned to treat the women they supervise as impersonally as they treat the men. But even when they are committed in principle to equal opportunity, the older men who make decisions about higher-level personnel still think of women in family terms. Many of them sympathize with young women on the job, who remind them of their own ambitious daughters, but women with the years of experience needed for really top-level jobs may stir up negative emotions about their wives and mothers.

"I don't want my office run by little old Jewish ladies like my mother-in-law!" the city attorney of Miami explained when he was discussing a list of employees to go in a downsizing. The remark was part of the testimony of Mikele Carter, a fifty-year-old policewoman who sued the city for age discrimination when she was fired. Her case was thrown out of court on appeal.

"You sound just like my wife," the vice chancellor of a western university recently told the only woman whose rank entitled her to attend policy discussions. She started keeping count of the times he interrupted her and discovered that she was the only policymaker he ever cut short.

"How strange it seems to work for someone who looks like my mother," one young man told his supervisor. Would he object to working for someone who looked like his father? And if he did, would he have felt free to say so to his face?

"You remind me of my mother," a young male employment interviewer said to an applicant he was turning down. Older men may actually hesitate to put an older woman in charge of men young enough to be just liberating themselves from their mothers.

Top managers approve of equal opportunity in principle. Most try to be impartial, when they think of it, but it's easy for them to disregard older women as office fixtures without ambition who really don't want or need their jobs. They may not consider promoting underpaid older women with long service who have made themselves as indispensable as the maiden aunts who used to help run big households. Traditionally, such women have literally been hidden in a back room.

In a suit against the Electro Switch Company of Massachusetts, a woman employee testified that the industrial relations manager denied her a raise on the grounds that she "made enough money and was one of the highest-paid women in the company." Another employee said she was told that "for a woman supervisor, you do very well." The court eventually ruled the remarks admissible as evidence of "an atmosphere conducive to sex discrimination."

Although managers have now been schooled to be careful what they say, a clever experiment devised by Ben Rosen, a business school professor at the University of North Carolina, shows that even the sophisticated readers of the *Harvard Business Review* continue to make decisions on the basis of traditional age and gender biases. Readers were invited to participate in a "Managerial Decision Making Survey" designed "to explore how managers digest facts, size up people and situations, and determine appropriate actions" when they have to make decisions "involving the behavior of other people." The situations required difficult decisions involving what to do about such personnel problems as a supervisor who resisted a new computer system, a sixty-three-year-old employee who refused an incentive to retire, a marketing manager who was disliked by young MBAs in the department, and a research scientist who might leave to follow a spouse to another city. Brief résumés and photographs were supplied for all the individuals involved.

What the managers filling out the questionnaire didn't know was that four questionnaires were sent out, identical in every way except for the ages and sexes of the individuals whose fate was at stake. This made it possible to calculate statistically the extent to which a pretty young woman was favored for the assignment of entertaining an important customer over an older woman or a younger or older man, or the handicap a younger woman faced in getting sent abroad to negotiate an important contract.

Rosen found that powerful stereotypes still influence managerial decisions across a variety of work settings, and that in some instances older women are the double victims of both age and sex stereotypes. "In one scenario," he wrote, "we depicted either a younger or older male or female manager who would be making an important presentation to a very big client. The client arrives unexpectedly on Sunday afternoon and indicates an interest in playing golf and talking business. Who does top management trust to entertain the important client on the links? Not the older female — even when it is noted that she plays an occasional round of golf. Specifically, 38 percent voted to send the older male manager, while only 26 percent recommended the older female manager."

"In a second case, a multinational company needed to select a marketing manager to join a team traveling to South Korea to negotiate a new joint venture. The negotiator needed to be assertive, technically expert, and tough. About two thirds of the responding managers were ready to send a male negotiator regardless of his age. Only 61 percent were willing to send a younger woman negotiator, and that number dropped to 51 percent when the female negotiator was older."

One tragedy of the glass ceiling is that older women who bump up against it are apt to be more ambitious than men their age. And it's not just postmenopausal zest. Many who have carried the double load of family and career are free to devote themselves singlemindedly to their work only at an age that strikes some employers as "too old." Virginia O'Leary, a plaintiffs employment lawyer in Indiana, tells about a woman pathologist who was refused promotion and expected to step aside for younger people just at the time in her career when her own children were grown and she was free to devote all of her energies to her work.

INVISIBLE UNEMPLOYMENT

Whether an older woman is more apt to be fired than a man, she is much less likely to be hired, and more likely to be paid less than a man for comparable work. In most professions — and especially in law, where the competition is keen — older women are seldom hired for a beginning job that can lead to promotion. A fifty-three-year-old widow with a degree in education says she had to work in a parochial school for less pay than she would get in a public school because the public school system wouldn't interview a woman her age. And even the Unitarian Universalist Church, which has pioneered age and sex equality, worries about a woman who is beginning her career in the ministry at sixty.

There was a time when most older women didn't need or want to work. Women are still less apt than men to be working after fifty-five (23 percent versus 39 percent). For years to come, men will be more likely than women to reach retirement age with a private pension, though every year more older women have to work because they have no husbands to support them or simply because their earnings have always been part of their family's income. At the same time, more older women have job skills they want to keep using. Those of us who are dyeing our hair aren't doing it solely out of vanity. When we're on our own in our later years, we think of ourselves not as displaced homemakers but as displaced workers.

Displaced workers are keeping unemployment high in the 1990s. They are the millions of middle-class people laid off in the down-sizing of the armed forces, defense industries, and big organizations, public and private. We hear about this happening to male

factory workers, but it also happens to women who have spent
years shuffling outmoded paperwork.

So what do they do when they can't find a job? Some go into
business for themselves. Others drop out of the labor force or
go into volunteer work.

Unemployed older women may account for the rise in small
business enterprises during the late 1980s and 1990s. Economists
look to small business to create new jobs, and women-owned businesses have been increasing faster than businesses owned by men.

Conservatives cite these statistics as evidence that prosperity
is at hand and that women are finally equal in the workplace.
But look at the numbers more closely and they suggest just the
opposite. The census definition of a business includes one-person
free-lancers. The vast majority of "businesses" are small, strug-
gling, one-person enterprises that are started strictly from hunger.
Their owners sound a lot like the door-to-door salesmen of the
Great Depression, who tried to eke out a minimal living by ped-
dling dime-store items to housewives.

Older women with work experience who can't find a decent
job when they need or want one become free-lancers or start up
a specialized service they see is needed, but as we have seen,
even the most creative are seldom able to support themselves at
it. Like teenagers working at McDonald's, they can work for very
low wages because they have other income.

The option is to quit looking for a job. Until recently, if you
stopped looking for a job because you didn't think you could get
the kind of job you wanted, you were counted out of the labor
force. For many years, this distorted the unemployment rate. When
jobs were hard to get, more seekers stopped looking, and since
they weren't counted in the labor force, unemployment was really
higher than reported. When times picked up, some of the discouraged took heart and started looking again, and before they
found a job they swelled the labor force, making the unemployment rate higher than it would otherwise have been. In 1994, the
Labor Department started counting these "discouraged workers"
as part of the labor force.

Whether you are a discouraged worker depends on the kind of job you think you can get at the time you're asked. It's a fine and shifting line, especially for older people who may be able to get by without a paycheck. When the Commonwealth Fund surveyed the paid and unpaid work of Americans over fifty-five in 1992, they found that older women were more likely to be discouraged than men: among those not looking for a job although ready and able to work, 66 percent of the women but only 42 percent of the men said they had stopped looking because no suitable jobs were available.

What do discouraged workers do when they're out of the labor force? Sociologists and students of the workforce have identified a number of situations that keep people out of the workforce. Middle-class young people may go back to live with their parents or get a student loan to go to college. Young women may decide to have a baby. But the growing number of "overqualified" women over fifty-five who have taken themselves out of the paid labor force have become the mainstay of social organizations that rely on volunteers.

Many of these people say that earning extra money is less important than doing something that helps, that relates them to other people, that is near home, that gives them control over their hours, and especially that they like to do and that is respected. Now all of us know some women who sincerely feel this way and have served their communities all their lives. As a matter of fact, they're the ones who do most of the volunteer work. But for many other older women, these claims could well be sour grapes.

Mixed motives can never be proved, but a case can be made that older women who would prefer paid employment if they could get it are being flattered, coaxed, and even shamed into working for nothing. Here's how the argument would go.

It may be coincidental, but nonprofit organizations embraced the virtues of activity in later life shortly after the young mothers on whom they used to rely deserted to the paid labor force. Not so long ago, the Red Cross wouldn't accept volunteers over sixty-five. But in 1986 the Committee on an Aging Society was talking

about a "vast reservoir of active, healthy, experienced, and educated retired persons" whose productivity might "be more effectively tapped, on an unpaid basis."

The Commonwealth Fund, traditionally concerned with older
people, took the lead. In 1988, it inaugurated a five-year effort
"to examine the productive potential of older Americans and . . .
identify the changes in existing attitudes and institutional practices
necessary to harness their tremendous capacity." While taking
primary aim at age discrimination in paid employment, a Commonwealth Fund study surveyed the extent of volunteering among
older people in order to dramatize their contribution.

The survey found that a fourth of all women over fifty-five
who are living alone volunteer to work for formal organizations,
and the percentage doesn't drop much for those over seventy-five.
In addition, millions of the single older women who responded
reported that they cared for sick or disabled relatives, spouses,
friends, and neighbors. Dr. Kevin Coleman, a health-care econo-
mist, assigned a dollar value to the hours and types of work the
respondents reported. His projections estimate that older women
living alone contribute *billions* of dollars' worth of work a year
that would otherwise cost somebody money. "The Untapped Resource" also reported the encouraging news that even more
women would like to volunteer than are actually doing it.

"The greatest challenge," said Robert N. Butler, the father of
the successful aging movement, "is to motivate older citizens to
take the first step." He advised treating volunteers better, giving
them more responsibility and flexibility, and applying "motiva-
tional concepts" to volunteer programs. Noting that "the very
fact of their unpaid status undermines their perceived competence
and value in the public mind," he advocated "educating the public
to appreciate the contribution and personal satisfaction of volunteering" — which was, of course, exactly what the Commonwealth Fund was doing.

During the 1980s, sociologists studied how best to recruit these
supposedly lonely, unappreciated older people by convincing them
of the psychological rewards of volunteering. A limited survey

of volunteers for the Senior Companion Program reported that they felt their help was vital, that the benefits in "personal growth" were beyond their expectations, and that they felt less lonely than they had before volunteering. Recruiters appealed to the strong work ethic of older people: "Just because you are retired doesn't mean you don't want to work."

Well and good — there's more to a job than the paycheck. But female volunteers, and especially the older women being recruited, were being shortchanged in psychological pay in exactly the same way they were being shortchanged in dollars. In hospitals, for instance, male volunteers were more apt to be making hospital policy as members of the board of directors while female volunteers were delivering mail to patients and answering their bells.

Women most often were the ones who were driving the sick to the doctor, comforting dying babies in hospitals, helping harassed teachers with paperwork, tutoring troubled schoolkids, staffing hotlines for people in various kinds of trouble, cooking for churches, collecting castoff furniture for battered women's centers, and doing everyone's filing, to name only a few of the miscellaneous, thankless, but essential tasks that there's never quite enough money to pay for. It was all noble, soul-satisfying, traditional woman's work.

Media praise for the contributions of older volunteers, some of it unconsciously patronizing, did not question the premises of the appeals the recruiters were making. But serious students began to have their doubts. In a Ph.D. dissertation that never received public attention, Susan Chambre questioned the appeals being made to recruit older volunteers and suggested that policy planners don't understand why people volunteer in the first place. In her 1993 roundup of existing information on older volunteers, Chambre pointed out that most people don't volunteer because they no longer have families; married people in her survey were more apt to volunteer than single ones. Dr. Lucy Rose Fischer, another investigator, points out that older people don't volunteer because they have time on their hands; employed older people are more apt to volunteer than retired ones. I would add that they don't volunteer because they "like to work." The work ethic may be strong among seniors, but there are also a lot of them who simply *don't* like to work.

Dr. Fischer is even blunter. In a 1991 study of older volunteers in Minnesota, she asked three embarrassing questions. First, are volunteers being exploited? So far as women are concerned, her answer is a flat yes. "Women have done unpaid work, in large part, because of their limited opportunities for paid work." And of course this is especially true for older women, particularly those forced out of paying jobs because of downsizing.

Second, how does the use of volunteers affect paid workers? "In a time of recession, workers might very well view volunteers as potentially taking away their much needed jobs."

Third, should volunteer work substitute for already existing entitlements? "One of the outcomes of encouraging volunteering is that there may actually be a decrease in public services."

In summation, if working without pay is Good For You, why don't we encourage young people to do it?

9

INVISIBLE
IN THE MEDIA
AND THE MARKETPLACE

T V IS A MIRROR, not of life as it really is (that's for high-brows) but of life as people *think* it is or ought to be. The trouble is that if you watch long enough, you take the world of the tube for right or real. If television fiction reflects what we think about older women, we think of them little, if at all.

Monitoring the people who flicker in and out of your homes is a little like counting moonbeams in a jar. Television deals with perceptions that are too subjective for accurate measurement; for instance, observers differ about whether they regard a character as "old." And even if we could find ways to be objective, it's a formidable task to monitor all the images that are being projected night and day.

What we know about the images we see on television comes from academic sociologists who monitor TV shows on the dubious assumption that they portray American values and, more often, from reformers in search of evidence that these values should change. Of these, the most serious researcher is Dr. George Gerbner, emeritus dean of the Annenberg School of Communications at the University of Pennsylvania.

A pioneer in the campaign against violence on television, Dr. Gerbner has been studying television since 1968. At his workshop in Philadelphia, researchers record the age, sex, characteristics, and situations of all the people whose images appear on various types of TV shows, not just during prime time. The data are organized so that if you are interested in older women, you can find out how they are portrayed and calculate how much time they get on the screen. In 1993, Dr. Gerbner's ten-year analysis of all kinds of television programming showed no real change.

"You have to look at all the hours and stations," Dr. Gerbner warns. "In spite of a few memorable programs, like *Murder, She Wrote,* older women are not only underrepresented, but they appear to be diminishing instead of increasing, as they are in real life. And our data show that as women age, they are more likely to be portrayed as unsuccessful. Especially in what children see."

More than twice as many older women are depicted in situations of failure on Saturday morning programs as on programs in prime time. Elderly women's rate of failure is four times that of elderly men, and the older women who do appear are at the bottom of what Dr. Gerbner calls the "lethal pecking order." About one in three gets involved in violent action, but only to be killed, or, as some programs graphically put it, "offed from the planet." "Symbolic annihilation" is what Dr. Gerbner calls it.

Are old women making any progress on television? If you are an avid televiewer, you can probably think of some examples. But the few studies we do have suggest that the improvement has been from virtual invisibility to gross underrepresentation.

In real life, older women outnumber older men, but the Older Women's League reports that a 1982 study found that in the world of the tube, men who appeared to be between forty and fifty-nine outnumbered women in that group by four to one, and among people who looked as if they were over sixty by an incredible twenty to one. In the real world, of course, it's the other way around: the margin by which women outnumber men rises with age.

An earlier study found that in the late 1970s, only 2 percent of the characters on television appeared to be over sixty-five, and of this 2 percent, only 9 percent were women, which works out to less than two tenths of one percent of the total number of characters. In the real world of those years, 11 percent of the population was over sixty-five, with women outnumbering men.

And while older women were always underrepresented on the screen, older men sometimes appeared more frequently than they occurred in the population at large.

The older women you saw on TV back then were generally portrayed as useless, helpless, or laughable. One media study found that males in prime-time television drama fail because they are evil but "females fail just as they age." During the 1970s, Maggie Kuhn's Gray Panthers enlisted volunteers — most of them older women — to watch the media for bias against older people. The instances they reported of demeaning, insipid dialogue and erratic behavior among older characters attracted some attention but failed to change what viewers saw or didn't see on the screen.

If programmers thought about it at all, they must have figured that viewers weren't interested in anything that happened to older women, no matter how provocative. And they might have been right. During the 1970s, a situation comedy about two elderly people living together without marrying so they could keep their Social Security benefits did poorly in the ratings and couldn't find a sponsor.

Since then there have been more older women on television, but it isn't at all clear that there has been an overall improvement. In the early 1990s, television lost several soap operas that portrayed rich and attractive mature women: gentle Miss Ellie of *Dallas,* beautiful Krystle Carrington and ruthlessly powerful Alexis Colby of *Dynasty,* and shrewd Angela Channing of *Falcon Crest.* In 1994 these kinds of older women have disappeared from television drama. Instead we have middle-aged, middle-class women who are having financial and family problems, like Roseanne. The only really attractive older women to be widely seen are Candice Bergen playing the role of Murphy Brown, a television newscaster in her forties, and Angela Lansbury as Jessica Fletcher, the well-off, smart, and sympathetic detective writer in *Murder, She Wrote.*

Older actresses find fewer television roles just when they have learned their trade and are hitting their stride. When Anne Bancroft was in her fifties, she identified personally with the role she played on TV of Mrs. Cage, a suburban housewife who shot an abrasive young career woman who made her own home-based life seem irrelevant. How could Bancroft feel that way herself? The reporter who asked got a tight-lipped answer: "My knees hurt. My hair is turning gray. And people tell me I'm irrelevant all the time."

As we have seen, a woman can be fired from television news-casting for being "too old" before she's forty. This is especially true of the "girl" reporters dispatched for live accounts from scenes of disaster. "I'm looking for a girl with lots of hair, a big smile, and a great sweater," a producer told a well-qualified field corre-spondent who was trying to switch jobs, while he traced the out-line that would fill the sweater. "You're getting a little too old for this." She was thirty-two.

Are things getting better? Women who have survived in the business beyond the first flush of youth say, "Yes, but." Marlene Sanders, the feminist who helped open network news to women in the 1970s, says that women have advanced from being excep-tions that prove the rule, like Barbara Walters and Betty Furness, to making up a third or a fourth of the correspondents at the three major networks. Gerbner's 1993 study found that 35 percent of news broadcasters were women.

But there's still a double standard. Jo Verne, who nosed out Jessica Savitch by six weeks as the first woman to anchor a local TV show, thinks a woman can be older but she can't be mediocre, and she has to have something more than standard good looks going for her — ideally, something memorable about her per-sonality. "At forty-six, Peggy Crone of Channel 5 in New York may be the world's oldest living girl reporter," Verne says, "but she's irrepressible. By comparison, the young male field corre-spondents are just portable mikes."

Everyone in the business takes it for granted that the women have to be better and look younger than the men with whom they compete. Competition is fierce, and everything counts. In 1990, thirty-five-year-old Meredith Vieria, the second woman to serve as an anchor on *60 Minutes,* was wondering how many years she had left at the network. She was socking away as much money as she could, "because when I'm forty, there'll be fifty twenty-year-olds, and will they really want me because of my talent and ability, or will they not want me because I have too many lines in my face?"

Lesley Stahl of CBS News, who is now in her forties, doesn't think that the women have a bigger age problem than the men, but she is taking no chances. "I will try not to age, but what can I do? I wear gobs of makeup. I get my hair done twice a week. I diet."

So there has been an improvement, maybe. But the rule still holds: visibly older women are underrepresented on television news.

There are magazines for people in every conceivable situation, no matter how small or fleeting. Young women are wooed by magazines like *Seventeen* and *Mademoiselle*, whose names suggest young women who haven't yet married. Other periodicals are directed to employed mothers and even to the small number of women who at any one time are nursing babies. But publishers have shied away from serving the rising millions of women over fifty-five. *Mirabella*, the fashion magazine, and *Lear's*, the two magazines directed to mature women, both ended by aiming at women who were willing to admit that they were forty, and neither singled out the special lifestyle situation of older women who are on their own.

It's much the same for books. Whatever happens to you, you can find books about it in any big bookstore or public library. Teenagers, young men, brides, parents, builders of model airplanes, hired guns who roam the world as soldiers of fortune, the newly retired, even old people are regarded as profitable markets for books. Robert N. Butler wrote *Why Survive? Being Old in America*, a groundbreaking attack on ageism, in 1975, and Alex Comfort wrote *Say Yes to Old Age* in 1976, but neither of these bestsellers was addressed especially to older women.

Books of advice for the widowed and the divorced are a publishing staple, and most of them are addressed to women. And while they may provide solace to individual widows, they don't appeal to most of the older women who acquired the habit of reading when they were young. These women tend to be veteran copers who do not respond to the oh-so-cheerful patronizing advice handed out in what the book trade calls "widow books," which are often written by social workers, psychologists, therapists, and financial advisers who make a living on the problems they describe.

Newspapers increasingly cover the achievements of older women on the same basis that they cover the achievements of older men, but feature articles are still appearing about obscure women whose sole claim to notice is that they have all their marbles at an advanced age. And it seems, at least to me, that octogenarian women achievers like Louise Nevelson, the sculptor, the dancers Martha Graham and Agnes de Mille, and the singer Sarah Vaughan have been singled out for special press attention because of their age.

Maggie Kuhn has a formidable intellect, but she is resigned to being described in the press as a cute old lady: "They love to describe my ninety-five-pound body, my half-moon bifocals, and my wispy bun."

In magazines, few women have wrinkles, pores, or expression lines around the eyes. Art departments don't bother to retouch photographs of older men, but they routinely make older women look as if they had been embalmed in their youth. Celebrities often control how they are depicted by providing photographs of themselves. Governor Ann Richards of Texas never retouches the photographs she sends out. The wrinkles frankly crisscrossing her vibrant face are part of the image that has made her popular.

Editors of the big women's magazines have a bad conscience about postmenopausal women. They are supposed to give their readers the information they need for their daily lives, but they'd much rather tell us how to reduce our thighs than how to cope with the loss of a husband or what to do when we're left with a house that's bigger than we need. In 1992, a major women's magazine that prided itself on providing the gory details of rape, child-molesting babysitters, high school drug peddlers, and incurable rare diseases rejected an article on how to prepare for the years alone "because most of our readers are under fifty and they don't like to think of such things." But most of its readers were over thirty-five.

The big-circulation women's magazines have a good business reason for shortchanging coverage of problems that affect older women. They depend on advertising of mass-consumed products such as toothpaste and breakfast cereal, and advertisers pay more money to reach young women, whose tastes for such products are forming. In the 1990s there are relatively fewer young women in the population, so magazines and television shows that depend on advertising compete desperately with each other to increase their share of the shrinking number of these prime prospects.

The rising age of readers is an embarrassment for all mass-circulation women's magazines. In 1993, when slightly more American women were over fifty than between eighteen and thirty-four (36.3 percent versus 36 percent), only 29.5 percent of the readers of *Good Housekeeping* were between eighteen and thirty-four. In an attempt to conceal the upward bulge, magazines are broadening the age brackets of their demographic profiles.

Good Housekeeping has used age breaks that conceal the increasing age of its readers. It reported that 62 percent of its readers were between eighteen and forty-nine, compared with 64 percent of all American women. Extending the bracket upward concealed how few of them were the young women eighteen to twenty-five whom advertisers want. The same result was achieved by another age break that raised the bottom end of the bracket to exclude them: 59 percent of *Good Housekeeping* readers were reported to be between the ages of twenty-five and fifty-four, compared with 57 percent of all women.

Women's magazines try to appeal to all age groups. They assume that their faithful older readers want to be treated as if they were young. But in spite of all their efforts, they haven't been able to attract enough readers under thirty. Generation X isn't a group of faithful readers. Its members scan magazines, if they pick them up at all, so editors clutter their covers with screams for attention, as desperate as those of television commercials.

The trick is to compete for the fickle young readers who bring higher space rates without turning off the faithful older ones who keep circulation high. One strategy that doesn't work very well is to segregate them. *Family Circle* tried running a column called "Potpourri Over 60" but discontinued it for "lack of pull." And *McCall's* has tried binding "silver pages" into copies mailed only to older subscribers.

Print and broadcast media supported by national advertising face the same business problem: how to hold on to the increasing proportion of readers or viewers over 50 while attracting the decreasing proportion of young people. The age preference can translate into significant dollars. Television shows have sometimes been able to sell younger viewers at two or three times the rate per thousand they get for viewers over sixty. The television season often starts with more new youth-oriented programs than can survive, in order to attract the young audience, and ends by restoring shows that appeal to older audiences, in order to keep the numbers of watchers from dropping. In 1992, NBC slipped to third place in the network ratings when it dumped popular shows like *Golden Girls* to attract more young viewers.

Television sometimes sounds as if it is deliberately trying to tune out older viewers. Sound bites are geared to the reaction times of youngsters, and so are the plots of sitcoms, which enact the "POW!" exclamations of comic strips. "We don't really need anyone over fifty years of age to succeed with our business plan," the head of Fox Broadcasting once proclaimed. The subliminal message is clear: old women, get out of our ratings!

Market researchers warned advertisers that they were going to need to appeal to older customers, and sooner than they imagined. In 1993, the oldest of the big crop of babies born after World War II were forty-seven, the youngest forty, and there

were fewer young women coming up behind them. But advertisers continued to look for those young women and magazines
and television shows competed to deliver them.

When advertisers looked at the figures, they knew that they
would have to sell to the aging baby boomers to stay alive, but
they are still chasing after the elusive Generation X like lemmings
that can't stop following each other over the cliff. Why?

According to Cheryl Russell, editor of *The Boomer Report*,
most businesspeople of the 1990s are too young to remember a
time when young adults were not the dominant consumer market.
Advertising is still a business for young people, and while women
are being hired as copywriters, the culture of the profession favors young men who have a talent for manipulating stereotypes,
including, of course, the stereotypes of age. Stereotypes yield
slowly to reality, but warning shocks are appearing.

Older women have no money, right? Media analysts were surprised to find that *Murder, She Wrote,* the most popular show for
women over fifty-five, pulled an audience with an average family
income of $60,000. Angela Lansbury is unhappy because adver-
tisers pay less per thirty seconds of commercial time on *Murder,
She Wrote* than for shows with a higher proportion of young
viewers. "The networks seem to be chasing people twenty and under," she complains. "Why? I don't know. They don't buy anything. They eat cereal. They drink Coke." When older women
were outnumbered by the younger baby boomers, it was easy to
forget that women have always had more money to spend when
they get into their forties or fifties than when they were young women
just starting out. Youth was where the money was only because
there were so many more young people when the baby boomers
were young. In addition, the recession of the 1990s left young
people relatively poorer than the boomers were at their age.

Older people are too set in their ways to switch brands or try
something new, right? Wrong, said a J. Walter Thompson research report. They switch brands as often as young people. And
you can't take "faithful" older customers for granted. Repeat customers had kept Chrysler afloat for years, but Madison Avenue

insiders say that they went elsewhere when Chrysler diverted its advertising dollars to attract young buyers, on the theory that its old customers were hooked and didn't need to be persuaded.

Advertisers kept on talking to the aging boomers as if they were young, on the sound Madison Avenue principle that you talk to prospects as if they were what they want to be. Older women clearly think of themselves as young, but do they respond to the same appeals that parted them from their money when they were in their twenties and thirties? Have they really learned nothing in decades of adult life?

The impending demise of the youth market created a golden opportunity for consultants and media advisers and a rash of experimental appeals to the mature market. Some favored a direct "stay young" approach. Pepsi tried addressing the aging Pepsi Generation with ads for "people who want to think and feel young," and Reebok portrayed an older woman race walking and saying, "I don't think seventy is old." Budweiser even tried a hip guitar-playing grandma who outrocked Stray Cats star Brian Setzer. Days Inns had a grandmother bringing a pony for her grandchildren into a hotel room while Grandfather sat quietly admiring her antics from the sidelines, for all the world like the traditional wife of a stumping politician.

Marketers have a hard time dealing with the miscellany of older consumers. Age, the traditional segmentation, is an unreliable predictor of the behavior of older people. It makes more sense to appeal to people on the basis of a common interest, showing people of all ages using a product, but market analysts have tried to preserve the age brackets by segmenting older people on the basis of lifestyle.

Market analyst James Gollub divides the over-fifty-five population into Attainers (the oldest and richest), Adapters, Explorers, Martyrs, Pragmatists, and Preservers (oldest and poorest). George Mochlis segments them on the basis of health and introversion, ranging from Healthy Indulgers, defined as extroverts in good health, to Frail Recluses, introverts in poor health. Soon there were supies (senior urban professionals) opals (older people with active lifestyles), and the much-sought woopers (well-off older persons). Promoters of upscale retirement real estate targeting woopers subdivided them into the go-goes, who are always traveling; the slow-goes, who go less often than they used to do; and the no-goes, who can't get out and about at all.

David Wolfe, one of the more thoughtful consultants, says that psychological development toward maturity is more important than lifestyle or demography. Some take longer than others, but with any luck, we become mature or, to use Abraham Maslow's term, "self-actualized" in our sixties. At that point we stop acquiring things or worrying about our status and identity and start thinking about where we stand in the big picture of community, society, and eventually all human life. We become less interested in buying houses and cars, or even having experiences that confirm the sense of self, and more interested in the esthetic, spiritual, philosophical, and caring experiences we can get from travel, education, religion, public service, and altruism. Appeals to altruism work better than appeals to status.

The best advice on what *doesn't* work comes from the advertising standards of *Modern Maturity*, the magazine that goes to the 33 million members of the AARP, who are all over fifty. In 1982 *Modern Maturity*'s advertising director, Treesa Drury, started turning down ads that were offensive to older people. Under the new guidelines, copy cannot, for instance, promise that a product will make you look fifteen years younger. There's a quota on ads for health-related products, and an absolute ban on impotence cures, dating services, adult diapers, write-your-own-will kits, and many other reminders of the seamy side of old age.

But even as they mull over such nonageist appeals, advertisers are taking no chances with the tried and true. Set in their youth-oriented ways, they continue to believe that the main interest of women over fifty is looking and feeling younger. Take, for instance, an ad for New Maybelline Revitalizing, the "age-denying makeup," whose light-reflecting coverage is supposed to diffuse fine lines: "With SKIN LIKE HERS, ask her age and she automatically SUBTRACTS 5 YEARS. If she slept well, maybe 6.

In love? Anything goes. Who does she think she's fooling? Everyone."

And just as the models in ads for baby products are always older than the children they represent, the models for products aimed at older women continued to be inevitably younger. In 1993, you could still buy out all the magazines on the newsstand without finding a woman with a line in her face. In spite of all the talk, visibly older women are all but invisible in ads.

Out of sight, out of mind. Retailers don't like to think about older women because these women are experienced shoppers and can cause them trouble. Older women love a bargain but know when what looks like a bargain isn't one. They expect expensive personal service. They are apt to know just what they want. Even those who have more money than they used to have don't buy on impulse.

It's easy to forget about such customers because they don't fit into a convenient niche where they can be sold special products by specialized pitches. They want what everyone else wants, starting with better customer service. Some marketers go so far as deliberately discouraging older customers, on the mistaken notion that they are going to cost more than their business is worth.

Maître d's at good restaurants can be conveniently blind, but they are especially good at not seeing an older woman alone until all the good seats are taken. And the computer systems that enable credit card companies and mortgage lenders to check applicants in a well-advertised hurry make no provision for older women who have neither a job nor a husband. They've been known to turn down newly divorced or widowed women with solid assets who have no personal credit history. After her divorce at forty-nine, Cynthia Coupe was turned down for a credit card in her own name because "people your age aren't very good credit risks."

Loan officers look at divorced older women with the banker's proverbial glass eye. Dana Hull's bank wouldn't give her a loan because they didn't think that restoring organs was a serious business, but she's grossing $25,000 a year at it anyway. A bank in Medina, Ohio, wouldn't lend Fay Porter $1,000 to fix up her house the year she was divorced, although she was drawing a teacher's pension. When she protested, they found that "there seemed to have been a mistake in your credit report."

Ralph Nader reports that the car insurance of a woman in her seventies was canceled because she made a claim for the theft of her car radio, her first in thirty years of paying premiums. The company's rationale seemed to be that older people average more accidents per mile driven than younger ones, but defenders of older drivers point out that they are just as good risks because they drive less.

Nader says older people are also discriminated against in the housing market. He cites the case of a landlord who quoted a lower rent to an applicant's son when he looked at the same apartment later. Older people are considered undesirable tenants because they may not be able to keep up the property or the rent payments, but it's the younger tenants who are more apt to wreck the place and skip without paying the rent.

Older women are invisible to mainstream business. "You don't see older women in ads," an advertising consultant explained, "because older women don't want to buy what advertisers have to sell." But where are the enterprisers who are supposed to find out what people want and give it to them? The answer seems to be that older women have been written off as wantless penny-pinchers who are too poor or apathetic to buy anything worth providing.

10

INVISIBLE
IN HEALTH CARE

"HE JUST handed me a prescription and walked out the door."

"He took phone calls and gave instructions to the staff about other patients while I was talking."

"He never looked straight at me."

These are typical of the complaints I heard from older women about their doctors. Most of them think their doctors don't take them seriously and are trying to get rid of them as quickly as possible. Research bears them out.

An Older Women's League report found that 65 percent of physicians think that women's complaints are influenced by emotional factors and that women make excessive demands. Even the vague symptoms that doctors dismiss when a woman mentions them are taken more seriously if a man presents them. A study of the medical records of couples treated by the same doctor showed that identical symptoms of dizziness, headache, and lower back pain were followed up more aggressively when presented by the husbands than by the wives. Other studies show that women with heart problems are less likely than men to receive sophisticated diagnostic tests, cardiac catheterization, and coronary surgery.

This is particularly disturbing when we consider that older women are the heaviest users of medical care. Women over sixty-five make more than three times the average number of visits to internists. Compared with those of men and younger people of both sexes, the most common ailments of older women are less likely to be studied by medical researchers, and treatment for them is less likely to be taught in medical schools or reimbursable under insurance rules. As of 1994, postmenopausal women under sixty-five were less likely than men of any age to be covered by health insurance of any kind.

Older women are the victims of a medical care system designed by and for young men. One female doctor will never forget her first cadaver. "She must have been a *Playboy* bunny," an instructor remarked before ordering the class to cut off the unwieldy large breasts and throw them into a can marked "Cadaver Waste." He implied that there was nothing to be learned from examining breasts.

As medical training proceeds, students are encouraged to use new high-tech methods for dealing with acute, interesting, and rare problems. But when they get out into practice, they are confronted day after day by a waiting room full of old women with chronic, dull, common conditions such as arthritis, for which there are as yet no exciting remedies.

Even worse, older women patients are being treated on the basis of medical research that excludes them. Although heart disease is the leading cause of death for postmenopausal women, doctors often ignore the symptoms because they've been taught that women aren't at risk. And why do they think so? Because what we know about heart disease has been learned from studying younger men. A review of seventy-five heart disease studies showed that most of them turned away subjects over sixty-five, the age at which heart disease most often strikes. New drugs have traditionally been tested on men because the hormones of women are supposed to mess up the findings, but if you're a woman, those findings don't help you at all. Women can't be sure that an aspirin a day will keep heart disease away, because the evidence is based on an experimental study of 22,000 men.

In 1992, Dr. Bernadine Healy, the first woman director of the National Institutes of Health, established a massive Women's Health Initiative to insure equality in research funding for conditions and diseases unique to women, such as menopause and breast cancer. The next year, the National Institutes of Health launched a fifteen-year, $625 million clinical investigation of 160,000 women aged fifty to seventy-nine. Among the reforms will be the requirement that drugs be tested on women as well as men.

Doctors are constantly being reminded that their patients are human beings and they ought to look at them and listen to them, but they can't afford to do it. Margaret Mahoney, president of the Commonwealth Fund, blames this on the insurance system. "Dealing properly with an older patient requires patience and time, but that time is not taken into account by insurance payment schedules," she explains. "Doctors feel that unless they reduce the amount of time they spend with older patients, they won't be able to make a living." Many doctors dread treating older women because they regard them as more talkative than older men.

Doctors have a number of tactics for defending their time. The simplest is to dismiss complaints as unimportant. "Of course you're tired. You're working," a doctor in Tucson told a fifty-three-year-old woman who had gone back to work, adding that "all women your age have mouth ulcers." It is even more common to blame the trouble on old age. But what seems trivial to a doctor may be devastating to a woman who hasn't come to terms with her own aging.

One woman who complained of arthritis pain can't forget that her doctor's response was a cheery "Welcome to old age!"

A woman who complained that her heart pounded when she ran upstairs was told that she "didn't need to run upstairs anymore."

A woman hospitalized in a strange city reported that "a doctor took one look at me, and without a question or a test pronounced me hopelessly senile."

"Old people are like old cars," a young male doctor remarked to a woman he had been treating for years. "Something is always acting up."

The high-tech way to deal with time-consuming complaints

is to prescribe a tranquilizer or ship the patient off to a specialist ("At your age you ought to have a complete blood workup"). If a workup discloses something beyond what is regarded as normal, expensive drugs and a new round of tests, visits, and referrals to specialists are in order.

Each tactic has its dangers. Dismissing symptoms can lead to ignoring treatable conditions. Brain tumors have been overlooked because doctors wrote off forgetfulness as the old medical garbage-pail diagnosis "senile dementia," and there's no telling how much serious illness could have been avoided if primary-care physicians had scheduled their older women patients for regular mammo-grams, Pap smears, eye exams, and hearing tests.

Ruth Combecker, the woman whose fatigue was attributed to working, happened to be an RN, and she knew enough about medicine to know that something was radically wrong. When she located the appropriate specialists, they found that she was suffering from Behçet's disease, a rare, painful condition produc-ing ulcers in the mouth, eyes, ears, and genitals in addition to fatigue. Once she had been diagnosed with an "interesting" dis-ease, she said, she got exemplary care.

When Helen Johnston was likened to an old car, she was com-plaining about a swelling belly to a doctor who had been treating her for cataracts, goiter, and knee problems. She reported that he ignored the swelling even after an ultrasound test confirmed that her uterus was enlarged. This was the case, he agreed, but the condition wouldn't bother her. She was soon in such pain that she walked unannounced into the office of a doctor whose sign said "Geriatric Medicine." She was rushed immediately to the hospital, where an emergency operation detected a cancer that had spread beyond control.

But there's also danger in the high-tech way of getting older women out of the doctors' hair. The increase in the number of specialists commanding higher fees makes it tempting for a pri-mary-care physician to refer someone with vague complaints to a series of doctors who are trained to see only part of the problem. And an increasing number of women have no primary-care physician to help them find the appropriate specialist.

When Lila Line complained of depression and mood swings, her female family doctor suggested she take antidepressants. She refused. She went to a psychiatrist. The female psychiatrist wanted to put her on Prozac, which Lila declined. She next went to a female mental health counselor, who suspected that the problem was physical and referred her to a male family practitioner. After exhaustive questioning and tests, the male doctor discovered a vitamin deficiency. Lila is fine now — and sold on megavitamins and a new diet.

When Phyllis Diller went to a top kidney specialist to find out why she had to get up so many times in the night, he ran all kinds of tests and pronounced her kidneys perfect. "You're so busy during the day that you just don't go," he explained. "You save it up and go at night." But he started to write a prescription for her anyway.

"Hold it," she said, tapping him on the arm. "I just don't take drugs. Every drug has a side effect. All I wanted to know was whether there was something wrong." So she paid him and walked out, a free woman.

Phyllis Diller is nobody's fool. According to Jacqueline Thea, a nurse, rehabilitation counselor, and volunteer spokesperson for the AARP, overmedication is a real danger to older women. More than a third of women over sixty-five are taking five or more prescription drugs a day. Usually these prescriptions are ordered by more than one doctor, so that no one keeps track of the drugs' interactions unless the prescriptions are all being filled by a conscientious pharmacist.

Then there's the problem of dosage. New drugs are usually tried on healthy young men, but dosages calibrated for a healthy, 180-pound, forty-year-old man may be dangerously high for a frail old woman. Thea explains that with aging, our fat-to-muscle ratio changes and our liver and kidney functions slow down, so it takes less of a drug to do more.

Overmedication is also likely to go undetected because doctors are apt to ascribe the side effects of drugs to depression or mental illness if the patient is an older woman. One study found that 15 percent of elderly women who had been admitted to a state mental hospital turned out to be suffering from drug toxicities that had been misdiagnosed as senility or mental illness!

Thea blames doctors for making drug addicts out of older women. She cites studies showing that two thirds of recently bereaved widows who go to physicians are given tranquilizers, antidepressants, and hypnotics, and quite frequently the widow keeps taking them to relax and get to sleep. Thea concludes that "more than any other age or gender group, older women appear to be at greater risk for physician-perpetrated drug abuse involving prescription psychoactive drugs."

Will the young women now rising in medicine make a difference? It sounds like a sexist remark, but it is probably fair to say that medical training does not wholly eradicate the well-established ability of women to listen and respond to other people. According to a roundup of important findings in 1993 by the *Journal of the American Medical Association*, women doctors spend more time with patients and give 40 percent more time to taking a medical history than male doctors.

This seems to be true all over the world. "Come back next week, we've all got it too" was what a young male doctor serving Peace Corps volunteers told Martha Peterson when she thought she was dying of dysentery in a little town on the Afghan border. She doesn't blame the doctor, because at the time he was busy dealing with wounded soldiers, but after she survived a second thirty-hour train trip, a female Pakistani doctor knew just what to do and even refused payment for the up-to-date medical treatment that cured Martha.

Both women and their doctors are victims of changing expectations. Older women complain to their doctors because they were brought up when patients paid doctors directly and had to be encouraged to incur the expense of consulting a physician about anything bothering them. And because we haven't been prepared for growing old, we ask the doctor about perfectly natural late-life changes in eyesight, hearing, joint mobility, balance, short-term memory, urination, and sleep. Like Phyllis Diller, we think these normal changes are a disease the doctor ought to cure.

Doctors know otherwise, but they haven't been trained to help women adapt to aging, or to respect palliative measures such as massage, exercise, chiropractic, and remedies outside of the tradition of mainstream medicine, which medical doctors often dismiss because they do no more than treat the symptoms of the chronic diseases that pile up in later years. The result is that the family doctor — or the internist, who is the modern equivalent — no longer takes responsibility for decisions such as whether it is safe for a forgetful eighty-five-year-old woman to live alone. With a clear conscience, the doctor can pronounce her in perfect health and wash his hands of the problems brought on by her failing memory. That's why we should probably forgive doctors when, bored and exasperated by continual demands for something they weren't trained to do, they dismiss what they can't fix with remarks like "Welcome to old age!"

By defining old age as a disease, we've loaded the old people onto the doctors by default. Dr. Carroll Estes, director of the Institute for Health and Aging at the University of California at San Francisco, calls this the "biomedicalization of aging." It results in monstrous and expensive nursing-home care for older people — predominantly women — whose principal problem is having trouble dressing and bathing themselves.

The same thing happened to childbirth. Once a natural process supervised largely by women, it is now usually treated with fancy apparatus and several medical attendants. Instead of being the principal actor, a woman in labor has become a patient who is expected to lie flat on her back on a narrow table designed for the convenience of the doctor, who until recently was invariably male. The psychological losses of this system are just now being addressed.

We have medicalized old age because doctors really do have good ways of dealing with the pathologies of this natural process, because older people do have more ailments that are properly subject to clinical attention than younger people, but principally, I would argue, because we can't accept aging as a normal life process. Medicalizing old age dooms us all to the eventual fate of being a mindless, passive patient, a ward of the medical system.

11

INVISIBLE

IN POLICYMAKING

POLICYMAKING IS the one job where it helps to have a few gray hairs, but unlike older men, older women are seldom seen in the halls of political or economic power. Although we are a growing part of the electorate, we are woefully underrepresented in Congress. Not only are there more of us, but more of us get out and vote than in the past. In the 1992 election, 69 percent of women over fifty-five voted, almost as many as the 73 percent of men that age, yet the supposedly youthful Congress elected in that "year of the woman" continued to be dominated by men over fifty. Women of any age held only 11 percent of the seats in the House and only 6 percent of the seats in the Senate.

We are even rarer at the top in big business. Women's faces now decorate business pages and women are highly visible guests on television talk shows, but the statistics tell a different story. In 1978, *Fortune* found only 10 women among the 6,400 individuals listed as top executives on the proxy statements of the 799 biggest American companies; in 1990, there were only 19 among 4,012 comparable listings. After twelve years of "progress," women had increased their presence at the very top from little more than a tenth to one half of one percent.

The special needs of older women on their own are seldom considered by traditional public and private social programs. We have been systematically ignored by historians, sociologists, medical researchers, philanthropists, and even by the activists who watch out for people who fall through the cracks of our changing society. This is beginning to change, but there's a lot of catching up to do.

GOVERNMENT-FUNDED PROGRAMS don't have anything against older women on their own. The problem is that the men who designed our Medicare, Social Security, pension, insurance, and health-care systems assumed that all older women would always be attached to a wage-earning husband, so the way to take care of her would be to take care of him.

Medicare was designed for acute ailments rather than the chronic but nondisabling conditions that affect so many older women. And it doesn't cover the long-term care required by those — mostly women — who outlive both their assets and a spouse who could help them through the activities of daily living.

Middle-aged women are no better off. During the years between forty-six and sixty-four, women are more apt than men to have no private health insurance. If they work, such women are less apt than working men (55 percent versus 72 percent) to have a job that offers health insurance. And if they have been covered as wives, they may have to fend for themselves when the marriage ends.

An older widow with a chronic ailment may find that she has a "preexisting condition" that makes it expensive or impossible for her to get covered at all. Because she was once diagnosed as suffering from multiple sclerosis, my stepdaughter couldn't get affordable health insurance when she was widowed. Her husband's law firm arranged to let her pay for the insurance she had had as a wife until she is old enough for Medicare to cover her. No wonder that continuing health insurance coverage for the woman has become an important issue in divorce agreements.

Social Security was crafted when women did not work for pay, and it tends to leave them with a lower monthly check than men usually get. A divorced wife sometimes has to get by on half what she and her husband would have received, although her living expenses may be almost as high. And in spite of corrective amendments, benefits are still based on earnings, so they still reflect the low-paid and less regular jobs that most older women have held. Also, many women worked in jobs that were not originally covered at all.

Female workers now of retirement age are much less likely to have a private pension than male workers their age. The women who flooded into the workforce during the 1970s, many of them mothers of small children, were more likely to work intermittently than women before and after them, and in those days, fewer firms had pension plans and vesting periods were longer. The result is that many of these women come of retirement age qualifying for no pension, or at best a very small one. Before large numbers of wives and mothers worked, the very small number of women in the workforce tended to be full-time long-term career librarians, editors, teachers, or civil servants who qualified for a pension because their work pattern was similar to that of men. According to Olena Berg of the U.S. Labor Department, private pension benefits received by men rose 6 percent between 1978 and 1989 in real dollars, but actually *declined* 17 percent for women. And some widows are still suffering because before 1985, a man could improve the pension he received during his lifetime by cutting his wife out of a survivor's benefit without telling her.

A little-known example of the built-in government bias against female dependents is the situation of military widows. The services have traditionally been generous to the dependents of our fighting men, on the theory that the welfare of their wives contributed to their morale, but there's no provision for military widows, who have outlived this particular kind of contribution to the national defense. The military pension system doesn't take very good care of widows, particularly if they have been divorced, and frequent changes in the laws haven't helped. For instance, Congress saved money by cutting the pensions of widows of military retirees who had taken a lower pension to provide for them, on the theory that they were entitled to Social Security. Some of these women wound up with less income than their husbands intended them to have.

The unequal impact of government programs on single older women is especially cruel because it is unintended. And it is getting worse. Budgets are being held steady while older women at risk are increasing in numbers. Among the many interest groups in Washington, the only voice they have is the Older Women's League.

PRIVATE PHILANTHROPY is a world outside of home that appeals to many women. Women have always done the bulk of the hands-on, one-on-one work of delivering help to individuals in need. They have always worried more than men about general health, education, and welfare, yet all but a tiny trickle of the $120 billion a year collected and spent by nonprofit organizations for the common good is controlled by cautious men, who decide who gets how much and how it's spent. Even when a big donation comes from a woman, she has all too often based her decision on a precedent set by the father or husband from whom she inherited the money or the men she allows to manage her nest egg for her.

The more money a woman has, the less likely she is to control it. Joanne Hayes of Hayes-Briscoe Associates, a consultant in fund development for nonprofit organizations, says that rich women have less power in their families than poor women, whose earnings are essential. For women rich or poor, money is to spend for things they use. For rich men, money is power — especially power over women.

Rich women have traditionally been allowed to buy anything they want for themselves or the household, providing they never forget where the money came from, even when it is legally their own. "My father would have wanted her to leave a little something to Vassar," an Ivy League son said in discussing the will of his widowed mother. "She's been a good steward of his money."

Fund-raisers in the past didn't bother to solicit rich women, even when the money was their own. All too often the women would say, "My accountant wouldn't let me." Brought up to feel that nice women didn't talk about money, they referred inquiries to male lawyers and managers. And according to Judith Barber, a Bay Area psychologist who edits *Family Money: A Quarterly Commentary on the Unspoken Issues Related to Wealth*, rich women have been brought up to feel that someone else will take care of them, so when they are on their own, they are more cautious than a man would be about giving money away, even to their own children.

Women have always owned more wealth than they have been allowed to control. Real estate and stocks have often been held in their names by fathers, husbands, and trustees, who make the decisions about buying and selling. Feminists back each other up in estimating that women really own 60 percent of private wealth, and the figure stands because there's no way to prove or disprove it, primarily because the ownership of wealth is almost deliberately shrouded in mystery.

We know a lot about who spends income that is used for consumption, but statistics on the ownership of wealth that can be used for power — real estate, securities, bank accounts — are lacking from government records. The only figures we have are extrapolated from the characteristics of the people whose lawyers and accountants haven't been able to keep their heirs from paying estate taxes when they die, and the IRS is so slow to analyze the characteristics of estate taxpayers that in 1994 the most recent breakdown was five years old. In 1989, 43.1 percent of the wealth subject to estate taxation was owned by women.

SOCIAL RESEARCH has traditionally underfunded studies on aging and the old. Old people of both genders have been left out of the schoolbooks from which most people get their first view of the wider world. Elizabeth Markson of Boston University found few references to aging or the existence of older people of either gender in ninety-one textbooks in biology, general science, health, government, history, economics, psychology, sociology, and home economics. She believes that textbook authors don't think of older people and so don't realize that they are leaving them out.

Old people aren't considered an exciting research specialty, and old women have held even less appeal for researchers than old men. Although they outnumber older men and have different problems and opportunities, older women have seldom been separately addressed in traditional studies on aging, and the most reliable one originally left them out entirely. Until recently, the benchmark Baltimore Longitudinal Study on Aging, which follows normal individuals for decades, was based exclusively on men.

Another example of inadvertent neglect of older women is the gap in our knowledge about the "oldest old," those who are over eighty-five. In this, the fastest-growing age group in America, there are five women for every two men. And although these people are more diverse than seventy-year-olds, it has only been in the 1990s that the *Statistical Abstract* has displayed age breakdowns beyond "over seventy-five."

"We know very little about this eighty-five-plus population," says Dr. T. Franklin Williams, director of the National Institute on Aging. "We don't know how they got to be that old, or why their survival rate is greater than among the general population. We know too little about their true medical needs . . . even how they are living."

It's hard to escape the conclusion that older women have been shortchanged in research design because research money is controlled by men. Feminists delving into the research budget of the National Institutes of Health discovered that Congress has appropriated less money to study medical problems affecting women only, and even to those that affect more women than men, than to those that affect men only. "People tend to fund what they fear," Patricia Schroeder, congresswoman from Colorado, explained on television, and the men who hold the congressional purse strings aren't afraid of menopause, osteoporosis, or cancer of the breasts, cervix, or ovaries. No fear, no money.

Even women's studies have paid no special attention to the postreproductive years of women's lives. At a meeting of the National Women's Studies Association, Barbara Macdonald denounced the omission as male thinking. "As the numbers of old women rapidly increase, the women you taught five years ago are now in the helping professions as physicians and social workers, because the jobs are there. They still call themselves feminists, but lacking any kind of feminist analysis of women's aging, they

are defining old women as needy, simple-minded, helpless —
definitions that correlate conveniently with the services and salaries they have in mind." And in the 1990s, women liberated in
the 1970s have discovered the issue of menopause without paying
much attention to the lengthening decades that follow it.

The evidence is overwhelming, and older women don't deny
it. Most of us are willing to admit that we are badly treated in
everyday life, at work, in health care, and by the movers and
shakers who make public and private social policy. But when I
pressed older women for examples, I usually got something that
had happened to somebody else. An older woman has to be exceptional in some way to admit that she has ever suffered herself.

The reason is pathetic. We'll do almost anything to avoid being
labeled "old." We'd rather be fired for incompetence than for
age. Virginia O'Leary, the discrimination lawyer, says her clients
would rather sue for discrimination on the basis of sex than age.
They understand sex discrimination, but they don't think of themselves as old and they don't want to admit that other people see
them that way.

Each of us knows in her heart that the emperor has no clothes,
but none of us wants to be the first to admit it. So we go on
kidding ourselves. Old women are badly treated at work, but that's
other women, not us, because we don't look or act our age. We're
not like those other old women. We're not old.

Why are old women invisible? Because we are supposed to
be ugly, weak, sick, slow, poor, helpless, and unpleasant.

12

OLD

IS UGLY

THERE ARE REASONS that no one likes to see or think about old women, especially about old women who are alone. Free-associate with "old women alone" and you get words like ailing, poor, institutionalized, sexless, predatory, forgetful, confused, senile, ignorant, incompetent, stupid, helpless, timid, rigid, old-fashioned, lonely, isolated, unhappy, bored, depressed, irritable, cantankerous, cranky, witchy, bossy, self-centered, complaining. People say these words out loud only on the rare occasions when they want to be unkind, but you can tell how often they think them by the lengths they go to get around them. Sometimes they express their dismal view by saying just the opposite.

You know you are old when acquaintances begin to say, "How well you look!" meaning "What, not sick?" Someday I'll muster the bad manners to retort, "How did you expect me to look!"

Some of the compliments you get make you wonder. When I told one of the women I was interviewing over the phone that I was seventy-eight, she said "You don't sound it. Your voice doesn't quaver." It should quaver?

Willard Scott, the weatherman on *The Today Show* who lays everything on with a trowel, is likely to describe a woman whom he greets on her hundredth birthday as a "pretty lady" when she isn't pretty in the usual sense of the word at all. This has always struck me as unbearably patronizing. How does he know that she even wants to be what he means by "pretty"?

"Confused," "ignorant," "incompetent." The expectation exposes those of us with wrinkles and a slower pace to attention we neither need nor deserve. A new train agent at Poughkeepsie held up the ticket line to inform me loudly and explicitly where to find the train to New York that I have been taking from the same track ever since my college days, which were long before he was born.

Sometimes the expectation of incompetence isn't concealed. "Do you get it, dear?" a social worker was overheard asking an older woman.

A woman who was taking her son out to dinner reports that the waiter ignored her and asked him, "What would she like to eat today?" Though slower to decide than waiters like, she was not an inanimate piece of baggage or incapable of reading the menu.

"Should we really be taking this road?" a young woman asked me when she doubted the directions of my eighty-four-year-old friend. Leslie is sometimes a little deaf, but her comment from the back seat was quick and logical: "Just because Susan is driving the car doesn't mean that she knows the way."

Doris Grumbach, the novelist and author, describes how a receptionist thought she was "deaf and, as we used to say, dumb" because she refused to budge when called by her first name. When the receptionist advanced and shouted "DORIS" in her ear, she stood up, forcing the misguided young woman to retreat. "Miss, I am Mrs. Grumbach. A stranger to you," she said. "About fifty years older, I would guess. Don't call me by my first name." And after that, the young woman didn't.

Gari Lesnoff-Caravaglia tells in her book *The World of the Older Woman* of a group of old people who were smart enough to worry about whether they would be able to get out of their group residence in the event of a fire. They asked for a fire drill but were told that they were too disoriented to profit by the experience and would simply be scared!

Robert Byrd of West Virginia seemed unaware of any disrespect to a sizable portion of his constituency when he said on the floor of the United States Senate that the balanced budget

amendment was "like your granny: cute, feisty, but no teeth."
Let him speak for his own granny. A lot of us are grandmothers
with plenty of teeth, both literal and figurative.

The word "grandmother" does not generally connote wisdom
and life experience. The Gray Panthers of San Francisco uncov-
ered a manual that proposed a "grandmother test" for prose. It
said that instructions should be written so simply and clearly that
even a grandmother could understand them.

The stereotype influences even professionals who are trained
to go by the facts. In a study of right-to-die decisions, Dr. Steven
Miles found that when judges had to construct the patient's preferences, women were consistently portrayed as less capable of
making rational decisions than men, and their wishes were less
often followed.

"Poor" is an adjective as firmly attached to "old woman" as
"damn" was attached to "Yankee" in the Old South. When I asked
my hairdresser about a cut-rate shop that had opened up next
door, he replied that he wasn't worried about losing profitable
business: "Once in a while I see a little old lady going in there
for a perm."

The "widow's mite" and the prudence traditionally required
of managers of the assets of widows and orphans are built into
the language. The poor old widow without a man to support her
has been an object of concern and charity since the days of the
Old Testament. Along with the perception that old women are
poor goes the comforting assumption that they have fewer needs
than everyone else. And discounts for senior citizens assume that
age alone makes a person poor and deserving of charity.

Rigid, conservative, old-fashioned, backward-looking, unable
to learn new things: these are more unflattering expectations that
are firmly attached to any visible sign of aging. "Dye your hair
and take up new interests," an older woman was advised to cure
something that ailed her. But why can't you take up new interests
without dyeing your hair?

The notion that the old are conservative, backward-looking,

and opposed to change is embedded in our language. "Young Turk" is our phrase for people of any age who challenge the entrenched power, or "old guard," of an institution. And the saying that a "good man" is radical in his youth and conservative in his old age assumes that political outlook changes with age.

Corroboration is hard to find. Studies haven't been able to establish that people swing to the right as they age, or that age itself is a useful predictor of political attitudes. Like young people, old people respond to changing events rather than changes in their bodies. According to Gloria Steinem, the women's movement was launched by middle-aged women who were able to see the restricted role of women when they were no longer in demand as sex objects.

Freud and other early psychiatrists assumed that older people couldn't profit from psychotherapy, but those in practice today say that older people do respond to treatment when it is offered to them.

Because employers think older people have so much trouble learning, they seldom invest in training them. American companies moving into eastern Europe have recently refused to hire local workers over forty, on the theory that they would be unwilling to learn new American ways of doing things. The theory was inadvertently put to the test when employees of all ages already on the payroll of stores that K mart was running were given psychological tests to determine which ones were suitable for promotion. K mart's director for eastern Europe was surprised to find that those over forty did as well as younger employees. "I was encouraged that women over forty with experience were happy to accept the change," he said.

Old women are supposed to be cranky, cantankerous, complaining, and hard to get along with, so it's news when they are not. "They weren't cranky old people at all," a neighbor told a reporter investigating the murder of a sixty-eight-year-old woman and her seventy-nine-year-old brother. "They didn't even complain when my son's rock band practiced in the garage."

Old women are supposed to be bored, depressed, and lonely. When James Whistler painted *Arrangement in Gray and Black: The Artist's Mother* in 1871, he was making an artistic statement about form and design. Art historians say he would be dismayed to find that "Whistler's Mother" later became a metaphor for the neglect and isolation of older women. Similar pictures of old women alone in a room have been used by social agencies to get sympathy and funds for programs for seniors. One social worker began an article about the need for more senior citizens' programs with an anecdote about an old woman who gets out of her lonely room by riding around all day on a bus.

Because doctors assume that old women are likely to be depressed, they put them on antidepressant drugs for a wide variety of vague symptoms. But depression is a serious clinical syndrome defined as a "disorder of mood in which a person feels unhappy and often has trouble eating, sleeping, or concentrating," and while it affects twice as many women as men and may have biological bases, it is not an inevitable consequence of aging. Instead, it's a preventable and treatable illness that doesn't seem to have much to do with the loss of the traditional female role. As a matter of fact, it's more common among women with children in the home than among women whose children have left home, and relatively uncommon among older women who have never married.

Feminists have not been shy about blaming the depression of women on what men have done to them, or, according to a public health report on women and mental health, on "such factors as 'learned helplessness,' the lower status of women, their greater dependency, and their more limited options."

Timid? Ask the soldiers in Moscow. At the attempted coup against Gorbachev, James Billington, then the librarian of Congress, watched while old women simply stood in the way of tanks and told the drivers to stop. "Tanks can't fight old women," he told Brian Lamb on C-Span.

If you're an old woman, your age can be used to explain anything you do. If it rains and you leave your raincoat at home, you're losing your memory, poor thing. If you take it and it doesn't rain, you've become a cautious old woman. When younger people make a mistake about raincoats, no one ascribes it to their age.

The problem with all the negative adjectives is that it's almost impossible to prove or disprove whether they describe any large class of people. Statistics verify that a majority of older women aren't poor, at least officially. Thanks to Social Security, most older women no longer live on incomes below what the federal government has defined as the poverty line for their family status. And the census tells us that fewer are living in long-term-care institutions than most people think. Most of the negative adjectives are subjective judgments. Rigid, timid, incompetent, conservative, even poor, compared to what? Social Security may have rescued old women from legally defined poverty, but it entitled the average woman to a lower benefit than the average man, a discrepancy that was not lost on the many older women who had no other source of income.

Erdman Palmore of Duke University is the authority on this can of worms. He began measuring the accuracy of attitudes toward old people in 1977, when he began giving his "Facts on Aging" quiz to students and other groups. He finds that people continue to overestimate the percentage of old people who live in long-stay institutions ("institutionalized") and the percentage living on incomes below the federally established poverty level ("poor"), but fewer make the mistake of regarding older people as "sexless" — an improvement he attributes to television shows like *Golden Girls.*

The myths of aging have been refuted time and again. Old people aren't necessarily poor, institutionalized, lonely, sexless, helpless, stupid, unhappy, ailing, more prone than younger people to absenteeism or accidents on the job, or especially self-centered and complaining. But lists that refute the stereotypes still qualify as news.

Why, then, do the myths survive? Primarily, of course, because old people are just beginning to be studied by and for themselves. Until recently, no one was interested in healthy old people who were making it on their own like other people. The aged have been studied primarily as problems. Most of what we "know" about older people, especially old women, comes from studies made by young people to help other young people cope with them — managers of nursing homes, social agencies and their fund-raisers, health insurance actuaries, retirement community managers and marketers, employers, even the subjects' own grown children.

Studies were undertaken to document the stereotypes because for these interest groups, the stereotypes can be blatantly self-serving. Negative images are still the most effective way in which advocates for the elderly can make pitches for funds and legislation. Employers have been using the notion that older people are happy to "disengage from society" to bribe people to retire from their jobs and make way for younger and cheaper workers. (Wouldn't you rather be taking it easy in Florida?)

The policy interests behind early studies made it easy to ignore glaring defects in the way the research was done. For the purposes of the studies, it didn't matter that surveys were based on people living in institutions. Those subjects were cheap and easy to find, and though they weren't typical of people their age, they resembled the old people who were causing the problems being studied.

Comparing the young and the old on a given payroll was a handy guide to deciding which workers to train. Young workers learned faster because they averaged more years of schooling. Employers would have chosen more accurately, perhaps, if they had gone by years of schooling, but age is a simpler yardstick, and it's right there on every employment record. The trouble is that these practices tended to confirm the false hypothesis: when an employer trains only the young ones, the older ones may really become less able to learn. The only way out of this circle is to spend the time and money to follow individuals over years to see what happens to people of varying educational and life experiences, but that doesn't solve an employer's immediate problem.

Finally, social research is methodologically biased toward stereotypes. It sets out to measure something someone expects to find. When we think about studying old people, we look for ways to measure loneliness, depression, and all those other bad things. And guess what? Most of the time we find it.

The result is that older women don't realize how much better off they are and will be than older women of earlier generations. Their health is better, their education is better, they've had job experience that widens their options, so they are less likely to wind up like the toothless, ailing, complaining, limited old parties of the stereotype. But no one has an interest in spreading this news, so women don't get much help in adjusting their sights to the realities of their situation.

The eye of the beholder is all-important when it comes to open-ended adjectives, so there is a suspicious silence about the group that is doing the seeing and the talking. Back when libraries catalogued their books on subject cards, I discovered drawers and drawers of cards for books under the general heading WOMEN and far fewer under the general heading MEN. A light bulb went off in my head: women were being seen and studied not by and for themselves but by and for men.

It's the same with old women. They are always described as the Other, not as Us. And who are we? The young, of course, and when gender is involved, young males.

The young standard is built into the language we all have to use. "Healthy" means young, or as one woman told me, "You aren't old as long as you're healthy." For a woman, "beautiful" means young and ready to reproduce. It is interesting to note that women are named April, May, and June, months associated with flowering. Men are not named for the springtime.

"Slow" means slower to react than young males. "Slower" is so generally taken to be worse that we forget that the slower response of older people on machine-scorable psychological tests may be due not only to changes in their nervous systems but to the greater likelihood that they will see more than one correct alternative. (Does this make them less rigid?) Palmore cites a study in which young people interpreted pictures of old people as depressed simply because the expressions on their faces were neutral or relaxed. Medical students should know better, but a group

discussing the likelihood that their own mental powers would decline wound up agreeing that 30 percent to 40 percent of the
elderly population shows signs of senility.

The young male standard is built into the environment in which
we all have to live. Old people seem slow and timid because curbs,
lighting, and steps are designed for the comfort of young males.
And are they more fearful of crime and less reckless drivers than
young males because of a change in the way they feel about hazards, or simply because the hazards are objectively greater for
people who are physically less able to get out of the way?

If some old people dwell on the past ("backward-looking"),
is it because they simply have more of it to dwell on and are denied
a meaningful role in the world around them, or is there something
about growing old that causes them to disengage from their sur-
roundings? The disengagement theory — that people voluntarily
cut down their activities and commitments when society pressures
them to retire — was standard doctrine for sociologists in the
1960s and 1970s and is favorably regarded in Europe even today.

The "objective" study of old people has always been done by
and from the point of view of the young. As Betty Friedan may
have been the first to point out, gerontologists think of old people
not as their present or future selves but as phenomena to study,
much as entomologists study ants. Brilliant psychologists like Skinner
have been willing to study themselves. O. E. Hebb's *Watching
Myself Grow Old* is a classic. But academic tradition decrees a
sharp separation between those who research and the "subjects"
they study. Researchers are normal. Subjects are problems. I did
not realize the force of this latent stigma until a semiretired social
scientist who is internationally known for her brilliant analyses
of survey data agreed to talk to me about the changes in her
own life — providing she did not turn up in my book as a case
history!

When it comes to the study of human beings, objectivity can
be disingenuous. Detachment seems easy and honest when we study
ants (What damage do they do? How best can we kill them?),
but we wouldn't expect the ants to agree, even if we could find

a way to ask them. And if we thought they could study us the way we are studying them, we would move heaven and earth to stop them.

We can't ask ants how they think of themselves, but when we ask old people, we find that while they subscribe to the stereotypes in general, they usually don't think the bad adjectives apply to them personally. Ask them about their own health, and a majority, including some who have serious health problems, say that it's excellent or good. A majority of people over fifty-five say that they are generally satisfied with their lives, even those coping with circumstances that many young people would find intolerable or depressing.

Old women don't think they are as bad off as young women think they are. Half the women under thirty who responded to a questionnaire in *New Woman* magazine said they were afraid of getting old, compared with only 17 percent of those over sixty; 15 percent of the younger group thought loneliness would be the worst part of being old, compared with only 8 percent of those over fifty. And "sexless" didn't describe all the older women. While 40 percent of women in their forties said that they were more interested in sex than ever before, so did 24 percent of women in their sixties.

Survey the elderly, and more of them will say that money, health care, and loneliness are problems for old people in general than will report them as personal problems. Matilda Riley, an authority on aging, concludes of such studies that "in every important life domain, age is positively related to satisfaction and negatively to perceived stress."

From the point of view of a young man, older women are pitiable because they don't know how pathetic they are. More accurately stated, they don't react the way young men think they would react if they themselves were stereotypical old women. Women *ought* to become crazy and depressed at menopause because they've lost the reproductive function that, in the young male view, defines them. They *ought* to be bored, sad, and at loose ends when their grown children and, worse, their husbands leave the nest, because, according to the young male view, nesting is their raison d'être. If they aren't, there's obviously something wrong with them. People used to worry about widows who *didn't* grieve.

Even early research failed to substantiate these expectations, but the findings circulated mainly by word of mouth among women themselves. It's only recently that we've been hearing the heretical evidence that losing a spouse is harder on a man than a woman, and that older women are often delighted to see their grown children leave the nest ("Thank God, nobody needs me!").

There are at least three reasons that women approaching their later years are going to be better off than the stereotypes that scare them. First, their generation is healthier, better educated, and more experienced than the old women they knew when they were growing up. Second, there are more possibilities for growth in later years than they have been taught to expect. Finally, they have going for them the interesting phenomenon that the psychologist Gilbert Brim described in his popular book *Ambition*.

What makes for happiness, Brim found, is not so much our situation in the absolute terms that can be caught in statistics, or how other people think we should feel, but how well we live up to our own expectations. And our expectations aren't fixed. If we are mentally healthy, our expectations for ourselves change with our capacity to meet them. Brim suggests that happiness consists of being engaged in overcoming what he calls "just manageable difficulties."

Brim and his sister, my friend Mary Hess, watched their father gradually adjust his interest in growing things to his declining strength. Just before he died, at 103, he was as content tending a windowbox as he had once been doing the strenuous outdoor tasks involved in tending several hundred acres of Connecticut farmland.

The up side of the stereotypes is that we may all be in for a pleasant surprise. Old age, when it finally comes, may not be as bad as we thought it would be.

13

WE DO IT
TO OURSELVES

OUR IDEA of what it means to be old may be a ghost, but we spend a lot of our precious energy fleeing from it.

Most older women say that they look and feel younger than their age. In one survey, older women said they felt an average of eleven years younger than their chronological age, while older men felt themselves an average of only seven years younger. All that means is that most of us don't feel the way we've been led to expect when we get into our later decades, so we assume that the bad stuff will come later.

And later and later. Ask women at what age they think they will begin to feel old, and the age recedes as they approach it. In one big survey, the average age of feeling old was fifty-two for women in their twenties, but seventy-one for those over sixty. "Gray hair says you're old when you're not," says a hair-coloring ad. One survey found women over eighty-five describing themselves as middle-aged. This increase in the chronological age at which we regard ourselves as old may mean nothing more than that we are healthier and stronger in our later years than we expected to be.

Lying about our age is more serious. A few of the women I talked with flatly refused to give the date of their birth. Some admitted to claiming that they were younger, but more have probably done it than will ever admit it. Lady Astor was at least honest about lying: "I refuse to admit that I am more than fifty-two, even if that does make my sons illegitimate."

I've heard of women who have lied about their age so often that they no longer know how old they are and have trouble qualifying for Social Security. My mother was a beauty who literally took the secret of her age to her grave, which was an embarrassment when it came to getting her death certificate.

The motives are as basic as sex and money. It's an open secret by now that very few postmenopausal women are eager to remarry. They don't want to wash an old man's socks. They don't want an old man who's going to need caretaking or expect to dip into their nest egg. Even those who loved their husbands discover, somewhat to their surprise, that they love their freedom. And as Ann Landers remarked after her divorce, "If it's sex that they want, they can get it without the laundry."

What single postmenopausal women seem to want from a man is remarkably like what single young men want from a woman: sex now and then with a younger, live-out partner who makes very few demands. Most of the women I talked with who wanted a relationship with a man were looking for someone within five years of their age, but those who wanted a younger man slightly outnumbered those who wanted an older one. Rich and famous older women like Liz Taylor, Ann Landers, and Phyllis Diller manage to achieve this. Older women looking for a younger man are likely to consider cosmetic surgery and spend half an hour every morning on their faces, and they don't like to spoil it all by advertising their age.

The other motive for denying your age is economic. A youthful image is essential to some of the most rewarding careers for women. Elizabeth Arden, the cosmetic queen, is said to have taken nine years off her actual age. And Grace Mirabella, founder of *Mirabella*, the women's magazine, is so coy about her age that in 1994, none of the one hundred guests surprising her on her "big birthday" were so tactless as to inquire which one it was.

Sue Mathias has always looked younger than her age. She was the mother of five children when she talked her way into a job as a weather "girl" in St. Louis. It was the job she liked best, so you can understand why she doesn't like to talk about her age now.

Old is bad for a career, but it's a bigger handicap for women than for men. When Lydia Brontë was studying people with long careers, she found that older women who had held on to low-level jobs wouldn't talk to her. One retail saleswoman in her seventies was so afraid of being associated with other people who had long careers that she hid in the stockroom when Lydia went to the store to find her.

"Staying young" sounds innocent and healthy, but some of what we do in its name can alienate us from our bodies, ourselves, our friends, and our own future. The embalmed look achieved by cosmetic surgery is a symbol of more than physical death.

More than 200,000 American women a year attempt to look younger by getting "eye jobs," to remove wrinkles, bags, and sags under their eyes; liposuction, to remove fat from waist, thighs, hips, buttocks, abdomen, calves, knees, ankles, and under the chin; facelifts, to correct sagging of the middle and lower face; silicone injections, to plump up wrinkles; tummy tucks; silicone implants, and more. These expensive and risky procedures cut a woman off from the messages her body is sending her and force her to live a lie in public. The lineless face doesn't match the hands that go with it, so who are we kidding? It is ourselves we are kidding.

Lying is worse than a waste of psychic energy. It destroys relationships. Let me tell you about a retired schoolteacher of seventy-five, whom I'm not going to name. Although worried about a potbelly, she told me that she looks much younger than her age. When asked how she felt about the image of older women on television, she said she was amused because she knew "women like that," but she wasn't outraged because she didn't think the caricatures applied to her. She felt she was too young to join an organization for older people, like the AARP, but she cares for the elderly through her volunteer work without identifying with them.

This "age passing" cuts women off from one another in more ways than they realize. "Oh, there are lots of people around here in their eighties," a seventy-five-year-old friend said while showing me around the posh facilities of her retirement community.

234 · THE INVISIBLE WOMEN

I remember the casual remark because she spoke of eighty-year-olds as people she would never know personally, and it set off a click in the back of my head.

All minorities have done it. Whenever they can, individuals try to escape discrimination by staying away from people who would otherwise be their normal associates. Blacks once tried to straighten their hair, and Jews their noses, and the lighter blacks and the less "Jewish"-looking Jews were often preferred in their own communities. Homosexuals are skilled in passing. Men who look straight are often preferred in the gay community.

Passing isn't new to women. All through history, some women have disguised themselves as men to get around one or another limitation of being female. In my youth, young women (and I am afraid I have to include myself) used to edge away from the other women at a party in order not to miss the supposedly more interesting things that the men were saying. Women who rise into the upper levels of business are still advised to take up golf and follow baseball so they can be less feminine and more like the people who matter.

Incredibly, that's the way a lot of older women feel today. "Other women my age are old, but I'm different. As a matter of fact, I have nothing in common with women my age." The name-withheld seventy-five-year-old wasn't the only older woman who told me that she was too young to join an organization for older people or to take advantage of facilities such as senior centers. This feeling is what marketers of luxurious senior housing have to overcome. The very idea of living with a lot of other people their age turns off the financially secure old people who are the best prospects for this kind of real estate.

Like all other victims of discrimination, old women cut themselves off from their natural associates and deny important parts of themselves. As Barbara Macdonald points out, even coloring your hair is a form of lying about who you really are. "To be surprised, time after time, by my own gray hair on the hairdresser's floor is to be cut off from direct knowledge of my identity," she writes.

But something else that happens to the age passers is even

worse. In order to stay forever young, they don't dare think about the future at all. They are so traumatized by the notion that the future has to be worse that they refuse to make any plans.

A few years ago I spent some time trying to persuade an eighty-five-year-old friend to accept some help in shopping, housekeeping, and repairing the house in which she had always lived alone. Her friends were terrified because she insisted on driving, and they even thought of disabling her car. I tried to get her to think about what she would do if she had to stop driving in the future.

"I don't see any point in planning ahead for something that may not happen," she would say. "Whatever comes, I'll deal with it the way I have always dealt with other catastrophes in my life."

I tried to explain that this catastrophe would be different. It would come precisely *because* she would have trouble coping.

My friend is a very bright woman. She was silent for a long time. "I guess I've been going on the assumption that I wouldn't change and the house wouldn't change," she finally said. Like Peter Pan, she was so sure that the next stage of life would be awful that she wanted everything to stay just as it was.

Staying forever young exacts a high price. It denies us not only control over our later years but hope for the positive growth that is possible. More than in other times and places, women in America have cut themselves off from their future.

Our culture leaves old women without a role. In traditional societies, few women survived to old age, and those who did were feared as witches or revered as wise women. The American frontier put a premium on women as childbearers, and the few who survived past the childbearing years were always needed by big families, if only for the incessant knitting required to keep all the children in socks. But as women's work went out of the home, women who were considered too old to earn were just in the way. "Granny bashing" became a way of telling them that they were burdens.

Other cultures make some sort of place for old women. European women often put on black and take a respected place in the family. The British don't expect their old women to disappear.

More than in New York, strangers on the streets of London are willing to give slow older people extra time and space; the cabs are easier to get in and out of, and even British actresses are able to continue beyond the first flush of youth. British-trained Diana Rigg, Angela Lansbury, and Vanessa Redgrave are among the handful of actresses who have found sympathetic older characters to play. And the British are especially sympathetic to old women who are eccentric.

American women are left with no generally accepted post-menopausal role. The old woman who wore purple in the poem appeals to older women because she makes a protest against their lack of a part to play in American life, but protest provides a full-time identity only for those who intend to devote their old age to a senior liberation movement. When Gloria Steinem looked for a role model for old age, she had to go to China, where old women are more respected than young ones. To remind her of what she would like to become, she keeps before her a photograph of a Chinese woman, "old, smiling, wrinkled, rosy, beautiful," who is belting out a Chinese opera to the sky.

The worst thing about stereotypes is that they tend to be self-confirming. Like my great-grandmother, who died because she thought she ought to, we all tend to live up or down to the expectations others have of us. If we don't stay in touch with our bodies and ourselves, we are in danger of *making* ourselves into the sad old women we are supposed to be.

PART IV

The Case for
Age Equality

14

WHAT IF: AN AGENDA
FOR AGE EQUALITY

RACISM. SEXISM. AGEISM. Once you name it, you know it's bad and on the way out. In 1967, the copy editor of *Born Female* wanted to know what I meant by "sexism," because she couldn't find it in the dictionary. I told her that it rhymed with racism and meant going by sex where sex didn't matter. She had heard about racism.

Ageism is newer. The *Oxford English Dictionary* defines it as "prejudice or discrimination against people on the grounds of age; age discrimination, esp. against the elderly. Cf. racism *b*, sexism" and says it first appeared in a *Washington Post* article of March 7, 1969, quoting Dr. Robert Butler, who defined it as "a form of bigotry we now overlook; age discrimination or age-ism, prejudice by one age group toward other age groups."

A few years later, sociologist Gari Lesnoff-Caravaglia was more explicit: "Ageism simply means that old persons are frequently resented, devalued, forgotten, ignored, and even openly disliked." More recently, Matilda Riley proposed a narrower definition: "the erroneous but stubborn belief in universal and inevitable decline because of aging."

Racism, sexism, ageism. The problem is not that the stereotypes behind these words are wrong. Sweeping generalizations are true often enough to serve as rough rules of thumb for dealing with the strangers we meet in the course of an uneventful day. The problem is that these rules of thumb are unfair to individuals. We make exceptions for individuals when we know them, but the most important decisions about individuals — hiring, promotions, loan approvals, even medical diagnoses — are increasingly made on the basis of impersonal rules that all too often incorporate the stereotypes. Older women on their own feel the pinch in these and many other areas of their lives.

The remedy is to base policy directly on the relevant characteristic. We no longer require firefighters to be male, on the theory that only men have the upper-arm strength required. Instead, we now require firefighters to demonstrate physical capabilities directly related to their ability to do the job. By this strict standard of relevancy, it's hard to think of anything but life insurance for which age is a bona fide qualification.

Decisions made on the basis of age are particularly inaccurate because the older a person grows, the more likely she is to be an exception. Yet we still allow the tyranny of the average to rule people in or out of jobs, housing, and social programs of every kind on the basis of their age. In some cases, we can't even identify the characteristic that age is standing in for.

Classifying workers and consumers on the easily determined characteristics of race, sex, and age was reasonably efficient in an industrial economy of mass production. But it had a fatal flaw: it encouraged people to live down to their classifications.

Segregation is the time-honored way to get the powerless to define themselves in terms of what the powerful want of them. Segregation of African-Americans in unskilled jobs encouraged them to think they couldn't do anything intellectually demanding. Women segregated in women's jobs bought the notion that they were biologically suited to limited tasks such as typing (women have nimble fingers), nursing (women are basically nurturant), and elementary school teaching (women naturally like children).

As with racism and sexism, so with ageism. Older women have been put into nursing homes simply because they can't get simple help with dressing, cooking, and shopping. Once institutionalized, they *become* helpless, just as surely as people incarcerated in a prison become hardened criminals. Armies, factories, and schools keep pounding down the nail that sticks up.

In an ideal world, essential products and services would be designed for the common use of people of all ages, sexes, races, and abilities. Variations would be relevant to the use of the product rather than symbols of a particular status, and they would be promoted on the basis of individual preferences.

A good example is congregate housing, which offers housekeeping, meal services, and recreational facilities for a group of apartments. This kind of living works for students as well as old people living alone and should be promoted to people of all ages and family statuses, including those caring for children. Once the stigma of being for the old is removed, congregate housing might prove the ideal solution for people who are lazy or during the short periods that crop up in almost everyone's life when it would be heaven to be relieved of the basic chores of daily living. Early in this century, when private rooms in hospitals were available to anyone who could pay for them, my father used to check himself into the Lawrence Hospital in Bronxville when he had a tough brief to write, because it was the one place no one would be likely to look for him.

Jobs, schooling, transportation, shopping, recreation, and sports could be provided on the basis of individual differences in such relevant characteristics as ability, taste, and income. This is the freedom everyone wants, and for the first time in human history we have the technology to make it widely available. Ingenious uses of cars, phones, television, and computers make it unnecessary for birds of a feather to flock together. Segregation by race and sex has become illegal in housing and education. We are making public places accessible to people of all physical abilities. Schools no longer administer IQ tests. They classify students on the basis of tests for what they call "cognitive ability" and try to mainstream children of widely varying abilities in the same classroom.

But segregation on the basis of age is increasing. We are creating special programs for older people in education, recreation, social services, sports, and jobs. Fewer old people than in the past live with their families, and more in new kinds of age-based housing. We tell them that they will be happier living in the kind of retirement community that Maggie Kuhn calls "padded playpens for wrinkled babies," and once there, they justify the move by living down to the fears that decided them to make it.

Most older women want to stay in their homes, even if the house is too old and too big for them. They want to go on living like everybody else. It's only when they are old, feeble, and alone that they discover that our vaunted standard of living was designed for strong, healthy young drivers living with other drivers, at least one of whom cheerfully undertakes such essential chores as taking out the garbage, repairing leaky faucets, and identifying the source of mysterious noises in the car.

As they become slower and weaker, women discover that it's harder and harder to live on their own. Even when they have the money, they can't find reliable people to help them drive, shop, clean, haul out the garbage, cut the grass, and make simple repairs. Incredible as it would seem in most other countries, some are forced into nursing homes or housing arrangements for the elderly by the lack of a little such help.

But what really forces many out of their homes is their dependence on the car. Most of the women I talked with said that they would have to consider moving when they felt it was no longer safe for them to drive. Except in inner cities, driving is almost the only way to get food in the house or to see a doctor.

It was not always thus. Back in the 1920s, a twelve-year-old could get to her music lesson on her own in most American towns, and her seventy-five-year-old grandmother could get to the doctor without making arrangements for a ride. In most towns and cities, a network of cheap, safe, accessible, nonpolluting trolley cars connected people of all ages, physical abilities, and incomes with stores, schools, friends, movies, churches, and doctors in their own town, and often took them to nearby towns as well.

Then Detroit changed all that. Cars drove the trolleys out of business, and the automobile industry saw to it that public transportation was starved in favor of public expenditure on highways for private cars. It succeeded so well that whole communities are now accessible only to people with wheels of their own. These communities are often small rural towns where old people are a majority because the young people have departed in search of jobs. Most Americans now live in a place where they need a car.

At the same time, more Americans are living in households of one. Depending on a car is hard when you are alone. Everyone at some time or another has felt what it's like to be without wheels of his or her own or has needed the kind of occasional help that neighbors used to provide before the wider contacts that cars provided cut them off from one another. But this car-dependent isolation is particularly hard on the weak and slow.

Special housing and special services for carless old people are the wrong answer. They divide people from one another and erode the sense of community essential to public order. Most old people don't need, and few of them want, to be segregated on the basis of their age. The benefits of mainstreaming are so great to everyone, young as well as old, that it's worth thinking about what we'd have to do to make the world comfortable for people of all ages, sexes, and marital statuses.

Let's try what Einstein used to call a "thought experiment" and imagine what the world would look like if we saw some changes in public policy and housing and transportation were available to citizens of all ages, speeds, strengths, and physical abilities.

◎ Compact villages and residential areas would replace the suburban sprawl of isolated houses and insular developments.

◎ Well-lighted residential streets would be served by clean, regular buses and vans with steps that would make them easy for children and old people to get in and out of. They might go slower and carry fewer people than vehicles designed for the impatient and athletic young, but they would serve more people of all ages while killing far fewer of them. And while I'm on the subject, I'd like to see private cars redesigned to provide more headroom.

◎ Roads serving outlying areas would be better lighted at night. Maps would indicate brilliantly illuminated thoroughfares as "brightways," for the convenience of people of all ages who don't like to drive in the dark.

- Houses would have skid-free surfaces, many conveniently placed electrical outlets, higher toilets, hand rails, levers instead of knobs on doors and faucets, ramps instead of steps, and garages that can be reached without going outdoors.
- Laws forbidding discrimination on the basis of race could be amended to forbid restrictions on the basis of age and family composition as well. Instead of communities for the elderly or the retired, housing with different levels of service would have to be available to all.
- Reverse mortgages and home equity loans that would allow older women to draw on the equity in their big old houses would be encouraged, rated by consumer groups, and regulated by appropriate federal and state authorities.
- Public transportation would be required in all residential areas of a given density. It could be supported by higher property taxes, which would discourage the suburban sprawl that isolates residents in areas unserved by essential public services and makes it hard for them to stay in their homes when they have physical problems.
- Building codes would mandate features that would insure the comfort and safety of ambulatory people of all physical abilities and require knockout framing for easy widening to accommodate wheelchairs and built-in reinforcement where grab bars might be needed in the future.

SHOPPING

The American standard of living, which is the envy of the world, is cheaper than the essentials of life in other countries in part because we've exported more and more of the work of shopping to the consumer. Supermarket shopping is efficient because it requires the shopper to have a car, and it requires strength and agility. In many places, you are expected to load the heavy bags into your car, keep the shopping cart out of the line of traffic, and get the bags out of the car into the kitchen when you get them home. Every time I shop I see poor or disabled people arriving in taxis or specially provided vans that add to the cost of their food. In less advanced economies, nondrivers can walk to stores where they can buy the essentials of life a few at a time and get them home on their own, even if they have to go every day. And the affluent of every age and physical ability find it easier to get their groceries delivered.

Until you are older and alone, you don't realize that the standard of living to which you have become accustomed is designed for strong, healthy young couples like the people in television commercials and catalogue ads. But there's a mismatch here. These healthy young couples are growing less representative of American consumers.

The census tells us that more people of every age are maintaining households on their own. And at some time or another, all of us have found ourselves, if only temporarily, without a car and/or the strength, acuity, or agility to buy and use common necessities. It's then that we discover that the alternatives are limited, especially in suburbs.

What changes would bring the necessities of life to consumers of all ages, whatever their situation?

- Makers of women's fashions would offer clothes for every figure and group them by function, taste ("high fashion," "classic"), and price instead of in departments for teens, misses, and women.
- Supermarkets would provide more help in locating items; label aisles in white on black instead of glare-producing black on white; arrange merchandise so that no one has to reach overhead, especially for large and heavy items; and label every item with an easily readable price tag. Phone-and-deliver service would be available everywhere for a fee to any customer, with subsidies based on need, not age.

246 · THE CASE FOR AGE EQUALITY

◎ Price tags, product labels, and instructions would be simply worded and printed in large, contrasting type, including special instructions for opening caps to bottles or jars when they don't yield easily on the first try. Artistic but faint labels on my computer printer make a secret of how to operate it. Business cards lettered in subtle colors beg to be thrown away. And instructions incised in the surface of things, such as in the metal of a shower control, should be against the law.

◎ Bottle openers, reachers, one-hand weed pullers, long-handled rakes, and other devices designed for easy manipulation would be displayed and advertised with items for the same purpose rather than in a section containing products of every kind for the elderly or handicapped. Plumbing displays should always include high toilets. Clothing displays should always include some garments with Velcro closings and deep armholes.

◎ Discounts based on means, quantity purchase, group affiliation, or a market-relevant characteristic would replace senior citizen discounts based solely on age.

◎ Credit ratings would be based solely on the individual's record of past payment of bills; discrimination on the basis of employment, age, marital status, and income would be outlawed.

PUBLIC PLACES

Public places in youth-oriented America aren't comfortable for anyone. Street crossing lights set to speed the flow of traffic raise the blood pressure even of young people.

What would we have to do to make all public places comfortable for people of all physical abilities?

◎ Automatic elevators, escalators, and street crossing lights would be set to give the average user a little more time than they do now.

◎ Curbs and steps, especially carpeted steps in airports, theaters, and hotels, would all be edged with a contrasting color that marks the depth of the risers. (In Japanese cities, pedestrians approaching a high curb trigger a chirping sound that warns them to watch their step.)

◎ Signs for streets, offices, and restrooms in public buildings and the location of merchandise in stores would all be big, placed according to rules intended to reduce glare and confusing clutter, and lettered clearly in contrasting colors.

◎ Lighting standards would prescribe more illumination than is now customary on urban streets and in the hallways of public buildings, especially in hotels and theaters, where changes in level are often deliberately concealed by carpeting. And in places where bright lighting is necessary, such as stores and the examining rooms of physicians, it would be designed so that people moving into it are not temporarily blinded by the glare.

There's plenty more to be done to make public places available to people of all ages, but you get the idea. The pity of it is that none of these modifications are especially difficult or ruinously expensive.

WORK

Our employment policies belong in *Alice in Wonderland*. Social Security and private pension systems pay older people to retire earlier and earlier while they are increasingly able and willing to work and needed in the workforce.

The most popular age of retirement is now sixty-two, and many companies offer retirement incentives to people as young as fifty-five. This has been happening while the health and vigor of older people has been improving and work has been becoming less physical. Most retirees say they would like to continue to do some kind of gainful work. But the financial incentives designed to get older workers out of the way of young ones burden pension systems, deprive the economy of productive human resources that could make it grow, and encourage older people to define themselves as useless when they are not. Youth-oriented policies inherited from the Great Depression are moving us in exactly the wrong direction.

It is a bitter irony that divorced and widowed older women are the only group that is bucking the trend to early retirement. Between 1972 and 1992, when there was a steady decline in the percentage of men over forty-five in the labor force, older women continued to work at about the same rate. Then, in 1992, more older women than in the past began to work or look for work, while men continued to drop out. The Bureau of Labor Statistics credits the sharp rise in the proportion of older women in the workforce to the rise in the number who are widowed or divorced. These women suffer from a double bind: whether they are surviving wives or workers, their pensions are lower than men's, and they have a harder time finding and keeping a job than men their age.

What would we have to do to reverse the disincentives to continue working past the ridiculously low retirement age?

- Strict enforcement of the Age Discrimination in Employment Act would require employers to hire and promote on the basis of skill, ability, and years of work experience and include older workers in training programs.
- Pension plans would be amended so they would not penalize workers who choose to continue working past age sixty-five or switch to lower-paid jobs.
- Pensions would be portable, so that older workers would be able to switch to more congenial work without losing their benefits.
- ERISA, the federal law regulating private pensions, would require covering the part-time work older people like to do.

◎ Health insurance would be available at a community-based rate, so that employers would not have an incentive to lower the average age of their workforce.

Some of these changes have been recommended by the middle-of-the-road Commonwealth Fund, but more controversial changes are going to be needed.

Social Security benefits are already scheduled to rise in the future, but is there any reason that benefits should be based on age instead of need? Why not allow an individual to drawn down benefits from earnings to finance a return to school or to raise a child and plan on working longer later on?

H E A L T H

Healthy young skin. Healthy young outlook. Healthy young appetite. Healthy means young to doctors, too. It's the standard by which they unconsciously ration medical resources away from relieving the chronic, "uninteresting," and "time-consuming" problems of the aging so that those resources can be spent on people with more decades of life ahead of them.

What would a truly age-blind health-care system look like?

◎ Medicare would be extended to the entire population, regardless of age. Doctors would have no incentive to favor one age group over another.
◎ Depression, arthritis, heart disease, and other conditions associated with old age would be treated regardless of the age of the patient.
◎ Medical ethicists would be asked to define an age-blind standard of health. They would have to decide whether changes that occur inevitably with age are the province of doctors or

whether they should be dealt with nonmedically, and if so, by which professions.

⊚ Medical ethicists might also be asked to take a second look at the living wills that people are being urged to make. Are we persuading or scaring people into deciding that they don't want to live under circumstances that they find hard to imagine? Nobody knows how she's going to feel about a quality of life she has yet to encounter. Her standard of what's tolerable may fall as her condition declines.

EDUCATION

Our formal educational system is designed to control the young and prepare them for life and work. But I believe that college is a holding pen and welfare program for many of those who don't know what they want to do with their lives or aren't ready to be adults when they graduate from high school. It is by now an open secret that college doesn't really prepare young people for work very well and that education isn't something that can be completed at any age. When it works, it becomes part of life from cradle to grave.

Meanwhile, what we call "adult education" or "lifelong education" to distinguish it from the system designed for the young is so essential to the economy's survival that it isn't being left to the educators. It's being done by employers, the armed forces, the media, psychotherapists, diet and exercise coaches, and non-academic commercial institutes and trade schools, among many others.

What we need to do is to make widely available to everyone opportunities not only for job retraining but for the personal development once reserved for those who could afford a liberal arts education. We need to do more than welcome older women who are returning to college or set up special programs for "nontraditional" students. (Traditional students are young.) We need to mainstream these people with "college-age" students for the benefit of young and old alike.

What do we have to do to make education really age-neutral? For starters, students would no longer be classified by age beyond the junior high school level. Instead of referring to "returning" or "nontraditional" students, we would have classifications describing the student's purpose in pursuing education, such as training, vocational, professional, or recreational. There would be no college courses designed especially for the elderly, such as those in the Elderhostel travel and study program, but lots of courses designed for people of all ages who are simply curious.

PUBLIC POLICY

Legal ages for school entrance, work permits, and marriage are administratively convenient and work only occasional hardship. Age is a bona fide qualification for life insurance because insurance depends directly on carefully compiled life expectancy tables; your age is directly related to how many more years of life you can expect. But in many other programs, age is not a bona fide or intrinsic qualification but a stand-in for something that is supposed always to go with it.

What would happen if we dropped every classification now made by age that couldn't be made by a more relevant characteristic?

◉ If the purpose of age qualifications for a driver's license is to insure safe operation of the vehicle, why not license all those who can pass a road test?

◉ If the purpose of age qualifications in car insurance is to set rates on the basis of the risk of accident, why not set rates on the basis of miles driven and other factors directly rated to a driver's chance of accident, rather than age and sex? Young males have more accidents than others, but they also drive more miles than females of all ages and older people. Old women who drive very little would be charged fairly on the basis of their risk.

Our welfare programs are almost as age-distorted as our educational system, but many of them discriminate in favor of old people — not just Social Security and Medicare, but a long list of tax breaks and subsidized housing, employment, and services. It looks at first as if age equality would leave old people worse off than they are now, and some of them will object to giving up their benefits. But these special privileges aren't unmitigated blessings. Before leaping to their defense, it's worth thinking about why they were started and the price the beneficiaries are paying for them today.

Historically, old people have always been ideal welfare objects: sick, poor, helpless, unable to work through no fault of their own, they were seen as suffering from the fate that awaits all of us. And it was easy and relatively cheap to help them. Cheating was difficult because application was by birth certificate. And in the past, at least, there weren't very many of them.

It went without saying that the programs couldn't do anything about age itself. They weren't aimed at making old people younger, but at relieving what was supposed to go with being older. The effect was to reinforce the stereotypes that were keeping old people down and prevent them from taking their natural place as functioning members of society.

It's interesting to imagine what would happen if we took age out of these programs and directed them to people of any age who were poor, sick, helpless, or unable to work.

⦿ Social Security would be based on years of employment regardless of age, with provision made for the years a parent was out of the workforce caring for children. Eventually, it might develop into a mandated unemployment insurance system, which would allow workers to draw an income based on former earnings while retraining for a new occupation or caring for family members.

◎ Services such as meal delivery, household help, hot meal centers, and transportation to doctors would be commercially available to anyone who wanted them for any reason. Subsidized reductions in the fees would be available for disabled, ill, or fragile old people who are now being served through social programs such as Meals on Wheels, visiting nurses, and home health-care services.

◎ There would be no senior citizens' centers. Instead, community centers would be open to any resident who needed or wanted the service, for a charge based on ability to pay.

◎ Programs like the Retired Senior Volunteer Program, for minimum-wage employment of the needy elderly, would be replaced by comprehensive public employment for people of all ages and abilities who could not find a job in the private sector.

◎ Subsidized housing now restricted to the elderly would be available to everyone on the basis of physical need and means.

◎ Tax breaks now based on age, such as property tax concessions, would be eliminated or extended to all on the basis of means. Social Security benefits would be taxed as regular income, eliminating the windfall for rich old people, and the one-time exemption from capital gains on the sale of a home now available only to people over fifty-five would be extended to everyone.

Special privileges based on age alone are as crippling to those who enjoy them as negative treatment based on race, sex, or age alone. There would be problems. We need to do some thinking and experimenting to see how real age equality would work out, and that's what the new discipline of gerontology should be addressing. But the obvious benefits of policies based on relevant factors rather than age are staggering.

Productivity would soar if employers had to go by what it really takes to do each job instead of using age as a proxy for ambition, stamina, and trainability. Sidelining everyone over sixty-two deprives every organization of qualities that take decades to build: a steady hand in crisis, experience in applying central values to new situations, a sense of community and continuity, an appreciation of the wide range of human capacities, a disinterested stake in the future. The very qualities more common in older people than younger ones are urgently needed. If we seem "too slow" for the current pace, it could be that the current pace is too fast for its own good.

The economy would get the shot in the arm it so badly needs if we tapped the productivity of retirees who are being arbitrarily prevented from working. That's what happened when we tapped the underused potential of people of color and women in the 1970s and 1980s.

Income would be distributed more fairly if the underpaid or unpaid work we expect women to do for their families or as volunteers for the community were recognized as work and paid for, if necessary by the taxpayers.

If retirement were based on ability, length of service, and inclination, men would retire earlier than women instead of the other way around, and both sexes would get their druthers.

If social life were organized by interests instead of age, life would be more fun for everyone.

Finally, there's no calculating how many lives would be saved if public transportation were generally available and public places were designed for people of every age.

Young and old, black and white, men and women, are all better off under policies based on factors more relevant than race, sex, and age. If we've learned anything from the civil rights and women's movements, it is that separate doesn't mean equal. I believe that segregation is bad for everyone.

Life could be safer, more productive, more fun, and fairer. Especially fairer. "Fat chance of getting fairness," I can hear you saying. But not so fast. In 1968, I ended *Born Female* with a case for equality for women that seemed outrageous at the time. In June 1994, a college classmate who had been invited to explain the American women's movement to an audience of college students in China called up to ask what had happened regarding the wild suggestions I had made. When we went through the list together, we found that most of them had been implemented and some had become irrelevant.

My friend reminded me that I had concluded that book with what at the time sounded like a forlorn hope. "Equity speaks softly and wins in the end," I wrote. "But it is expedience, with its loud voice, that sets the time of victory."

I was right about expediency. In retrospect, our impassioned rhetoric would never have been heard if so many of us had not been finding ourselves, for the first time in our lives, the recipients of paychecks of our own. It started me wondering whether expediency with its loud voice could be working for older women now.

15

A PROGRESS
REPORT

OLD WOMEN have made a lot of progress without trying. We've fallen heir to better health and more money than our mothers had. Technology compensates for physical handicaps that used to restrict older people. Diversity of products and lifestyles means there is room for us. Gone are the days when fashion decreed the same look for women of every figure; the loose-fitting clothes we need have become uniforms for active people of both sexes and all ages.

The social changes of the past thirty years have freed us, too. In 1961, I was a maverick because my second child was born a full twenty-six years after my first, without noticeable ill effects on any of us. In those days, everyone was expected to move through life on a predictable timetable. But young people now delay marriage, children, and good steady jobs. People divorce in midlife and build new nests at an advanced age. The example of individually paced life courses makes it easier to start a new life on our own in our sixties, seventies, and eighties, and if we lie about or conceal our chronological age, it's easy enough to disappear into the landscape. Nobody who gets to be seventy thinks that seventy is old anymore. It's just the number that keeps us down.

Age may have become just a meaningless number, but it is written into so many policies that we are going to have to fight to get rid of it. Stereotypes die hard, but they are not immortal.

It's early days in the fight against ageism, but we may be able to see what's ahead by looking back at the stages we have gone through in the fight for racial and sexual equality.

Disproving the stereotype with case examples is the easiest part, but it has to come first. Black scientists and women enterprisers made news and started everyone thinking, even when they were presented as freaks. Before the civil rights movement, many African Americans tried to look, think, and act like whites. Before women's liberation in the 1970s, the biggest compliment you could pay an ambitious woman was to say that she "thought like a man."

Differences were an embarrassment to both groups. In the women's movement, we were always talking about the broad overlap in strength between men and women as evidence that women could do most physical jobs. Civil rights advocates emphasized that blood types were the same for all races and even today ascribe the higher mortality rates of blacks to poverty and discrimination, even though the rates for blacks are higher than those for whites in the same income and educational brackets. .

In the second stage, the stereotype-busting role models inspire others to follow. Ambitious African Americans and women get together to talk about their goals. Local consciousness-raising groups spring up and network with one another until there is a grassroots basis for a national protest movement.

In the third stage, the movement wins some well-publicized victories. Laws are passed. Policies are changed. Then, when victory seems inevitable, the movement splinters into factions, the rank-and-file members drift away, some of the most talented leaders take advantage of new opportunities to pursue a mainstream career.

But the battle is not finally won. In the fourth stage, those who feel threatened begin a sneaky backlash. I would argue that crime has become the nation's number-one political issue because "crime" is a code word for resentment of inner-city blacks, just as "family values" has become a code term for the good old days when women served men at home. Susan Faludi's *Backlash* became a bestseller in 1992 because working women everywhere instantly recognized the phoniness of the arguments and statistics being peddled to convince women that they really didn't want careers and were paying much too high a price for job equality.

Fortunately, the backlash is a lost cause. Blacks and women aren't equal yet, but they have achieved enough political and economic power to command attention as individuals rather than as stereotypes. The same thing happened when we stopped demonizing the Japanese after World War II. If you were an adult during that war, you recall how the Japanese were portrayed as all alike, and how they began to look "whiter" and different from one another after the war was over and Japan became prosperous.

Now let's see how well this track applies to progress toward age equality. We're getting out of stage one, disproving the stereotypes. Women still make some afternoon papers for continuing to function in their nineties, but the best publications no longer treat active old people as newsworthy curiosities. Crude jokes about old age are in bad taste, although they have yet to become as politically incorrect as jokes about people of color and Jews. And just as we once attacked psychiatrists like Freud, who based their theories on the passivity of women, so Betty Friedan now reproaches gerontologists for ignoring active old people and concentrating on the declines of age instead.

Stage two is just beginning. Most old women aren't ready to organize a protest movement. The only national organization that even pretends to represent all of them is the Older Women's League, which watches legislation affecting them and tries to mobilize them politically. What's left of the Gray Panthers has moved into other social issues. Both are woefully underfunded.

But on the far horizon you can see a cloud forming, a cloud that is now no bigger than the size of a man's hand. All over the country, older women are getting together to talk about the uncharted stage of life in which they find themselves and the way they feel about how they are being put down and left out. As we have seen, they write for each other in an underground press that parallels the rhetoric of the women's liberation movement of the 1970s. Some of these authors are early feminists who have found a new cause in the indignities they suffer because of their age.

So far, the organized protests of older women have been directed not against their treatment at work, the issue that rallied younger women to the feminist cause in the 1970s, but against the patriarchal values of traditional Christian and Jewish faiths. The possibility that God could be a woman, or have feminine aspects, is dividing mainstream Protestant churches.

Some of these women are resurrecting pagan goddesses and witches (etymologically related to "wit"), who symbolize the special wisdom of older women. In many communities, they meet to celebrate this ancient wisdom in covens (etymologically related to "convents," the medieval housing solution for husbandless women). Croning ceremonies welcome an older woman into the Wise Woman stage of life, which in ancient mythologies followed the stages of Maiden and Mother. Women who participate draw comfort from a ritual that recognizes a stage of life beyond childbearing.

Stage three in the fight for age equality is yet to come. As of 1994, there were few policy victories in this battle. Such gains as we have made have generally been the unintended side effects of moves made for other reasons. A good example is a 1994 regulation by the New York City Commission on Human Rights prohibiting discrimination on the basis of age in public places. The measure was aimed at insuring access for children and young people, but it also prohibited the exclusion of older people from activities like exercise classes that are of importance to old women.

We have the aggressive movement for the rights of the disabled to thank for ramps and high toilets in public places, which make access easier for us, too. And health insurance reform promises to take care of formerly married women who have lost the coverage they had as wives before they are old enough for Medicare.

On another front, there has been limited recognition of the discriminatory potential in the journalistic convention of identifying individuals by age. There once was a time when newspapers always identified the race of a black (but not a white) and the marital status of a woman (but not a man). Now the best usage is to use these identifiers only when they are relevant to the story, but the most conscientious news editors don't see age identifiers as inherently discriminatory in the same way. Asked whether identification by age was less common than it used to be, J. Russell King, deputy news editor of the *New York Times,* said that this "might well be the case," adding that the *Times*'s rule of thumb is "to mention the age of people in the news when it seems pertinent . . . and our inclination is to view it as pertinent most of the time."

In the workplace, the last of the age caps on the Age Discrimination in Employment Act (ADEA) was finally removed. Since January 1994, tenured college professors have been free to continue working as long as they please. ADEA has been so badly enforced that, as we have seen, few women have brought suits against employers for the special kind of discrimination that is practiced against older women. The whole field of age discrimination has been so underlitigated that there have been no landmark decisions insuring age equality like those that forced real progress toward sexual equality and civil rights.

In medical care, researchers are beginning to pay more attention to the ailments of postmenopausal women, but it takes a long time for new studies to be made and even longer for their findings to filter down to patients.

In spite of the low profile of these gains, there seems to be a stage-four backlash against the very idea of age equality. I began to suspect it in 1993, when Tracy Kidder published a book called *Old Friends.* Why, I wondered, would the Pulitzer Prize–winning author of *The Soul of a New Machine,* a thrilling account of the team that created a computer, choose to write about life in a nursing home?

Kidder said he did it "partly because so much well-meaning commentary on old age depicts white-haired people in tennis clothes — a tendency, it seems to me, that inadvertently denigrates the lives of the many people who haven't drawn such lucky hands." He argues that an old age free of pathology isn't really normal, but ideal. "More than a million live in nursing homes now," he wrote in a *New York Times* op-ed piece. "The celebration of successful aging leaves out all of them. Ultimately, of course, it leaves out everyone."

He seemed to be taking direct aim at me. Celebrating later years was exactly what I was doing. And he even had a name for it. Whether I knew it or not, I was part of a school of thought called "successful aging." Although his book is not intended to be scholarly, the single authority he quoted is a clue to his own point of view. It was Thomas R. Cole, who wrote *The Journey of Life: A Cultural History of Aging in America.*

Cole turned out to be the editor of "Aging and the Human Spirit," a slim quarterly published by the Institute for the Medical Humanities at the University of Texas medical branch at Galveston. The issues I found there concerned *spiritual* grounds! The implication was that fighters against stereotypes of age were preventing people from coming to terms with their own mortality. "Accumulation of individual health and functioning remains the norm," Cole complained in one of the quarterly's editorials, "as if death had nothing to do with life except to mark its end." My feelings about death exactly.

Kidder did not go unchallenged. In a letter to the *New York Times,* Gene D. Cohen, deputy director of the National Institute on Aging, protested that looking for "successful" or "ideal" aging in a nursing home was "like spending a year in a children's hospital and asking 'What's this myth about healthy, active kids?'" And he went on to restate the secular case for the undeniable improvement in the health of older Americans.

But you don't have to be religious to recognize that "successful aging" is suspiciously silent about the large number of women who *aren't* aging "successfully," and it should not be politically incorrect to mention them. Instead of "Why do gerontologists ignore the old people who are functioning very nicely, thank you?"

perhaps there is room in the world for those who ask, "What are we going to do with the growing number of old people who are eventually going to be unable to care for themselves?"

Luckily, we may be entering the final stage, in which expedience, with its loud voice, insures the victory. Widowed and divorced women are now likely to reach their later years with enough economic power to command recognition as individuals, the treatment white males have always regarded as a birthright. More old women than ever before have the buying power that commands respect in the marketplace, and the education and professional experience that command respect in the workplace.

The economic power of older women isn't immediately apparent. Social workers have an interest in reminding us that many older women alone have incomes just above the poverty line, where money means groceries. But less is said about what's happening at the other end, where money means power. The data are sketchy because the rich don't like to talk about their money and they have the power to keep it quiet, but it looks as if more of the money that means power is winding up in the hands of single old women.

Quiet long-term economic and demographic trends are working for them. Women are living longer, and since they outlive men, they stand to inherit more of the wealth now owned by men. The increase in the proportion of single women over fifty-five in the population suggests that more of the nation's wealth is flowing to older women through inheritances, divorce settlements, and the sale of family businesses. And more and more of the two thousand women a day who now turn sixty are either earning money or can look forward to a pension.

Upscale markets are beginning to feel the spending power of older women. A few straws in the wind:

⊚ In show biz, older actresses are doing well at the box office. In the spring of 1994, Broadway had fifty-five-year-old Diana Rigg starring in *Medea* and fifty-seven-year-old Joan Rivers starring in *Sally Marr . . . and Her Escorts,* an autobiographical play of her own, while in Washington fifty-two-year-old Barbra Streisand was kicking off her first paid concert tour in twenty-eight years. At seventy-six, Lena Horne produced a new album, and one critic proclaimed that she was "rhythmically more daring than she used to be."

◉ In fashion, "beauty" still means "young," but "young" is being redefined for higher ages and for mental and moral rather than physical qualities. People talk about being "young at heart" or having a "young outlook" as well as looking younger. Many women said to me that the best way to stay young was to take up new interests or go to college.

We are being reminded a little more often that feminine beauty is more than skin deep. According to the essayist Roger Rosenblatt, "Beauty depends on the effect of character on experience." Forget aging gracefully, he advises. "Age ferociously instead . . . Seize everything valuable within reach . . . The face will follow. All the cosmetic surgeons in the world could not produce such a face."

Avant-garde fashion designers are experimenting with radical redefinitions of what women should look like. Maybe it's better to look interesting than young. Maybe it's more important to look like yourself whatever your age. Or, even more radical, maybe old is intrinsically more beautiful than young, suggesting a pride in age.

This message is beginning to be beamed at sophisticated older women through ads that feature women who are frankly and starkly old. In 1993, the *New York Times Magazine* carried four full-page ads, a back and a front head shot in stark black-and-white of a man and a woman with long straight hair. The faces were blown up so big that sagging flesh was sharply outlined, and you could almost see the pores. There were only four words of print: "American Beauty" and under that, in bigger type, "Banana Republic," the name of a clothing store. Although unnamed, the man was Paul

Cadmus, a painter who would be recognized by older women because he was popular in the 1940s, and the woman was Sissie Guest, a New York socialite. Many older women took the ad to mean "Old women can be beautiful," while others took it to mean "Interesting people can be old."

In sophisticated circles, it's becoming a bit more popular to separate beauty from youth. Some people admire women whose beauty comes from within, beautiful women who just happen to be old, and even women who take a positive pride in being old and looking it.

Some women are defiantly refusing to color their gray hair. Some have made their white hair a signature, a symbol of age and experience. We may even one day have women proclaiming their age as a badge of honor, but in the 1990s, the fashion and beauty industries are still defining their older customers as women who are "staying young" by spending a lot of time every morning on their faces and dressing in defiantly vivid colors, which have become a signal of advancing old age. According to Jutta Heckhausen, a researcher on life stages at the Max Planck Institute in Berlin, "The German and maybe also general European stereotype of elderly American women pictures them as typically putting on too much makeup and dressing too brightly for European taste." She thinks that continental women are less afraid of growing old and more willing to dress their age.

But growing old is beginning to come out of the closet. A full-page picture of "Venus, older than when Botticelli painted her," illustrated a *New York Times* roundup of fashion ads featuring older models. The feature was stimulated by the release of a film called *Real People Face Aging*, produced for an ad campaign by Clinique, a division of Estée Lauder, around the theme "Beauty isn't about looking young."

Fashion houses and catalogues are beginning to use and publicize models who are (gasp!) nearly fifty, although they are careful not to look it — which is, of course, exactly what the customers are trying to do. "It's not about age and not about demographics," said Calvin Klein. "It gets boring just looking at eighteen-year-olds, and it's time to appreciate the view that when a girl becomes a woman, she really becomes beautiful."

Television commercials are trying to attract older consumers by using older models to act out their supposed dreams. One Days Inn commercial aimed at encouraging older people to travel to see new babies in the family had a grandmother kicking her shoes straight up to the ceiling to demonstrate her delight at the prospect of meeting her new granddaughter.

The market power of older women is clearly growing, but there are interesting signs of progress in the workplace, too. The women who got their start during the women's movement of the 1970s are more apt than their working mothers to be covered by pensions or to have built a business that gives them substantial assets of their own. Much of what comes naturally to them is managing human relationships: counseling, mentoring, nurturing, networking, matchmaking, mediating, getting people to work together. A nurse who understands patients and doctors sets up a little business to handle insurance reimbursement and manage the offices of doctors who have no taste for these chores. A retired Foreign Service officer helps an international organization place foreign visitors in American homes. A retired secretary takes on writing a newsletter that keeps other retirees in touch with one another. A high-powered corporate officer emerges from retirement every year to help her successor set up the company's annual meeting.

Older women become membership secretaries of their professional associations, recruiters and directors of volunteers, ombudsmen for colleges and universities, church secretaries who help arrange weddings and funerals, and, very frequently, town clerks, who mediate between local government bureaucracy and the taxpayers.

These are the roles that older women have been playing for centuries. They created the European salons of the eighteenth century, which enabled artists and intellectuals to exchange ideas. As self-appointed hostesses, they defined and ruled the "high society" of every nineteenth-century American city. In almost every culture they have been the keepers of the extended family, and they are still the genealogists, conveners of family holiday celebrations, and organizers of family reunions, which may now assemble kin from every part of the world.

This person-to-person work is becoming critical now that organizations are being restructured. Even in stable times, bureaucracies have never done it very well, if at all. The older women who undertake these traditional roles can be the pinch hitters who save the whole game.

A newer road to power for older women is in philanthropy. Not all the women who are coming into more money than they need are willing to let their male relatives and advisers tell them what to do with it. Proof is hard to come by, but there is reason to expect a substantial increase in the wealth older women are going to control in the future.

Many women don't come into money of their own until later in their lives, so it wasn't until the 1990s that women who developed a social conscience in the 1960s, learned independence in the 1970s, and achieved career success in the 1980s were able to become serious donors. These women aren't innocents in the world of big money. Many have pursued professional careers, and like Muriel Seibert, the pioneer stockbroker, a few have earned their own fortunes.

These women are a threat to established philanthropies. Up to now, big nonprofit organizations have been run by men who share the business ethic of the rich men who founded them or whose donations now support them. But women who make their own decisions about giving may not respond to appeals that have always worked on men.

Striking differences emerged in what women and men told Sondra Shaw, who was assistant vice president for external affairs at Western Michigan University when she was studying women donors. She learned that women give because they genuinely enjoy being able to help people in need. In contrast, men give to match what others are giving, to repay what they have received in the past, or to attain the influence and reputation they hope to have in the future.

Women are repulsed by the idea of getting any advantage for themselves out of a gift and often give anonymously or in the name of a family member. Unlike women, men love to see their names on buildings.

Women are often turned off by sophisticated planned giving schemes that sometimes attract men whose primary motive is tax evasion. Women give to help others, not themselves.

Women are more apt to give their money to an organization for which they have worked as a volunteer. Men are more apt to accept an honorific volunteer post as a reward for a big donation.

Women want to know exactly how their money will be used. They want to fund specific projects, such as making a building accessible to the handicapped. Men give to support the institution in general.

Women want to see and interact with the people they are helping. Men are willing to delegate the actual work to a bureaucracy, as they do in their offices.

As fund-raisers get the message, they no longer dare to ignore or patronize female donors. They are finding that older women respond better to an appeal from another woman than to the nice young men and smooth older men traditionally assigned to "doing widows."

But it's not just fund-raising techniques that are changing. Women who make their own decisions are funneling their money to organizations that haven't attracted big contributions from men. One woman told Sondra Shaw that she was "inclined to give to organizations that are having trouble raising money rather than to the Red Cross or the big art organizations that have a lot of visibility." Another said she was skeptical of appeals from the American Cancer Society.

These women may be more likely than men to give their money to organizations working for social change and helping groups that have been left out or mistreated — children, minorities, the handicapped, and especially women. And because many of them do not have much to give, they are joining together to support projects that are too small, too radical, too local, too specialized, or merely too inexperienced to get support from the established philanthropies.

These special-focus or alternative funds are dedicated to change, not charity that shores up the status quo, and women outnumber men in supporting them. Growing fastest of all are the women's funds springing up all over the country to address issues like spousal abuse, employment discrimination, lesbian rights, and sex stereotyping in schools and colleges — issues traditionally ignored by the big endowed foundations. Small, local, specific, and easy to monitor, they attract women because it's easy to see the faces of the people who are being helped. For instance, the Minnesota Women's Fund provides legal and financial advice to women who are managing farms and supports a local program called Women Hurt in Systems of Prostitution Engaged in Revolt (WHISPER), which helps women who are leaving prostitution.

These funds are an echo of the grassroots women's movement of the 1970s, organized by many of the same women, now a generation older. What they lack in money (some of the grants are pitifully small) they make up in enthusiastic support from a large number of watchful donors, many of whom are newcomers to giving and need help in how to do it. After Tracy Gary gave away most of her own Pillsbury fortune, she set up a Center for Resourceful Women in San Francisco, offering seminars, networking, and encouragement to women who have substantial assets to donate.

Sondra Shaw likens the wildfire rise of women's funds to the movement to set up settlement houses spearheaded by Jane Addams and Helen Hull a century ago.

The best hope for the future is the example that today's older women are setting for their daughters. Women tend to think of what their own mothers were doing at their age. Many found themselves telling me about the new lives their mothers had created as widows, usually out of sheer necessity. These mothers had seemed to give them permission to strike out on their own.

Mary Jean Tully told me that although her husband fully supported her feminist activities, she decided in the late 1980s that she wanted an independent life. She recalled that this was about the age at which her mother was widowed. "I did on purpose at sixty-one what my mother did inadvertently at sixty-four — become an unmarried woman, in effect, although the marriage was still there legally. I feel very strongly that this was the right thing for me, and I think it's probably the right thing for a lot of women at this age and at this stage in their lives . . . to take charge of your own life at long last."

Think how many more of our daughters will be taking charge of their own lives when they get to be our age!

APPENDIX
*An Encyclopedia
of Salty Secrets*

NOTES

BIBLIOGRAPHY

INDEX

Appendix

AN ENCYCLOPEDIA OF
SALTY SECRETS

EVERYONE'S ENERGY is finite. Kids waste most of their seem-
ingly inexhaustible supply. When they grow up, they learn to use
their heads to save their heels. Growing up and growing old are
parts of a continuous process of directing the energy at your disposal
most efficiently to what matters most to you. And you can be
even more efficient when you have only yourself to consider.

Goals change and energy levels change, but coping skills continue to improve. Women get more practice than men at coping
because so much of the nitty-gritty work of everyday life has
been dumped on them. They become virtuosos in the art of getting the most out of the least, and everyone can profit by the
strategies they have invented for dealing with the little hassles
of everyday life in contemporary America.

Some strategies require learning what you don't need to worry
about. When I asked women, "What's the main thing you've learned
in the past ten years?" the honest answers ranged from great big
general things, like "I learned how to be patient with myself,"
to specific little insights, like "I learned that my grandchildren
like the presents I send them even though they don't write to
thank me." My own list included taking things in steps, sleeping
on big decisions, and reading the instructions for new equipment
— all things that I could have learned earlier. But better late than
never.

Most of the strategies boil down to ways of simplifying your
life.

CUT IT OUT

Freedom is knowing what you don't have to do: letters you don't have to write; phone calls you don't have to make; things that don't have to be cleaned; gadgets that aren't worth buying, unpacking, servicing, and the trouble of eventually getting rid of them.

CUT IT DOWN

Less can be more. Buy fewer clothes to take care of, but keep them in meticulous condition and be sure they are in style — maybe one good outfit a year. Eat less food, but tastier — maybe one cookie for dessert, but homemade (keep the rest in the freezer, so you have to defrost to nibble). Substitute a space-saving electronic keyboard for the piano you don't use enough to justify its taking up space but don't want to be without. Send Christmas cards only to people you are willing to write a personal note to, *not* a general letter addressed to everyone.

DO IT AT HOME

New technology cuts down the energy we all used to spend on driving around. Everyone has learned to keep up with friends by phone instead of visiting, and the latest movies are often available on cable in your own bedroom.

The secret of the "secrets" is that each addresses a specific problem and works regardless of age. None of them works for everyone. Some are so automatic and intuitive that you may be surprised to find that they are news to anybody. The list is intended to remind you that you too may be able to invent a way around something that is bothering you.

BATHING SUITS

◎ Two-piece suits with halter tops that close with fasteners are easier to get on and off than one-piece models.

CHILDPROOF MEDICINE CAPS

◎ Save regular caps of different sizes and use them after you get the pharmacist or a visitor to open the safety model mail-order pharmacies insist on sending.

CHILDREN

Most older women want their grown children to treat them as equal friends and companions rather than as dependents or sources of money and babysitting. We want our grandchildren to remember us for ourselves rather than as legendary present givers, feeders, spoilers, and allies against the tyranny of parents.

One problem is that the traditional grandmother was a dependent. But thanks to Social Security and pensions, in the 1990s, more money and support flows from parents to grown children than the other way around. Another problem is that the relationship is not symmetrical: you want to give advice and companionship, but your children may want logistical help such as money and babysitting. If you want them to be friends, you are going to have to learn to let go and give them more room.

◎ Let them know exactly what's expected of them. Keep them up-to-date on the state of your health and finances, and plan to get out of this world with as little trouble for them as possible. A good way to get these obligations out of the way of the relationship is to write a letter telling them the location and date of your will, the executor, where you want to be buried, what you want done with archives and heirlooms; you can also enclose a living will for your medical care.

◎ Let them know that you have an independent life of your own. Don't make their old rooms into shrines. Use the space for a project of your own unless they specifically say they may someday want it.

◎ Give them room for the parts of their lives that cannot include you. For instance, try not to call them more often than they call you. Wait for them to tell you about their plans and ask for your advice.

⊚ Limit visits. Think twice about staying with them for more than three nights. Program time with a married daughter on neutral ground where the two of you can enjoy something you both like that wouldn't interest her husband or children. I try to serve my daughter shellfish because her husband doesn't like it.

⊚ If a grown child comes "back home" to live, be prepared to treat him as an adult. Make it clear for how long and on what terms he will stay. If he's to do chores for his keep, spell them out. If he expects to entertain friends, lay down ground rules.

⊚ If you are invited to live with a grown child, try to arrange separate quarters. Families with space sometimes set up a house trailer or build a separate small house in the back yard for their parents.

Finally, a list of don'ts and do's:

Don't respond to what your children tell you with anecdotes, however fascinating to you, about how we used to do it in the old days. These stories may be more interesting to you than they are to them, and they accentuate differences that do nothing to promote a relationship of friendly equality.

Don't give them advice. If they ask for it, they may really be asking for an ear. If they want your opinion on an event, ask, "How did that make you feel?"

Don't pass judgment on what they tell you.

Do listen wholeheartedly to anything they are willing to say. Ask questions if you don't understand it.

Do ask their advice on and help with new technology or customs that puzzle you.

Be *their* support system.

CLOTHES

◎ Clean out your clothes closet once a year and give away anything you haven't used since the last weeding. Decide *then* what you need to buy and what you'd grab if your rich nephew phoned you to meet him at a fancy restaurant. This rule not only makes it easier to choose what to put on in the morning, but forces you to get rid of outfits that are hopelessly outdated.
◎ Shun back zippers, tiny buttons, tight jackets, and other styles that are hard to get into and out of. Look for knits, big armholes, Velcro closings, and dresses with front buttons or zippers all the way down. Choose comfortable, roomy pants in a larger size. Some women find wraparound skirts easier to manage than pants.

CRIME

People are victimized by crime less frequently as they grow older, largely because they don't go out as much. But many of us, especially older women living alone, are more afraid of it. Here's the advice that some women give:

◎ Keep your former husband's name on the mailbox and in the phone book, and use a male voice for the message on your answering machine.
◎ On streets and in parking lots, walk as if you know where you are going.
◎ When attending parties at night, ask your hostess if any other guest could pick you up on the way. But take a taxi home so you can leave independently.
◎ Check the references of a new houseworker or repair person and demand identification from any sales or service person before you let him into the house. He could be casing the place for a future burglary.

◎ Keep your credit cards concealed and close to you when a strange home health-care worker is in the house. Services that provide home health-care workers investigate and bond them, which is one of the reasons that they cost you more than workers you hire yourself.

CROSSING BUSY STREETS

◎ Don't hesitate to ask for the arm of a stranger waiting to cross if you're afraid you won't be quick enough to dodge the traffic. Even thugs and drug addicts will be delighted to see you safely across.

CROWDS

◎ Plan ahead to avoid them. Arrive and depart a little early at an event that is going to cause parking problems, or wait until the jam thins out.

DOCTORS

◎ Ask your doctor to explain or repeat instructions you don't understand.

◎ Don't hesitate to ask a doctor about his or her training and experience in treating your specific problem. Request a second opinion, and switch to another doctor if you don't like the treatment you are getting. Many women prefer a woman doctor. According to one survey, women are twice as likely to have a Pap smear or mammogram if their family doctor is a woman.

◎ Ask your doctor about future checkups and note them on your calendar, so that you can take the initiative in demanding the checkup when the time comes. Many primary-care physicians forget to tell women on Medicare about mammograms and other recommended tests, and many are not set up to remind them when a checkup is due. Dentists, who are paid directly, never fail to remind you of when you are due for a checkup.

◎ If your regular M.D. seems bored with chronic problems such as arthritis, depression, pain, or allergies, ask him or her to suggest a chiropractor, medical masseuse, herbalist, biofeedback coach, acupuncturist, or another alternative health specialist, or consult one on your own. Some can be Medicare-reimbursed.

◎ Ask your doctor to refer you to a physical therapist to prescribe an exercise program for your physical condition or a change in your exercise program after an illness.

◎ Demand and keep copies of all your medical records. Your doctor may quit or you may outlive him or her, and you can no longer rely even on your principal doctor to keep track of all the specialists you may eventually need.

DRIVING

Cars, roads, and signs are designed for the young. As you age, you cannot respond as fast as you used to. You have more trouble hearing and seeing, especially out of the sides of your eyes at night and in glaring lights. It's harder to switch your attention from near to far and pay attention to more than one thing at a time. Dashboards are cluttered and standardized, and 15 percent of older women can't see over them. Older people have fewer accidents than younger ones because most of them are sensible enough to cut down on driving, but *per mile driven*, people over sixty-five have more accidents than any group but teenagers.

The physical changes come at different ages for different people and so slowly that you have to start compensating for the declines as soon as you suspect them.

◎ Ask someone whom you respect to tell you whether she has noticed any change in the way you drive.

◎ Ask your ophthalmologist whether you need special glasses for driving.

◎ Keep your car repaired even if you don't drive much.

◎ If you're buying a car, choose power steering and brakes, a simple dashboard without bells and whistles, and doors that make it easy to get in and out. White is more visible and safer than any other color.

◎ Take a defensive driving course and save on your car insurance.

◎ Visualize the route in your mind before you set out so you don't have to stop to think on the road, even if you're in familiar territory.

◎ If you haven't been to a place before, consult a map, and if possible, take along a friend who can navigate for you.

◎ Don't talk or listen to the radio or even music tapes while you drive.

◎ Go around the block to avoid a turn across traffic or get the protection of a traffic light.

◎ At night, look to the right of the road to avoid the glare of oncoming headlights.

◎ Raise the driver's seat with a cushion if you have trouble seeing over the dashboard.

◎ Avoid heavy traffic. Sunday morning is a great time to shop at the supermarket.

◎ Don't drive on any road that rattles you. Secondary roads are less nerve-wracking than highways, especially those that require you to change lanes to get on and off them. I don't like the idea of driving across the Mid-Hudson Bridge, so I figure out a way to avoid it.

◎ Finally, although neighbors will give you a lift to concerts and meetings, and friends will go with you on shopping trips, you should be willing to spend a little money on a driver. I contract with a college student to drive me in my car for day trips, to the airport where time pressure adds to the strain, and to the doctor when he is going to do something that may mean I need more assistance than I feel like asking of a cabdriver. And I plan errands like food shopping, banking, shoe repair, gasing up and washing the car, and other chores so that a college student or neighbor can do them at an hourly wage on one afternoon every other week.

EATING ALONE

You need to eat regular meals at regular hours even if you are alone.

◎ Set up a "dinner club" of single friends who rotate playing hostess.
◎ If you work, make your main meal lunch, which occurs at a regular time.
◎ Time meals to the news or a regular TV show.
◎ Read while you eat. A plastic book holder protects reading matter from food splatters.

EXERCISE

Inactivity shortens life and speeds up the declines of aging. Regular exercise improves blood pressure, breathing, resistance to disease of every kind, and your outlook on life. It is no accident that almost all of the women I contacted were among the tiny minority of older people who have a regular exercise program.

Experts advise you to choose activities you like, program them into your day, vary the routine to exercise all parts of your body, and start slowly and work up gradually. It takes willpower to outwit the obstacles that the lazy part of you is always saying are insurmountable.

◎ Get expert help in setting up your program. Don't just ask your doctor whether it's okay to exercise. Get him to prescribe a session with a physical therapist, who can tell you exactly which muscles and abilities need attention. Next, get a personal fitness coach to recommend specific exercises to accomplish what the physical therapist suggests. Your local Y can do this for you.

◎ If you need company, try exercise classes at a Y or a commercial spa. But if time is more important, ask the Y to recommend a certified personal trainer, whom you can pay to come to your house and give you stretching and strengthening exercises to do every morning. In addition, do aerobic walking, swimming, or sports on a regular basis.

◎ To maintain a walking schedule, make a date with a friend to walk with you every morning. On bad days, when there's risk of falling, try walking in a shopping mall or in the basement of an apartment house with a Walkman in your ear for company. As a last resort, try setting up an exercise machine in front of your TV.

◎ To maintain a swimming schedule, vary your stroke as your strength declines, and choose times when the pool isn't crowded. Arthritis has reduced me to the backstroke, which makes me a hazard to other swimmers, especially since I can't steer because one arm is weaker than the other, but other swimmers have been surprisingly cooperative since I summoned the courage to explain the situation.

◎ Slow down, but don't give up an exercise or a sport that is becoming too hard for you. Your personal trainer may have practical suggestions for ways to keep swimming, skiing, or playing golf or tennis. If you used to compete in them, there may be a senior competition you can join.

◎ Look into line dancing, race walking, golf, or one of the many sports that don't take sudden bursts of breath.

FALLING

Personal emergency response systems, which summon help through an electronic device you wear around your neck, are expensive, cumbersome, and sold by dubious high-pressure tactics. Most falls can be prevented.

- Keep shoes, steps, and floor coverings repaired.
- Keep things put away so you don't trip on them.
- Eliminate small rugs or back them with adhesives.
- Keep furniture in accustomed places, especially on the route to the bathroom at night.
- Take a cellular phone when you go outside in winter.

FORGETTING

Everyone is always forgetting and losing things, so don't worry about it. A lot of the remedies suggested cause as much trouble as the forgetting itself. The trick is to organize your life so you don't have to do so much remembering.

- Everyone forgets names, so don't let it embarrass you. Prompt someone you know whose name escapes you by giving your name first and then asking for help on hers.
- Keep extra pairs of eyeglasses and cases stashed around the house to use until the ones you've mislaid turn up.
- Stick to a routine. It saves thinking.
- Have a place for everything and put things back after every use so you don't have to remember where you left them. Get rid of things you don't use every day, to reduce the clutter.
- Finish one thing before starting another.
- When two things pop into your mind at once, jot key words for each on the nearest piece of paper so you don't forget the thought you can't pursue at the moment.
- Keep yourself reminded of things you should do by writing a Post-It note to yourself and sticking it where you should be

doing them: the computer screen, the windshield, the fridge door, the bathroom mirror, even the dining room table.

◎ Keep lists of people to call or write, things to buy, books to read, jobs for a helper, favors to ask of your support system. Jot them down on the nearest Post-It pad when you think of them, and consolidate once a day, transferring the urgent ones to your calendar. Keeping your lists, calendar, and letters on a computer takes a load off your mind and gives you a "find" key for multiple clues to a name that escapes you.

◎ Keep a calendar and update it every day.

FRIENDS

Women are more important to one another as they grow older, especially when they are alone. When you embark on a new life, it's worth taking the trouble to stay in touch with age mates you've known for years while you are making friends with new women.

◎ Keep up with old friends by sending them birthday cards, planning trips, joining for simple pleasures such as a game of Scrabble, a morning walk, or a favorite TV program, and taking an interest in their children.

◎ Make friends with young women around a common interest or something you can do for them, if only lending a nonjudgmental ear.

◎ Make new friends by getting a job, joining a church or club, or working for a cause where you will encounter like-minded people.

◎ Talk to people on trains, in buses, in doctors' waiting rooms. If nothing else, they'll keep you posted on what's going on outside your immediate world.

GETTING NOTICED

- Adopt a trademark hairdo, scarf, or unusual piece of heirloom jewelry, or, like Bella Abzug, an imposing hat.
- Do something unexpected, like flying a kite.
- Speak up when people think you haven't heard them.
- Wear expensive clothes if you can afford them. This works especially well with headwaiters who avoid seeing women.
- Don't get out of the way of people who pretend they don't see you on the street. Make them blink.

GETTING UP

As you get older, your blood pressure doesn't adapt as quickly to change in elevation as it used to, and your knees aren't as quick to correct your balance. You can't change yourself, but there's a lot you can do to get around the problem.

- Get up slowly, especially from bed.
- Buy a higher bed that is easy to get in and out of.
- Install a higher toilet seat.
- Add high, hard seating in a room that has soft, low sofas and chairs.
- Use a wheeled chair at dining and work tables, which will save you from getting up for something you can't reach easily.
- Take showers instead of tub baths.
- Get up and walk around for a few minutes every hour, especially if you are reading or working at a desk.

GRANDCHILDREN

Grandmothers are liberating themselves from the roles of babysitter, present giver, spoiler, overfeeder, and family icon and finding ways to become their grandchildren's special friend.

◎ Treat your grandchildren as adults as much and as soon as possible.

◎ Avoid anything that sounds like criticism of their parents, and explain that the rules their parents have laid down apply when they are with you, too.

◎ Invite each grandchild to visit alone, so you get a chance to have one-on-one time together.

◎ Keep up with each grandchild's current favorite TV programs, sports, and interests so you have something to talk about.

◎ Write each grandchild separate letters or cards. Everyone likes to get mail in his or her own name. Personalized stationery is a good gift that encourages a child to write.

◎ Take each grandchild in turn on a trip alone when he or she is between the ages of eight and twelve. Find a place or an event that will interest both of you.

◎ Spend more time with grandchildren whose parents are separating.

◎ Listen. You can be a young person's safest and only audience.

HEARING

◎ Ask people to speak up, speak slowly, face you, and repeat something you didn't catch.

◎ Try to talk to one person at a time.

◎ Turn off the TV during conversations.

HOMEMAKING

◎ Weed. Little by little, and with a hardheaded helper, clear out closets and drawers. Throw away broken appliances and outdated medicines, cosmetics, magazines, and foodstuffs. Donate clothing, appliances, furniture, and household goods you aren't using to a charity, and be sure to get a receipt for the deduction on your income taxes. Sell the rest at a garage sale. Store seldom-used items in sturdy, well-labeled cardboard boxes.

◎ Simplify. A quilt is just as good as a top sheet and easier to manage. You don't have to cook to have company; the local deli will oblige.

◎ Standardize. You don't have to have three nutritious meals you like that are different every day. Having the same things every day makes it easy to cook and shop. Frozen dinners can be ideal.

◎ Rearrange. Keep things you use every day where they're easy to reach.

◎ Get someone else to do it. Keep a list of the occasional chores you can't do yourself and have it handy when a friend incautiously asks, "Is there anything I can do?" My list includes changing ceiling bulbs, opening tight caps on jars, and sweeping cobwebs off the ceiling.

◎ Identify specific tasks you can no longer do yourself and contract with a neighbor or a high school student to do them. This includes things like getting the garbage down to the road, washing the outside of windows, filling the birdfeeder, and running the vacuum down steps.

HOSPITALS

◎ When you are admitted to a hospital, take a friend along to check the ward, act as your advocate, and see to it that you don't get lost in the bureaucracy.

◎ Refuse to take the mental-status exam hospitals give to classify you. When they ask you something you aren't sure about, say, "I'm anxious and sick and can't remember."

HOUSING

Over 40 percent of women over sixty-five live alone, and that's the way most of them want it, but they are seldom in housing designed for their new lives. Some single older women live in retirement communities or congregate housing, which offer various levels of services and restrictions, but many are stubbornly sticking it out in a house they've inherited.

For those who have more house than they need, there are really two problems. First, how do you live safely alone for the longest possible time in a house that is too big, too outmoded, and too hard to maintain? Second, how do you know when to move to housing that supplies some of the services you need, and where and what kind do you choose?

There are many ways to make out in the big old house you think of as home:

⊚ Get help, company, and sometimes a little financial aid by sharing it with children, elderly parents, or a friend.

⊚ Remodel to create a rental unit in unused space and/or to make the house safer and easier for you to keep. If necessary, finance with a reverse mortgage or home equity loan.

⊚ Before remodeling, research the changes architects recommend for older people, such as eliminating steps by moving your laundry room out of the basement; building a ramp on outdoor steps; attaching the garage to the house, so that you can get to the car without going outdoors in bad weather; installing a higher toilet and reinforcements in the bathroom wall, so you can later install grab bars and hand rails; widening doors and hallways for future wheelchair access; installing remote controls for lights; relocating electrical outlets higher from the floor; and replacing doorknobs with levers. Many are inexpensive if they are all done at once.

⊚ Start building a support system of people you can pay to help you with shopping, cleaning, banking, cooking, and the more strenuous activities of daily living (see "Support Network").

Investigate community resources you can use to continue living in your house if you become unable to bathe, dress, cook, clean, shop, or drive.

However you feel about moving, it doesn't hurt to start thinking ahead about what you'd like. For instance, I would like a climate that is kind to arthritis, a congregate living facility with housekeeping services and easy access to a pool, and a college town that is also an airline hub.

◎ Explore the many alternatives, insofar as possible, by visiting and talking to women who live there. Visit as many congregate living facilities as you can and talk with female residents. Take your time. Many high-profile facilities want a sizable chunk of your assets up front. The arrangements are so complicated that you'll need to pay a lawyer or real estate specialist to look at the contract before you sign it.

INCONTINENCE

Don't worry if you occasionally lose control of your bladder. It happens to more than 20 percent of older women who aren't institutionalized (how many more, we don't know, because so few are willing to talk about it). But you can prevent and remedy it.

◎ Ask your doctor to tell you how to do Kegel exercises, which strengthen the muscles that control urination, and program them into your day. I do them in bed before getting up.

INVESTING

You have to take responsibility for investing your own money, but the best way to do it is to consolidate the management of stocks and bonds in the hands of a single professional you can trust.

◎ Know how your investment adviser is paid. A money manager who makes all the decisions and sends you a check every month may cost you 2 or 3 percent of your assets.

◎ Before signing up, ask other clients of your professional adviser about her strengths and weaknesses.

◎ Keep your adviser informed of changes in what you hope she will achieve. Be sure she knows how much risk you are willing to take and how you intend to monitor her performance. An annual meeting in her office to go over reports is more productive than having lunch together.

LONELINESS

Loneliness seems to be a combination of silence and lack of response that is not confined to the newly widowed or divorced. There are many ways of snapping out of it.

◎ Take a walk in your neighborhood.

◎ Plan a structure for your day.

◎ Set yourself a practical short-term goal, such as cleaning a closet, and a long-term goal, such as visiting a place you've always liked.

◎ Think of someone who may be lonelier than you and call her up to say hello.

◎ Write your feelings down in a diary.

◎ Write letters to distant friends and relatives.

◎ Join a club and go to meetings.

◎ If you don't have a pet or a job, look for one.

MEDICATIONS

◎ Ask the prescribing doctor what each drug will do, what side effects are common, whether you should take special precautions such as avoiding alcohol or driving while you are on it, and whether it will interfere with any other drugs you are taking. If the doctor has prescribed a brand name, ask whether there is a generic equivalent that will save you money.

◎ Avoid drugs that interfere with each other by informing each prescriber of all the other medications you are taking.

◎ Take all your prescriptions to the same pharmacist and ask him or her to check for conflicts.

MEN, SEX, AND REMARRIAGE

You're not likely to replicate the relationship you had with your former husband, but that doesn't mean that you're through with men and sex. Some older women are surprised to find themselves enjoying the best sex of their lives after losing an older husband whose libido was winding down.

Single older women greatly outnumber the available older men, but the imbalance doesn't really cause heartache. Doing laundry, taking care of someone else, and having a man put a claim on their assets are powerful reasons why older women feel like reversing the famous advice "Men in single state should tarry, while women, I suggest, should marry."

Fortunately, there are other options.

◎ Occasional sex with a friendly man who lives elsewhere was the most popular option among the women I interviewed, and some of them were set up with a younger man whose sexual appetite matched theirs.

◎ Regular sex with a housemate or a new husband is also popular. If you wish to remarry, the best bets for husbands are old beaus and the widowers of women friends. But be sure to safeguard your assets with a prenuptial agreement.

◎ Some women have a regular male companion with whom they don't have sex but do have romance. An example is the crusty old doctor on *Murder, She Wrote,* who is something more than a friend but less than a lover to detective writer Jessica Fletcher.

The best bets are inveterate bachelors who have had to learn to be charming.

MONEY

- Simplify banking by using ATMs and all automatic deposit and debit opportunities available.
- Simplify your home records by leaving stock and bond certificates with your broker or financial adviser.
- Forget standard budgets and learn to spend money on what you want for yourself.
- Get used to spending more on help, such as a house cleaner or yard worker, and less on things, such as a car that you may find yourself driving less and less.
- If you own a house outright, investigate a reverse mortgage, which allows you to tap your equity. The older you are, the more income you can expect from a reverse mortgage or annuity.
- Discuss your financial affairs with your heirs. They may be counting on your money, but it is just as likely that they would rather have you come out even by using all your assets for yourself.
- Your power of attorney, living will, will, and instructions about burial should be in a place known to several people who are likely to be nearby for a long time.
- Find out how estate planners and financial advisers who offer you free advice are paid.

MOVING

Moving to smaller quarters takes planning and a wrenching reassessment of the priorities of your new life.

- Start giving away pieces of furniture you know you won't need to children and friends when they visit.

◎ Start looking for a new home for a pet you can't take with you.

◎ Sell or give away anything you've always hated and mentally tag what means most to you.

◎ When you've chosen a new place, think where each item you want to save will go. If things won't fit, tag those you most want to keep and offer the others to family and friends. Dispose of the rest at a yard sale.

◎ If you possibly can, keep the old place for a few months while settling into the new one. One woman rented a room in her old house from the new owner and stacked her overflow stuff in it so she could weed it out at her leisure. If this doesn't work, you can rent low-cost space for a few months.

SALES PITCHES

"Little old ladies living alone" are prime targets for high-pressure sales pitches, outright scams, and con games.

◎ Hang up on telemarketers without compunction.

◎ Especially beware of pitches for investment schemes, personal emergency response systems, home improvements such as driveway blacktopping, furnace inspections, and pesticide services, especially those offering free inspection. Comparison shop before you sign.

SEEING

◎ Put higher-watt bulbs almost everywhere, especially in reading lamps and lights over steps. Use fluorescent ceiling lights in kitchens, bathrooms, and workrooms.

◎ Install night-lights between bed and bathroom.

◎ Read with a spotlight over your left shoulder, and turn off room lights to avoid cross-lighting.

◎ Mark the most used place on hard-to-read controls with red nail polish. This works on showers, ovens, measuring cups, and computer printers.

SHOPPING

Some women love shopping. Others are waiting for the day when everything, including groceries, can be bought by telephone and delivered to the house.

If you like shopping, make something of it. Go with a friend who feels the same way. If you're against shopping, there are ways around it.

◎ Buy in bulk to avoid shopping trips. Visit a discount warehouse, taking some young muscle along, and stock up on imperishables, or write to the manufacturer and have a carton delivered.
◎ Hire someone to shop for you, preferably a friend who loves it.
◎ Shop from catalogues. You know what clothes work for you, and if you aren't sure about the size, order several sizes, do the trying-on at home, and return the wrong ones.
◎ If you have a milk delivery service for perishables, you can cut down on supermarket trips.

SLEEPING

Don't fight bouts of wakefulness in the middle of the night. Use the time to do something interesting or useful. When I was learning Greek, I used the time to conjugate Greek verbs — a sure way to get back to sleep. Now I keep paper and pencil beside my bed so I can write when I wake up. But there are many other possibilities.

◎ Plan the next day.

◎ Call up someone in a time zone west of you.
◎ Catch a late-night television program.
◎ Keep tapes handy to play your favorite music.
◎ Get up and walk around.
◎ Try another bed in the house.

SLOWING DOWN

When aging changes first creep up on you, things just take longer to do than you think they're going to take. You're tempted to hurry, but that's the worst thing you can do.

◎ Give yourself extra time for appointments or everyday tasks.
◎ Think ahead of time about how to deal with predictable encounters with faster-moving young people on trips or at parties and events, paying particular attention to the location of bathrooms, steps, and taxi stands. Before going on a TV program, I figure out answers to the questions interviewers are likely to shoot at me.
◎ Choose exercises, puzzles, handcrafts, and knitting patterns of just manageable difficulty.
◎ Beat the telephone tag game by calling people instead of waiting for them to call you. They're sure to call when your mind is on something else or your body is sunk in a chair it's hard to jump out of.

"STAYING YOUNG" (A.K.A. AGE PASSING)

◎ Stop trying to *look* young. Cosmetics don't fool anyone, and the attempt calls attention to your worst features. Everyone agrees that what keeps you young is enthusiasm.
◎ Learn something new. Going back to college is often a good idea, particularly going back to college with "college-age" people.
◎ Find a cause you believe in enough to want to work for it:

the environment, a political campaign, your college, anything that moves you.

◎ Take up painting, sculpture, music, a foreign language — something demanding that you've always wanted to do.

◎ Vary your schedule if it gets too comfortable. Visit a place you've always been curious about. Sample a TV program you've always avoided, at least long enough to be sure you really loathe it.

There are some practical steps you can take, too.

◎ Give yourself extra time for operations you now do slowly, so you won't be conspicuous getting into coats, going up steps, or finding a parking place or a seat at a public meeting.

◎ Get people to talk about themselves when you want to divert their attention from the problem you are having getting out of a soft, low chair or walking up a steep staircase.

◎ Buy coats with big armholes so you don't attract attention getting them on and off in public places.

◎ Stop complaining about aches, pains, and Young People Today (YPT).

STIFF JOINTS

Joints simply wear out. Arthritis can be relieved with anti-inflammatory drugs and exercise, but it eventually forces you to change your ways.

◎ Do stretching exercises *every* day, even if they hurt, or your joints will freeze up for good. Take Tylenol a half-hour before stretches to relieve the pain. If you have trouble getting up from the floor, do floor exercises on a bed; if necessary, put an old door on top for solidity.

◎ Reduce, but don't omit, practicing a handicraft that forces you to use your joints, such as knitting, pottery, and gardening.

◎ Learn to use a word processor or computer to write letters.

The keyboard is easier on your fingers than writing by hand or on an old-fashioned typewriter.

◎ Get a podiatrist to cut your toenails.

◎ Avoid soft pouch handbags, especially those you sling over your shoulder. Pesky little things like lipsticks can't escape your fingers in a hard handbag. Cut down on what you must carry and save your shoulders by putting it into a hand-held briefcase.

◎ Reorganize your cupboards and refrigerator so you can retrieve items you use most often without reaching.

◎ Buy easily lifted quarts of milk instead of half-gallons when you stock up to avoid supermarket trips.

◎ Locate the nearest full-service gas station so you don't have to pump gas yourself.

◎ Use an electrically heated bedpad to comfort your arthritis in winter, rather than an electric blanket, which is hard to manage if you have problems turning over.

◎ Investigate reachers, dressing hooks, bottle cap unscrewers, and other gadgets designed to help you do common tasks. Try them before you buy them to be sure they work for you. Some are more trouble than they are worth. A pliers with expandable jaws beats most of the elaborate jar-top unscrewers on the market.

SUPPORT NETWORK

Women who continue to live on their own past their seventies almost always do it with the help of a support system of paid and unpaid helpers for shopping, banking, making repairs, providing rides to parties or the doctor, heavy cleaning, or just plain gossiping. They may be friends, relatives, neighbors, colleagues, or fellow members of a church, club, political party, or interest group. Networks can be extended to friends and children of any of these people. The best support systems are established long before they are needed, but they all require continuing care and feeding.

The trick is to see that other people get something they want out of helping. Most people really enjoy helping if they like the task and can do it when and where it's convenient. Find out who to ask to do what by listening to what people tell you about their lives.

◎ Listen to everybody who comes to your house to see if there's something you can do to help them. It pays to make friends with your plumber, electrician, yardkeeper, and handyman.
◎ Pay people who go out of their way to help with a homemade quilt or sweater, a batch of homemade cookies, or the gift of something they've admired that you no longer need.
◎ Try bartering a skill such as typing, tax preparation, or tutoring for home repairs, heavy cleaning, or a professional service you can't afford. When my husband discovered that his dentist was trying to write a book, he traded editing it for a set of false teeth.
◎ Get hold of a list of college or high school students who are willing to do errands, yard work, heavy cleaning, and other chores for a little bit of money. If you pay a dollar an hour more than the going rate, you'll be sure to get attention. Friends with children in school are the best source, but most colleges and high schools have employment services.
◎ Don't be discouraged if the people who say they want to help you aren't available when you need them. You should have a roster of twice as many as you'll ever use.

WORK

◎ Keep doing something you define as work.
◎ Look for work with an old employer, or find work through an offshoot of an old job or a hobby.
◎ Omit age on résumés but emphasize your responsibilities and willingness to work on a contract basis.
◎ Retrain for work that interests you.

◎ Try working for a temporary service.
◎ Speak up if you are put down for your age.
◎ Consider teaching something you know at a local community college.
◎ If you're willing to volunteer, shop for opportunities that use a skill or talent you enjoy.

Notes

After seventy, losing a wife shortens the lives of men, but losing a husband does not significantly shorten the lives of women. See p. 22 of "Marital Status and Health Among the Elderly," a paper presented at the 1994 annual meeting of the Population Association of America by Noreen Goldman, D.Sc., professor of demography and public affairs at Princeton University's Office of Population Research (21 Prospect Ave., Princeton, NJ 08540).

Health Risks, by Elliott J. Howard, M.D. (Body Press, Tucson, 1986), contains a longevity test for individuals of both sexes and all ages that gives numerical scores for factors that add to or subtract from life expectancy. In 1994, Dr. Howard adapted the items on his original test to apply to women over fifty. Factors that add to life expectancy on his score are listed below with a plus; those that subtract, with a minus.

1. FAMILY HISTORY
   Parents over 75, no cancer/heart disease   +
   Heart disease in a parent before age 50   −
   Stroke before age 60 in both parents   −
   Cancer in parent or sibling   −
   Heart disease, diabetes, in both parents   −

2. SMOKING
   Never smoked or quit over 5 years ago   +
   Quit less than 5 years ago   −
   Live or work in polluted air   −
   Smoke more than a pack a day   −

3. WEIGHT
At or near ideal weight   +/−
Over 20% above or below ideal weight   −
Over ideal with extra at waist   −

4. PHYSICAL ACTIVITY
Sports, aerobics, brisk walking, gardening, or other
    exercise 3 days a week   +
Less than 3 days a week   −

5. EATING HABITS
5–7 servings vegetables/fruits/cereals a day   +
antioxidant vitamins   +
3–5 servings vegetables/fruits, limited fat   +/−
less than 3 servings vegetables/fruit, little
    high-fiber cereal   −
bacon, processed meat, whole milk, butter, cheese,
    ice cream, and saturated fats   −

6. DRINKING HABITS
Less than 1.5 oz. hard liquor, 12 oz. beer, 5 oz.
    wine once or twice a week   +
Same amount almost every day   +/−
Same amount or more every day   −

7. MENTAL ATTITUDE
Usually upbeat, smiles easily, energetic   +
Enjoys work, busy with many projects   +
Needs tranquilizers, headache medication, stomach
    antispasmodics   −
Few if any projects, feels worthless   −
Usually depressed, unhappy at work   −

8. BLOOD PRESSURE
Systolic (first number)
    100 to 120   +

121 to 140   +/−
Over 140   −
Diastolic (second number)
     60 to 70   +
     71 to 85   +/−
     Over 85   −

9. HEART DISEASE
No sign of heart disease by EKG or stress test and
     parents lived to 75   +
Mild to moderately high blood pressure   −
Mild to moderately high cholesterol   −
Abnormal EKG and/or angina   −
Enlarged heart and/or abnormal EKG   −

10. CHOLESTEROL
Total cholesterol/HDL ratio
     3:1 or less   +
     4:1   +/−
     5:1 or more   −

11. OSTEOPOROSIS
A blood relative with osteoporosis and any of
     these conditions   −
thin bones
postmenopausal, no estrogen replacement
smokes
uses cortisone
thyroid disease
excessive alcohol, caffeine intake
underweight
uses diuretics
sedentary
low calcium intake
diabetic on insulin
uses antacids with aluminum

12. DIABETES

Blood sugar normal, no diabetes in parents or
  grandparents   +
Diabetes, treated by oral medication and diet or
  insulin and diet   —

2. WHAT REALLY HAPPENS WHEN YOU GROW OLD

The best quick source that puts aging into context is *Human Development*, by Diane E. Papalia and Sally Olds (McGraw-Hill, New York, 1994). Constantly revised, it has a meticulous bibliography.

Biomarkers: The Ten Keys to Prolonging Vitality, by William Evans and Irwin H. Rosenberg (Fireside, New York, 1992), has practical suggestions for prolonging life through diet and exercise, based on research at the U.S. Department of Agriculture Human Nutrition Research Center on Aging at Tufts University.

We'll know more about what happens to individuals as they age when we get the results of the Health and Retirement Study conducted by the University of Michigan's Institute for Social Research for the National Institute on Aging. It is following eight-thousand respondents aged fifty-one to sixty in 1992, and their spouses, for the next ten or twelve years to check on changes in their employment, health, mental ability, income, net worth, retirement plans, and much more.

3. THE SALTY OLD WOMEN AROUND US

The women who volunteered their experiences for this book came from many different places. I started with women readers of *Modern Maturity* who had responded to my 1988 questionnaire on second careers, and with women whose names were suggested by friends. Others were recruited through appeals in publications. In addition to appearing in Bard Lindeman's "Prime Time" column, appeals and ads for volunteers appeared in *Broomstick* and

Encore, periodicals written for and by older women; *Hot Flash,* the publication of Jane Porcino's National Action Forum for Midlife and Older Women, Inc.; *The Hotline,* a bulletin of career, educational, and re-entry information and opportunities for returned Peace Corps volunteers; the *OWL Observer,* a national newspaper of the Older Women's League; and the *Vassar Quarterly.* Some names came from *Legacies,* an anthology of personal stories by new writers sixty and over edited by Maury Leibovitz and Linda Solomon (HarperCollins, New York, 1993).

Other women responded to speeches I made on women and aging from platforms ranging from the Dutchess County chapter of OWL and the Dutchess County Mental Health Association to the Women's Center of St. John's Medical Center in Steubenville, Ohio, the Senior Options Expo in St. Paul, sponsored by the Minnesota Senior Federation, and the Chancellor's Breakfast at the University of Nebraska at Omaha.

Still others came through organizations such as the Women's Initiative of the American Association of Retired Persons; the Giraffe Project, a nonprofit organization based in Langley, Washington, that honors people who "stick their necks out" to help others; the National School Board Association; the Joint Training Partnership Council of New York State; the National Network of Women as Philanthropists; and the Thanks Be To Grandmother Winifred Foundation.

Some came from published sources, especially Lydia Brontë's *The Longevity Factor: The New Reality of Long Careers and How It Can Lead to Richer Lives* (HarperCollins, New York, 1993), but also from magazines and newspaper accounts and the writers of letters to their editors.

4. CUSTOM-MADE ROLES

On adventure: An issue on risk-taking in the quarterly *Update on Human Behavior,* published for helping professionals by Susan Sturdivant (Human Services, Inc., 6060 N. Central Expressway,

Suite 224, LB 719, Dallas, TX 75206), reports that older people are not more timid than younger people. "When given a choice of safe and risky options in a variety of situations, the elderly chose safer alternatives no more than their younger counterparts, suggesting that it is the situation itself and not the age of the risk-taker that determines choices."

Carl Jung, the psychoanalyst, advised older people to continue taking risks in order to keep growing, but he was thinking of psychological risks and spiritual, moral, and religious growth. Once career and family challenges have been met, people should explore a meaning of life that will prepare them for death.

Peace Corps applicants must have a college degree and/or work experience, preferably in agriculture or natural resources; business or accounting; engineering; health, nutrition, or nursing; industrial arts or technical education; primary or secondary education; special education, science, or math; skilled trades like carpentry or metalworking; or teaching English as a second language. In addition, an applicant must be a U.S. citizen, in good health, free of legal and financial obligations, and willing to serve two years after three-month preservice training. For an application, write to the Peace Corps Recruiting Office, Washington, DC 20526.

For opportunities to volunteer your services abroad, write to:

⊚ Global Volunteers, 375 E. Little Canada Road, St. Paul, MN 55117-1628; phone 612-482-1084, fax 612-482-0915 or 1-800-487-1074.
⊚ American Association for International Aging, 1133 20th St. NW, Suite 330, Washington, DC 20036; phone 202-833-8893.

For volunteers with academic credentials, consult Earthwatch, 680 Mount Auburn St., P.O. Box 403, Watertown, MA 02172; phone 617-926-8200, fax 617-926-8532.

On doing good: You can get a list of all the boards that oversee professions for which citizens can volunteer from the secretary of your state.

For opportunities in domestic volunteer work, consult the National Center, 1111 North 19th St., Suite 500, Arlington, VA 22209, or look for Volunteer Center or Voluntary Action Center in the white pages of your telephone book.

Dr. Colter Rule, a New York psychoanalyst, believes that women are biologically conditioned to be more nurturant and caring than men.

Richard Graham's proposal for a third women's movement is detailed in "America's Third Women's Movement and the Uses of Gender," published in a special issue of *Proteus, A Journal of Ideas* devoted to gender in America.

On sharing wealth: The National Network on Women as Philanthropists is housed in the School of Family Resources and Consumer Sciences, University of Wisconsin, 1300 Linden Drive, Madison, WI 53706; phone 608-262-1962.

Gloria Steinem lays out the case for the "masculinization of wealth" in "The Truth about Rich Women," an essay in *Moving Beyond Words*, her most recent book.

Ruth Crocker, a historian at Auburn University who is working on a biography of Olivia Sage, generously shared her findings on this little-known benefactress.

On creating art: The works of the following writers are most easily obtained from their publishers:

◎ Lila Line, *Waterwomen*, Queen Anne Press of Wye Institute, Cheston-on-Wye, Queenstown, MD 21658.
◎ Frances Weaver, *The Girls With the Grandmother Faces* (and her subsequent titles), Midlife Musings Publishers, P.O. Box 970, Saratoga Springs, NY 12866.
◎ Jane Poulton, *A Better Legend: From the World War II Letters of Jack and Jane Poulton*, University Press of Virginia, P.O. Box 3608, University Station, Charlottesville, VA 99208.
◎ Helen Crosswait, *Reflections of a Paleface from Rosebud*, Paleface Productions, 333 Pine St., Chadron, NE.
◎ Ellen Paullin, *Ted's Stroke: The Caregiver's Story*, 1988. Seven

Locks Press, P.O. Box 27, Cabin John, MD 20818; phone 301-320-2130.

- Ruth Jacobs, *Be an Outrageous Older Woman* (and her other recent books), Knowledge, Ideas & Trends, Inc. (KIT), 1131-0 Tolland Turnpike, Suite 175, Manchester, CT 06040.
- Jane Porcino, *Living Longer, Living Better: Adventures in Community Housing for Those in the Second Half of Life* (and her other books), Continuum, 370 Lexington Ave., New York, NY 10017, or Jane Porcino, c/o National Action Forum for Midlife and Older Women, Box 816, Stonybrook, NY 11790-0609.

Small publications for and by older women include *Broomstick: Options for Women Over Forty* at 3543 18th St., #3, San Francisco, CA 94110; *Encore*, P.O. Box 1599, Mariposa, CA 95338; and *Hot Flashes*, c/o Jane Porcino, NAFOW, Box 816, Stonybrook, NY 11790-0609.

The Legacies writing contest invited persons sixty years and over to submit a brief story that they would want their grandchildren to know. The best stories were published by Harper-Collins in 1993 in the book *Legacies*.

7. INVISIBLE IN EVERYDAY LIFE

Evidence that even children sit farther from old people than from middle-aged people comes from "Mediation of Interpersonal Expectancy Effects: Expectancies about the Elderly," the report of a study by Monica J. Harris and her colleagues at the University of Kentucky published in *Social Psychology Quarterly* 57, 1(1994): 36–48.

8. INVISIBLE IN THE WORKPLACE

For an overview of laws against job discrimination, see *Your Rights in the Workplace*, by Barbara K. Repa (Nolo Press Self

Help Law, Berkeley, CA, 1993; phone 510-549-1976), or a similar handbook in your local library.

Employment law is so complicated and there are so many statutes and venues that if you think you have been the victim of illegal discrimination, you had better start by consulting an employment lawyer who specializes in representing plaintiffs. If there is no listing for the National Employment Lawyers Association in your city directory, send a stamped self-addressed envelope to the National Employment Lawyers Association, 600 Harrison St., #535, San Francisco, CA 94107. You may qualify for advice from the local Legal Aid Society.

Women bring fewer lawsuits than men but win more of them. A report entitled "An Evaluation of the Impact of Age Discrimination in Employment Legislation," made by Syracuse University's All-University Gerontological Center and School of Management for AARP's Andrus Foundation in 1985, found that white males filed most of the ADEA claims and that employers won most of them. But in a hearing before the Special Committee on Aging of the U.S. Senate on August 2, 1991, the following colloquy occurred between Senator William S. Cohen and Lou Glasse, testifying for the Older Women's League:

> COHEN: Yet the record would indicate that women are becoming much more successful in applying those discrimination claims than men.
> GLASSE: I'd like to know, sir, where this data comes from?
> COHEN: The study was conducted by researchers at Syracuse University's School of Management. The study looked at the enforcement of the Age Discrimination in Employment Act by the EEOC and found that although more claims have been filed by men, women have been more successful by percentage.

The estimate on the value of volunteer work contributed by women over fifty-five was made for the Commonwealth Fund by Kevin A. Coleman of Lewin-VHI, a public policy research firm in Arlington, Virginia, that specializes in health-care financing. Under Margaret Mahoney, the Commonwealth Fund has commissioned a series of studies on older people, their problems, and their contributions to American life. Its most recent study is entitled "The Nation's Great Overlooked Resource: The Contributions of Americans 55+." It is based on a national survey conducted for the fund between October 1991 and January 1992 of 2,999 Americans (1,069 men and 1,930 women) age fifty-five and over. Dr. Coleman was kind enough to break down details of the data for me by age, sex, and marital status. He is the author of a study entitled "The Economic Value of Older Americans to Society."

9. INVISIBLE IN THE MEDIA AND THE MARKETPLACE

George Gerbner, dean emeritus of the Annenberg School for Communications, University of Pennsylvania, developed his rigorous methods for monitoring television in order to document the incidence of violence in programs watched by children. In 1993, his cultural indicators research team issued *Women and Minorities on Television*, a report on the period between 1982 and 1992, funded by the Screen Actors Guild and the American Federation of Radio and Television Artists. An update of a similar study covering the period 1969 to 1978 convinced Dr. Gerbner that in spite of memorable programs, there has been little overall change. He has summarized his conclusions in "Learning Productive Aging as a Social Role: The Lessons of Television."

Dr. Gerbner is particularly concerned about the images in programs beamed to children. Some of them drive a wedge between generations. One television researcher reported that a child said, "I won't grow old. It's too terrible." Asked where old people come from, another child thought that they were born to other old people.

10. INVISIBLE IN HEALTH CARE

The comments on the large breasts of a cadaver were related by Adriane Fugh-Berman, M.D., in "Tales Out of Medical School," *The Nation*, January 20, 1992.

Evidence of the neglect of older women in health care is summarized in the 1992 Mother's Day Report of the Older Women's League, entitled "Critical Condition: Midlife and Older Women in America's Health Care System."

Practical advice on the health problems of older women is available from the *Parent Care Advisor*, a monthly newsletter published by LRP Publications, 747 Dresher Road, P.O. Box 980, Horsham, PA 19044-0980; phone 215-784-0860.

11. INVISIBLE IN POLICYMAKING

For the status of women in both public and private pension systems, see "Women, Pensions, & Divorce: Small Reforms that Could Make a Big Difference," a 1993 publication of the Women's Initiative, American Association of Retired Persons.

For specific information, consult Pension Rights Center, 918 16th St. NW, Suite 704, Washington, DC 20006, or their publication *Your Pension Rights at Divorce*, by Anne E. Moss (1993).

"Personal Wealth, 1989" by Barry W. Johnson and Marvin Schwartz, in *Statistics of Income Bulletin* 12, 4 (Spring 1993), Publication 1136, estimates that women made up 42 percent of the 3.4 million top wealth-holders in 1989. Neither the census nor the Internal Revenue Service has figures on the percentage of all personal wealth now held by women, but development specialists at the University of California at Los Angeles, the National Network on Women as Philanthropists, Judith E. Nichols, a development consultant, and Ann Kaplan, editor of *Giving, U.S.A.*, newsletter of the American Association of Fund-Raising Counsels, agree that women own at least 43 percent. Published estimates have run as high as 60 percent.

12. OLD IS UGLY

According to the *American Heritage Dictionary*, the word "stereotype" means "1. A conventional, formulaic, and oversimplified conception, opinion, or image . . . 2. One that is regarded as embodying or conforming to a set image or type . . . To characterize by a stereotype: *Elderly Americans are the neglected sector of the fashion industry, stereotyped by blue hair and polyester pantsuits.*"

The sociologist Matilda Riley was the first to define attitudes toward aging as stereotypes.

Some stereotypes persist in spite of evidence that they are the reverse of the fact. In later years, for instance, losing a spouse is more lethal for men than for women. According to a Swedish study, the mortality rate of widows during the first three months of bereavement is 22 percent higher than that of married persons between seventy and seventy-four, while the mortality rate of widowers is 48 percent, or twice as high.

13. WE DO IT TO OURSELVES

More than six thousand women responded to "Women Growing Older," a detailed questionnaire printed in the January 1993 issue of *New Woman*. The results, printed in the November 1993 issue, reported that half of the women under thirty were afraid of growing old, compared with only 17 percent of those over sixty. Fifteen percent of the women under thirty but only 8 percent of those over fifty thought that loneliness would be the worst part of growing old. As for sex, 30 percent of the women in their forties and 24 percent of those in their sixties said that they were more interested in sex than ever before.

14. WHAT IF: AN AGENDA FOR AGE EQUALITY

Architects and designers know how to make buildings, public places, and products comfortable for people of all ages, but their recommendations have not been widely publicized.

One example is the contributions to an Invitational Conference on Life-Span Design of Residential Environments for an Aging Population convened by the Forecasting and Environmental Scanning Department of the AARP in 1993. Another is the OWL Model Bill on Accessible Housing.

Technical information is available from the following experts:

- ◎ Lenny Rickman, National Association of Home Builders Research Center, Upper Marlboro, MD.
- ◎ Ron Mace, president, Barrier Free Environments, Inc., P.O. Box 30634, Highway 70 West, Water Garden, Raleigh, NC 27622; phone 919-782-7823.
- ◎ Elaine Ostroff, Adaptive Environments Center, 374 Congress St., Suite 301, Boston, MA 02210; phone 617-695-1225.
- ◎ Leon A. Pastalan, director, National Center on Housing and Living Arrangements for Older Americans, College of Architecture and Urban Planning, University of Michigan, 2000 Bonisteel Boulevard, Ann Arbor, MI 48109-2069; phone 313-763-1275.

For practical suggestions, write for the AARP's free publication "Perfect Fit: Creative Ideas for a Safe and Livable Home," AARP #D1444823 AARP EE0768, AARP, 601 E. St. NW, Washington, DC 20049.

The Sixth Sense: Understanding Sensory Changes and Aging is a practical checklist for evaluating how well an older person's environment is adapted to aging changes. It is available from the National Council on the Aging, Inc., 600 Maryland Avenue SW, West Wing 100, Washington, DC 20025.

For the timing of crossing lights, see Russell E. Hoxie et al., "The Older Pedestrian," *Journal of the American Geriatric Society* 42, 4 (April 1994).

APPENDIX

A few sources on "secrets":

On driving, write to the AAA Foundation for Traffic Safety, 1730 M St. NW, Suite 401, Washington, DC 20036, and ask for *Concerned About an Older Driver*, by James L. Malfetti and Darlene J. Winter.

On grandchildren, write to GrandTravel, 6900 Wisconsin Ave., Suite 706, Chevy Chase, MD 20815, or call 1-800-247-7651, for the current edition of *Grandtravel: Very Special Vacations for Grandparents and Grandchildren*, which suggests trips designed to interest both grandmothers and school-age children.

On health, phone the hotline of the Arthritis Foundation at 1314 Spring St., Atlanta, GA 30309, for quick answers to simple questions about this common problem. The numbers are 800-283-7800 or 404-872-7100.

On homemaking, write for "The User-Friendly Home: Older Nevadans Share Ideas for Easier Living," compiled by Barbara A. Gunn and Patricia A. Tripple, Geriatric and Gerontology Center, University of Nevada at Reno; phone 702-784-1800.

For information on incontinence, write to AHCPR Publications Clearing House, U1-P, P.O. Box 8547, Silver Spring, MD 20907, for a booklet entitled, "Urinary Incontinence in Adults: A Patient's Guide," published by the Agency for Health Care Policy and Research.

Bibliography

Aburdene, Patricia, and John Naisbitt. *Megatrends for Women.* New York: Villard, 1992. See the account of the goddess movement.

"Aging Survey Report." *New Woman,* November 1993.

Alexander, Jo, ed. *Women and Aging.* Corvallis, Ore.: Calyx, 1986.

Anson, Ofra. "Evidence that Elderly Women Living Alone May Be in Better Health than Their Counterparts." *Sociology and Social Research,* vol. 72, no. 2, January 1988.

Arber, Sara, and Jay Ginn. *Gender and Later Life: A Sociological Analysis of Resources and Constraints.* London, Calif.: Sage, 1991.

Armitage, Karen J., et al. "Response of Physicians to Medical Complaints in Men and Women." *Journal of the American Medical Association,* vol. 241, no. 20, May 18, 1979.

Baehr, Helen, and Gillian Dyer, eds. *Boxed In: Women and Television.* New York: Pandora, 1987.

Baltes, Paul B., and Margaret M., eds. *Successful Aging: Perspectives from the Behavioral Sciences.* New York: Cambridge University Press, 1990.

Binstock, Robert H., and Linda K. George, eds. *Handbook of Aging and the Social Sciences.* New York: Academic, 1990.

Bishop, James M., and Daniel R. Krause. "Depictions of Aging and Old Age on Saturday Morning Television." *The Gerontologist,* vol. 24, no. 1, 1984.

Block, Marilyn. *Women Over Forty: Visions and Realities.* New York: Springer, 1991.

Borenstein, Audrey. *Chimes of Change and Hours: Views of Older Women in Twentieth-Century America.* Rutherford, N.J.: Fairleigh Dickinson University Press, 1983.

Borges, Marilyn A., and Linda J. Dutton. "Attitudes Toward Aging: Increasing Optimism Found with Age." *The Gerontologist*, vol. 16, no. 3, 1976.

Brim, Gilbert. *Ambition: How We Manage Success and Failure Throughout Our Lives*. New York: Basic Books, 1993.

Brontë, Lydia. *The Longevity Factor: The New Reality of Long Careers and How It Can Lead to Richer Lives*. New York: HarperCollins, 1993. A report of a study of 150 eminent individuals who continued to work and achieve beyond normal retirement age.

Brothers, Joyce. *Widowed*. New York: Ballantine, 1992.

Brown, Helen Gurley. *The Late Show: A Practical Semiwild Survival Guide for Every Woman in Her Prime or Approaching It*. New York: Morrow, 1993.

Brubaker, Timothy H., and Edward A. Powers. "The Stereotype of 'Old': A Review and Alternative Approach." *Journal of Gerontology*, vol. 3, no. 4, 1976.

Butler, Robert N., and Herbert P. Gleason, eds. *Productive Aging: Enhancing Vitality in Later Life*. New York: Springer, 1985.

Chamberlain, Letitia. "The Experience of Leisure, Time, and Meaning in Daily Life among Retired Professional Women." UMI Dissertation Service, 1990.

Chambre, Susan M. "Volunteerism by Elders: Past Trends and Future Prospects." *The Gerontologist*, vol. 33, no. 2, 1993.

Chopra, Deepak. *Ageless Body, Timeless Mind: The Quantum Alternative to Growing Old*. New York: Harmony, 1994.

Chudacoff, Howard P. *How Old Are You? Age Consciousness in American Culture*. Princeton, N.J.: Princeton University Press, 1992.

Cole, Thomas R. *The Journey of Life: A Cultural History of Aging in America*. New York: Cambridge University Press, 1992.

Comfort, Alex. *Say Yes to Old Age*. New York: Crown, 1976.

Commonwealth Fund. *The Untapped Resource: The Final Report of the Americans over 55 at Work Program*. New York: Commonwealth Fund, November 1993.

Dail, Paula W. "Prime-Time Television Portrayals of Older Adults in the Context of Family Life." *The Gerontologist*, vol. 28, no. 5, 1988.

Davis, Richard H., and James A. Davis. *The Television Image of America's Elderly: A Practical Guide for Change*. Lexington, Mass.: Lexington Books, 1985.

Day, Alice T. *Remarkable Survivors: Insights into Successful Aging among Women*. Washington, D.C.: Urban Institute Press, 1991.

Doress, Paula, Diana Siegal, and the Midlife and Older Women Book Project. *Ourselves, Growing Older: Women Aging with Knowledge and Power*. New York: Touchstone, 1987.

Dychtwald, Ken. *Age Wave: Choices and Challenges for Our New Future*. New York: Bantam, 1990.

Elliott, Joyce. "The Daytime Television Drama Portrayal of Older Adults." *The Gerontologist*, vol. 24, no. 6, 1984.

Estes, Carroll L., and Elizabeth A. Binney. "The Biomedicalization of Aging: Dangers and Dilemmas." *The Gerontologist*, vol. 29, no. 5, 1989.

Estes, Clarissa. *Women Who Run with the Wolves: Myths and Stories of the Wild Woman Archetype*. New York: Ballantine, 1992.

Evans, William, and Irwin H. Rosenberg. *Biomarkers: The Ten Keys to Prolonging Vitality*. New York: Fireside, 1992. Practical suggestions based on Tufts University research.

Faludi, Susan. *Backlash*. New York: Crown, 1992.

Fischer, Lucy Rose. "Older Volunteers: A Discussion of the Minnesota Senior Study." *The Gerontologist*, vol. 31, no. 2, 1991.

Friedan, Betty. *The Fountain of Age*. New York: Simon and Schuster, 1993. Groundbreaking attack on ageism as it affects both sexes.

Gaitz, Charles M., and Judith Scott. "Analysis of Letters to 'Dear Abby' Concerning Old Age." *The Gerontologist*, February 1975.

Gerbner, George. "Women and Minorities on Television: A Study in Casting and Fate." A report to the Screen Actors Guild and the American Federation of Radio and Television Artists, June 1993.

Golant, Stephen M. *Housing America's Elderly: Many Possibilities, Few Choices*. Newbury Park, Calif.: Sage, 1992.

Grumbach, Doris. *Coming into the End Zone: A Memoir.* New York: Norton, 1991.

————. *Extra Innings: A Memoir.* New York: Norton, 1993.

————. *Fifty Days of Solitude.* Boston: Beacon, 1994.

Healy, Bernadine. "The Yentl Syndrome." *New England Journal of Medicine,* vol. 325, no. 4, July 25, 1991.

Holland, Barbara. *One's Company: Reflections on Living Alone.* New York: Ballantine, 1992.

Hollenshead, Carol, and Berit Ingersoll. "Middle-Aged and Older Women in Print Advertisements." *Educational Gerontology,* vol. 8, 1982.

Hot Flashes, Newsletter for Midlife and Older Women. National Action Forum for Midlife and Older Women, Inc.

House, James S., Karl R. Landis, and Debra Umberson. "Social Relationships and Health." *Science,* vol. 241, July 29, 1988.

Howard, Elliott J. *Health Risks.* Tucson, Ariz.: Body Press, 1986.

Hoxie, Dr. Russell E., Dr. Laurence Z. Rubenstein, et al. "The Older Pedestrian." *Journal of the American Geriatrics Society,* April 1994.

Huckle, Patricia. *Tish Sommers, Activist, and the Founding of the Older Women's League.* Knoxville: University of Tennessee Press, 1991.

Jacobs, Ruth. *Be an Outrageous Older Woman: A RASP: Remarkable Aging Smart Person.* Manchester, Conn.: Knowledge, Ideas & Trends, Inc., 1994.

Kaiser, Susan B., and Joan L. Chandler. "Audience Responses to Appearance Codes: Old-Age Imagery in the Media." *The Gerontologist,* vol. 28, no. 5, 1988.

Kaplan, George A., et al. "Mortality Among the Elderly in the Alameda County Study: Behavioral and Demographic Risk Factors." *American Journal of Public Health,* vol. 77, no. 3, March 1987.

Kidder, Tracy. *Old Friends.* Boston: Houghton Mifflin, 1993.

Kuhn, Maggie. *No Stone Unturned: The Life and Times of Maggie Kuhn.* New York: Ballantine, 1991.

Lear, Frances. *The Second Seduction*. New York: HarperPerennial, 1993.

Leibovitz, Maury, and Linda Solomon, eds. *Legacies*. New York: HarperCollins, 1993.

Lesnoff-Caravaglia, Gari. *The World of the Older Woman*. New York: Human Sciences Press, 1984.

Lewis, Myra I., and Robert N. Butler. "Why Is Women's Lib Ignoring Old Women?" *Aging and Human Development*, vol. 3, 1972.

Lopata, Helena Znaniecka. *Women as Widows: Support Systems*. New York: Elsevier, 1979. Lopata updated this classic in "Feminist Perspectives on Social Gerontology," a paper presented at the 1993 American Sociological Association meeting.

Macdonald, Barbara. "Politics of Aging: I'm *Not* Your Mother." *Ms.*, July-August 1990.

Maddox, George L. "Aging Differently." *The Gerontologist*, vol. 27, November 1987.

Madsen, Axel. *Chanel: A Woman of Her Own*. New York: Holt, 1991.

Manton, Kenneth G., et al. "Estimates of Change in Chronic Disability and Institutional Incidence and Prevalence Rates in the U.S. Elderly Population from 1982, 1984, and 1989 National Long Term Care Survey." *Journal of Gerontology*, vol. 48, no. 4, 1993.

Martz, Sandra, ed. *I Am Becoming the Woman I've Wanted*. Watsonville, Calif.: Papier Mache Press, 1994.

———. *When I Am an Old Woman I Shall Wear Purple*. Watsonville, Calif.: Papier Mache Press, 1987.

McCarthy, Kathleen. *Lady Bountiful Revisited: Women, Philanthropy, and Power*. New Brunswick, N.J.: Rutgers University Press, 1990.

Moen, Phyllis, Donna Dempster-McClain, and Robin M. William, Jr. "Successful Aging: A Life-Course Perspective on Women's Multiple Roles and Health." *American Journal of Sociology*, vol. 97, no. 6, May 1992. Proves the advantage of having multiple roles.

Moore, Alinde J. "'Getting By': An Exploration of Late-Life Adaptation in Elderly Women." Paper presented at a conference entitled "The Enduring Spirit: Women As They Age," University of Nebraska at Omaha, April 1–3, 1993.

Moore, Pat, with Charles Paul Conn. *Disguised.* Waco, Tex.: Word Books, 1985.

Morris, Desmond. *The Book of Ages.* New York: Viking, 1984.

Moss, Anne E. *Your Pension Rights at Divorce: What Women Need to Know.* Washington, D.C.: Pension Rights Center, 1991.

Mossey, Jana M., et al. "Self-Rated Health: A Predictor of Mortality Among the Elderly." *American Journal of Public Health,* vol. 72, no. 8, August 1982.

National Institutes of Health. *Opportunities for Research on Women's Health.* Hunt Valley, Md., September 4–6, 1991.

O'Bryant, Shirley L. "Older Widows and Independent Lifestyles." *International Journal of Aging and Human Development,* vol. 32, no. 1, 1991.

O'Leary, Virginia. "Age Discrimination in the Workplace and Its Effect on Women." Paper presented at the "Enduring Spirit" conference, University of Nebraska at Omaha, April 2, 1993.

Palmore, Erdman. *Ageism: Negative and Positive.* New York: Springer, 1990. Includes the results of the author's quiz on stereotypes of aging over the past quarter-century.

Papalia, Diane E., and Sally Olds. *Human Development.* New York: McGraw-Hill, 1995. Constantly revised. A meticulous bibliography of recent research.

Perlmutter, Marion, and Elizabeth Hall. *Adult Development and Aging.* 2nd ed. New York: John Wiley, 1992.

Petersen, Marilyn. "The Visibility and Image of Old People on Television." *Journalism Quarterly,* vol. 50, 1973.

Pifer, Alan, ed., with Lydia Brontë. *Our Aging Society: Paradox and Promise.* New York: Norton, 1986.

Porcino, Jane. *Growing Older, Getting Better: A Handbook for Women in the Second Half of Life.* New York: Continuum, 1991.

———. *Living Longer, Living Better: Adventures in Community*

Housing for Those in the Second Half of Life. New York: Continuum, 1991.

Repa, Barbara K. *Your Rights in the Workplace*. 2nd ed. Berkeley, Calif.: Nolo Press, 1993.

Riley, Matilda White, et al., eds. *Aging in Society: Selected Reviews of Recent Research*. Hillsdale, N.J.: L. Erlbaum Associates, 1983. Riley updated her views in "Longevity and Opportunity: The Future for Women," a paper presented at the Radcliffe Conference on Women over Fifty: Living Longer and Smarter, Cambridge, Mass., April 3–4, 1992.

Rodin, Judith. "Aging and Health: Effects of the Sense of Control." *Science*, September 19, 1986.

Roosevelt, Eleanor. *On My Own*. New York: Harper & Brothers, 1958.

Rose, Phyllis, ed. *The Norton Book of Women's Lives*. New York: Norton, 1993.

Rosen, Benson, and Thomas H. Jerdee. *Older Employees: New Roles for Valued Resources*. Homewood, Ill.: Dow Jones-Irwin, 1985.

Rosenthal, Evelyn. *Women, Aging and Ageism*. Binghamton, N.Y.: Haworth Press, 1990.

Rowe, John W., and Robert J. Kahn. "Human Aging: Usual and Successful." *Science*, July 10, 1987.

Rubinstein, Helena. *My Life for Beauty*. New York: Simon and Schuster, 1964.

Russell, Cheryl. "Ageing As a Femininist Issue." *Women's Studies International Forum*, vol. 10, no. 2, 1987.

Sacks, Oliver. *Awakenings*. New York: HarperPerennial, 1990.

Santmyer, Helen Hooven. . . . *And Ladies of the Club*. New York: Putnam, 1982.

Sarton, May. *Encore: A Journal of the Eightieth Year*. New York: Norton, 1993.

Scott, Anne Firor. *Natural Allies: Women's Associations in American History*. Chicago: University of Illinois Press, 1991.

Scott, Hilda, and Juliet F. Brudney. *Forced Out: When Veteran Employees Are Driven from Their Careers*. New York: Fireside, 1987.

Shahtahmasebi, Said, Richard Davies, and G. Clare Wenger. "A Longitudinal Analysis of Factors Related to Survival in Old Age." *The Gerontologist*, vol. 32, no. 3, pp. 404–13.

Shaw, Sondra. *Reinventing Fundraising: Realizing the Potential of Women's Philanthropy.* San Francisco: Jossey-Bass, 1995.

Sheehy, Gail. *Passages: Predictable Crises of Adult Life.* New York: Bantam, 1976. For Sheehy's view of the passage of women to later life, see her article "Ordinary Women Inventing Extraordinary Lives," *New Woman*, November 1993.

Skinner, B. F., and Margaret Vaughan. *Enjoy Old Age.* New York: Norton, 1983.

Smith, Jessie Carney. *Epic Lives: One Hundred Black Women Who Made a Difference.* Detroit: Visible Ink Press, 1992.

Stearns, Peter. "Old Women: Some Historical Observations." *Journal of Family History*, Spring 1980.

Steinem, Gloria. *Revolution from Within: A Book of Self-Esteem.* Boston: Little, Brown, 1992.

Taeuber, Cynthia M. *Sixty-Five Plus in America.* U.S. Bureau of the Census, Current Population Reports, Special Studies, Series P23-178. Washington, D.C.: Government Printing Office, 1992.

U.S. Senate Special Committee on Aging. *Aging America: Trends and Projections.* Washington, D.C.: Government Printing Office, 1991.

Walker, Barbara. *The Crone: Woman of Age, Wisdom, and Power.* San Francisco: Harper & Row, 1988.

Witt, Linda, Karen M. Paget, and Glenna Matthews. *Running as a Woman: Gender and Power in American Politics.* New York: Free Press, 1993.

Wolf, Naomi. *The Beauty Myth: How Images of Beauty Are Used Against Women.* New York: Doubleday, 1992.

Wolfe, David B. *Serving the Ageless Market: Strategies for Selling to the Fifty-Plus Market.* New York: McGraw-Hill, 1990.

Women's Research & Education Institute. *The American Woman 1992–93: A Status Report.* New York: Norton, 1992.

Index